TREES OF TEXAS

RED MA

EASTERN REDBUD *Cercis canadensis*

ASHE JUNIPER *Juniperus ashei*

GREEN HAWTHORN *Crataegus viridis*

AN EASY GUIDE TO LEAF IDENTIFICATION

TREES OF TEXAS

Carmine Stahl and Ria McElvaney

TEXAS A&M UNIVERSITY PRESS *College Station*

Second Printing, 2012

The paper used in this book meets the minimum requirements of the American National Standard for Permanence of Paper for Printed Library Materials, z39.48–1984.
Binding materials have been chosen for durability.

∞

LIBRARY OF CONGRESS
CATALOGING-IN-PUBLICATION DATA

Stahl, Carmine A.
Trees of Texas : an easy guide to leaf identification / Carmine Stahl and Ria McElvaney.—1st ed.
p. cm.— (W. L. Moody, Jr., natural history series ; no. 34)
Includes bibliographical references and index (p.).
ISBN 1-58544-242-9 (hardcover : alk.paper)
ISBN-13: 978-1-60344-515-3 (pbk.)
ISBN-13: 978-1-60344-684-6 (ebook)
1. Trees—Texas—Identification.
2. Trees—Texas—Pictorial works.
I. McElvaney, Ria, 1958– II. Title. III. Series.
QK188.S72 2003
582. 16'09764— dc21

2002152758

To those nearest our hearts who keep the wild alive inside

GOLDEN RAIN TREE
Koelreuteria paniculata

MEXICAN BUCKEYE *Ungnadia speciosa*

CONTENTS

ACKNOWLEDGMENTS   X

INTRODUCTION   xiii

HOW TO USE THIS BOOK   xvii

MAP OF VEGETATION REGIONS   xxi

KEY TO LEAF SHAPES   xxii

TREE PROFILES   1

APPENDIX A: TREE FAMILIES   243

APPENDIX B: SCIENTIFIC AND COMMON NAMES   245

APPENDIX C: INTRODUCED SPECIES   254

APPENDIX D: TREES BY REGION   255

APPENDIX E: BUTTERFLY HOST TREES   260

APPENDIX F: LIGHT AND WATER REQUIREMENTS   261

APPENDIX G: RECIPES FOR WILD EDIBLES   267

GLOSSARY   269

BIBLIOGRAPHY   271

INDEX   275

ACKNOWLEDGMENTS

RED MAPLE *Acer rubrum*

TRAVELING THIS BIG STATE to collect foliage, flowers, and fruits from trees in every region required the help of a lot of people. We cannot express enough thanks to the park staff, property owners, nurseries, naturalists, arboretums, and just plain friendly, interested people for the kind and gracious help we always received.

Special thanks go to David Riskind, Natural Resources Director of the Texas Parks and Wildlife Department, and to the fine personnel of the state park system. Among the parks where we received extra help were Balmorrhea, Davis Mountains, and Martin Dies state parks and the Big Bend State Natural Area.

The staff of the Valley Nature Center in Weslaco were also very helpful, particularly René Ruiz, who spent many hours with us over the course of our several trips there. Jesse H. Jones Park and Nature Center and the Mercer Arboretum and Botanic Gardens in Humble afforded valuable help with many trees. Likewise, the personnel of the San Antonio Botanic Gardens were considerate and helpful. Our grateful thanks go to the Robert Vines Science Center in Houston and the National Audubon Society's Sabal Palm Grove Sanctuary in Brownsville.

Mike and Patsy Anderson of Mike Anderson Nursery in Houston provided superb assistance with specimens and their phenomenal knowledge of the locations of native trees and plants. We appreciate the help of Mark and Laurie Garretson

of Earth Works Nursery in Victoria and the Ted Doremus Nursery in Warren; and the access given by Betty's Bloomers Nursery in Kountze, Gerald and Kay Deppe of Woodville, and the Mitchell Oil Company to its Lake Creek Field. Marc and Marianne Eastman of Fort Davis gave invaluable information about the trees of their region and allowed us to collect specimens on their property.

Oscar Mestas, urban forester in El Paso, supplied us with a number of specimens. Many thanks, Oscar. John Watson, urban forester with Harris County Flood Control District, gave us useful information on the location of some difficult-to-find trees in Central Texas. Ronnie Ponder helped with vital specimens. Monique Reed of the Texas A&M University Herbarium gave us important technical information, particularly on current classifications and ranges of native trees.

Margaret Lambert of Kingwood generously shared her fine collection of native trees. Jim Kingery, director of Moundbuilders State Memorial Park in Newark, Ohio, provided us with a wealth of information about the historical uses of many tree species. My son Ralph, who resides in Washington state, and my daughter Merry Carol, who lives in Ohio, also helped with some hard-to-find specimens.

And to those who have worked long and hard before us to describe the trees of Texas, we offer special thanks. Among them are Robert

Carmine Stahl

Vines, Benny Simpson, and Paul Cox and Patty Leslie, whose works are listed in the bibliography. Times and classifications change, but we always appreciate the foundations.

I've been privileged to know and work with some of Texas' greatest plant people, among them Lynn Lowrey and Robert Vines; with outstanding anthropologists and archaeologists like Lou Fullen and Roger Moore; and with a host of fine naturalists and ornithologists like John Tveten, Fred Collins, Gary and Cathy Clark, Howard Peacock, and so many others who have graciously and gladly shared their knowledge. All nature is related, and all the naturalists we know are generous with their insights. We are grateful to those who have left this legacy and to those who continue to build upon it.

The enthusiasm and help of Texas A&M University Press Natural Sciences Editor Shannon Davies have been incomparable. We deeply appreciate her gracious, prompt assistance and the wisdom and help of all the staff at the press.

Finally, to our patient and loving spouses, Rick and Mary Lou, who have never complained while we have chased wild trees all over Texas, and to Ria's children, Kate and Tess, who have grumbled but borne it well: Thank you, our dearest and nearest.

And thanks to all our friends who have encouraged us over the past several years and asked, "How's the book coming?" Here it is, *compañeros*.

PRAIRIE FLAMELEAF SUMAC *Rhus lanceolata*

YELLOW TRUMPET *Tacoma stans*

LEAVES: Semi-evergreen
HEIGHT: To 40 feet
GROWTH: Fast
VALUE: Dye, landscape, wildlife
FAMILY: Sweet Leaf (Symplocaceae)
REGION(S): 1

*T*HE COMMON NAME OF THIS tree comes from the sweet taste of the almost evergreen leaves, which are greedily eaten by deer and livestock. Its popularity with horses inspired another appellation: horse sugar. The species name *tinctoria* refers to a former use of the leaves to produce yellow dye.

A small tree growing in scattered locations around the southeastern quarter of the United States, including East Texas, sweet leaf appears chiefly near streams or in moist woods. *Symplocos* boasts about 350 species worldwide, but only this one occurs in North America. Most of the others grow in tropical regions.

This tree occasionally reaches up to 40 feet in height but usually tops out at about 15 to 20 feet. The fragrant, yellowish clusters of spring flowers mature into small orange-brown drupes that are a favorite fall and winter food of birds. The thick, persistent leaves make sweet leaf a good landscape plant, but few nurseries offer it, and it rarely survives transplanting.

LOQUAT

Eriobotrya japonica

*D*ESPITE THE SPECIES name *japonica*, this tree actually originates in China. Homeowners plant it for ornamental value over much of the southern United States and in many other warm countries. Near the Texas Gulf Coast it reseeds itself and naturalizes.

Loquat takes a classical small-tree form and sports large, tropical-looking leaves, densely covered with rusty hairs on their undersides. The flowers appear in early winter, and the edible fruits ripen within a couple of months thereafter.

These yellow pomes taste pleasant enough when eaten raw. They produce their best flavor, however, when made into jellies, jams, or wine. Growers cultivate loquat for the market mainly in the Middle East, Israel being the world's number one supplier. Birds and other wildlife enjoy the fruits as well.

LEAVES: Evergreen
HEIGHT: To 25 feet
GROWTH: Moderate/fast
VALUE: Edible parts, landscape, wildlife
FAMILY: Rose (Rosaceae)
REGION(S): Non-native

Quercus laurifolia and Diamond leaf oak (*quercus obtusa*) **LAUREL OAK**

*L*AUREL OAK DERIVES its name from its laurel-like leaves, usually just slightly wider than those of willow oak (p. 3), especially in the middle. Today, botanists include the diamond leaf oak, which has leaves even wider at the middle, in the same species.

Laurel oak likes well-drained sites in Southeast Texas, but the diamond leaf form prefers wet areas. With water oak (p. 17) and willow oak, this species forms a complex in the black oak group that produces various hybrids.

Laurel and diamond leaf oaks are good trees for landscape and shade, depending on the drainage in your yard. Their almost evergreen leaves and spreading branches form a nice rounded crown. The acorns provide valuable wildlife food, and the wood serves for fuel and charcoal.

LEAVES: Semi-evergreen
HEIGHT: To 80 feet
GROWTH: Fast
VALUE: Landscape, shade, wildlife
FAMILY: Beech (Fagaceae)
REGION(S): 1

DESERT WILLOW

Chilopsis linearis

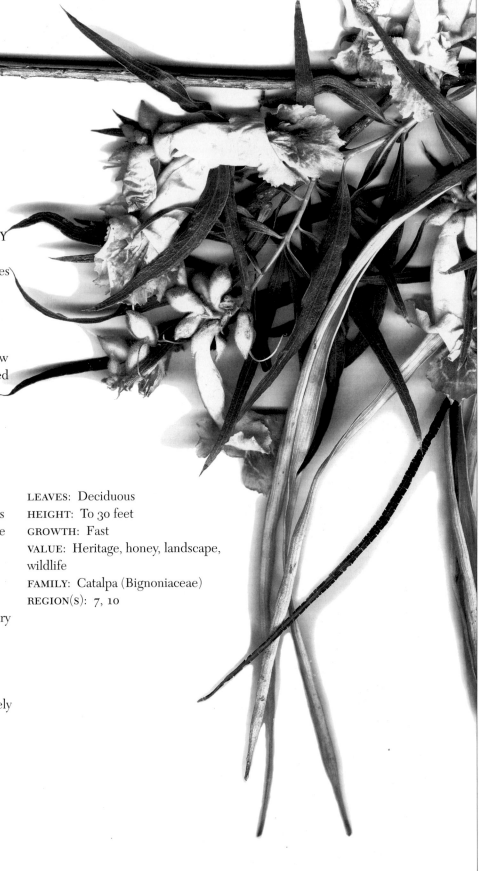

*T*HE GRACEFUL BEAUTY of this arid-country tree commands notice. For several weeks it produces delicate trumpet-shaped flowers, colored lavender, white, and violet, which attract both bees and hummingbirds. Long thin pods, each containing a number of seeds, follow the flowers. These seeds are equipped with feathery edges, designed for dispersal by the wind.

Despite its name and its narrow, linear leaves, this tree is not a true willow but rather a member of the catalpa (p. 128–9) family, which includes the trumpet creeper vine (*Campsis radicans*). The tree shares one of its common names, as it once shared a portion of its habitat, with the *Mimbres or Mimbreño* Indians who settled in New Mexico about 750–1250 A.D.

Desert willow grows alongside dry washes throughout the American Southwest, including West and southwestern Texas, but people often plant it elsewhere. The highway department utilizes it extensively for beautification and soil stabilization. Its chief requirement for success is a well-drained location.

In Mexico, craftspeople use the branches for weaving. Native Americans once favored them for bow wood, and birds eat the winged seeds.

LEAVES: Deciduous
HEIGHT: To 30 feet
GROWTH: Fast
VALUE: Heritage, honey, landscape, wildlife
FAMILY: Catalpa (Bignoniaceae)
REGION(S): 7, 10

Salix nigra

BLACK WILLOW

$\mathcal{W}$ILLOWS HAVE BEEN used medicinally from prehistoric times to relieve headaches, reduce fevers, and heal wounds. Through most of the nineteenth century, physicians prepared their own willow bark potions. In the 1880s, scientists synthesized the compound derived from willow bark, acetylsalicylic acid, into the pill we call Aspirin. In a pinch, willow bark even provides sufficient nutrition to serve as a survival food, but it will always taste bitter.

Black willow wood, too, was put to several interesting uses in the past, including the manufacture of artificial limbs, polo balls, and a special charcoal used to make gunpowder. Native Americans employed the roots for red, orange, and yellow dyes. They utilized the roots and young branches in basketry and mat weaving.

Many species of willow grow across Europe, Asia, and North America. In the eastern half of the United States, black willow predominates. It proliferates along streams throughout its range and performs a great service by holding soil banks against erosion. While black willow makes an alluring landscape feature, the tendency of its roots to invade plumbing and the seed litter produced by the females discourage its use in most cases.

LEAVES: Deciduous
HEIGHT: To 80 feet
GROWTH: Fast
VALUE: Dye, erosion control, heritage, landscape, medicinal
FAMILY: Willow (Salicaceae)
REGION(S): 1–10

YEW LEAF WILLOW

Salix taxifolia

*T*HE STREAMBEDS AND
dry washes of far West Texas form a
rugged contrast to this delicate little
willow growing here and there along
their margins. Thriving at elevations
of 4,000 to 5,000 feet, yew leaf willow
graces the rocky edges of Limpia
Creek near Fort Davis, Calamity
Creek south of Alpine, and a few other
select locations in the Trans-Pecos.

Both its common and scientific
names derive from its narrow, silvery
green leaves, which resemble those
of the yew tree (*Taxus* spp.), and
which, together with its diminutive
yellow blossoms, imbue this tree with
definite landscape potential.

Although rare in Texas, yew leaf
willow flourishes in Mexico and
Guatemala. It also grows in southwestern New Mexico and southern
Arizona.

Settlers once used the branches as
brooms, and Indians in Mexico
concocted a malaria remedy from the
bark. Ranchers say the leaves offer
good browse.

LEAVES: Deciduous
HEIGHT: To 30 feet
GROWTH: Fast
VALUE: Heritage, landscape,
medicinal, wildlife
FAMILY: Willow (Salicaceae)
REGION(S): 10

BLUEJACK OAK

LEAVES: Deciduous
HEIGHT: To 35 feet
GROWTH: Slow
VALUE: Wildlife
FAMILY: Beech (Fagaceae)
REGION(S): 1–3

*T*HIS TREE'S COMMON name reflects its blue-green foliage, which has densely wooly, grayish white undersides to conserve moisture. The scientific name *incana* refers to this fuzzy growth.

A tough little tree, bluejack oak thrives in dry locations in East Texas and in the Post Oak Savannah. The tree adapts especially well to such places as the deep sands of Roy E. Larsen Sandylands Sanctuary in the Big Thicket, which accounts for another nickname: sandjack oak. From there its habitat spreads westward to Georgetown.

The acorns present a boon to wildlife, and the wood makes good fence posts. But bluejack oak has little other commercial value because of its rare occurrence and because of its small trunks, which often lean dramatically.

COMA

Sideroxylon celastrina

SOME HERBALISTS in Mexico attribute aphrodisiac powers to the fruits of this small tree. Coma blooms in late fall with tiny greenish white flowers. The small, oval, black fruits mature in late spring to feed birds, small mammals, and apparently the occasional would-be lover. Carpenters sometimes use the heartwood in cabinetwork.

Coma, also called saffron plum, thrives in the coastal counties from Matagorda through the Lower Rio Grande Valley and westward into deep South Texas. This little tree also grows southward all the way to Colombia and Venezuela.

Its thorny branches stretch to 20 feet or more in height. Often, however, it occurs as no more than a shrub. Coma has lumpy twigs and small, smooth leaves with a blown-back appearance.

LEAVES: Evergreen
HEIGHT: To 20 feet
GROWTH: Moderate/fast
VALUE: Wildlife, wood uses
FAMILY: Sapodilla (Sapotaceae)
REGION(S): 2, 6, 7

Diospyros texana

TEXAS PERSIMMON

LEAVES: Deciduous
HEIGHT: To 35 feet
GROWTH: Slow
VALUE: Dye, edible parts, landscape, wildlife, wood uses
FAMILY: Ebony (Ebenaceae)
REGION(S): 2–7, 10

*T*HE LITTLE BLACK FRUITS of Texas persimmon rival those of the common persimmon (p. 41) for sweetness and flavor. Settlers used the juice to dye leather, and woodworking enthusiasts value the hard, heavy wood. Only one in many specimens is a female, fruiting tree, but these attract myriad birds and mammals.

Another tree named for Texas, this persimmon rates as one of the state's most attractive natives. Its smooth, peeling bark in shades of gray and sometimes pale pink renders it highly ornamental. Small leathery leaves add an eye-catching feature.

Texas persimmon can attain about 35 feet in height, but it sometimes forms invasive, shrubby thickets. Most common on the Edwards Plateau, it also grows on outcrops of limey sandstone on the Blackland Prairies, in South and West Texas, and in Mexico. Usually evergreen in South Texas, it sheds its leaves in colder areas.

LEAVES: Deciduous
HEIGHT: To 30 feet
GROWTH: Moderate/slow
VALUE: Edible parts, dye, heritage, landscape, wildlife
FAMILY: Buckthorn (Rhamnaceae)
REGION(S): 2, 3, 6, 7

SMALL, BRIGHT GREEN leaves set among thorny twigs give this tree a glossy appearance and make it an attractive ornamental. The little blue-black fruits taste sweet and juicy and could be used to make jelly if the tree produced them more abundantly. Squirrels, raccoons, opossums, and many birds relish them.

The wood, which appears red, reportedly yields a blue dye, and pioneers made red ink from a decoction containing brazil wood chips.

Also called bluewood condalia, *capul negro,* and a host of other names, this tree presents a common and striking sight throughout southern parts of the Edwards Plateau and southward to the Rio Grande. It can grow to 30 feet and often forms thickets.

The species name commemorates the eminent botanist Joseph Dalton Hooker (1817–1911), who succeeded his father, William Jackson Hooker, in the directorship of Kew Gardens and who served as confidant to Charles Darwin and friend to Asa Gray and Thomas Henry Huxley.

HIS MOST COMMON OAK of East Texas lives life in the fast lane, growing rapidly and dying young. It achieves a massive size in 60 to 70 years and takes only 12 to 15 years to become a significant shade tree. Developers often plant it because of its fast growth. Few water oaks live much beyond 100 years, however.

Powerful storms, such as hurricanes, topple this tree more than any other. Once exposed, the remarkably shallow root system looks completely inadequate to support the tree's impressive size.

Water oak prefers damp places, such as flood plains and lowlands. Deciduous in cold winters, it remains at least partly evergreen in mild years. With or without leaves, horizontal bands of lichen on the trunk offer a clue to identification.

A prolific crop of acorns provides a bounty for squirrels, deer, hogs, and other foragers, and the fissured bark of old trees contains a good supply of insects for a variety of birds, including woodpeckers, nuthatches, and creepers.

Water oak sometimes hybridizes with the graceful willow oak (p. 3) or with live oak (p. 77), making semi-evergreen blends. The leaves of saplings and fast-growing branches often do not look like those of the mature tree. They can be lobed, like those of red oak (p. 110) or white oak (p. 93), or elongated like those of willow oak, further complicating identification.

LEAVES: Semi-evergreen
HEIGHT: To 80 feet
GROWTH: Fast
VALUE: Shade, wildlife
FAMILY: Beech (Fagaceae)
REGION(S): 1–3

GUM BUMELIA

Sideroxylon lanuginosum

LEAVES: Semi-evergreen
HEIGHT: To 40 feet
GROWTH: Slow
VALUE: Heritage, landscape, wildlife, wood uses
FAMILY: Sapodilla (Sapotaceae)
REGION(S): 1–8, 10

ALSO CALLED woolybucket bumelia, wooly buckthorn, and a number of other common names, this small tree grows in all regions but the Panhandle and, with rare exceptions, far West Texas. It survives in rather poor, dry soil and boasts several varietal forms throughout the state. A few nurseries offer gum bumelia as an ornamental.

This tree can reach a height of 40 feet or more with a trunk of about one foot in diameter. It often protects itself with sharp thorns, and new leaves emerge silvery green. When the tree sustains a scrape or wound, it exudes a gum that children once chewed, resulting in the tree's common name. The wooly undersides of its leaves, reflected in the species name *lanuginosum,* suggest several other nicknames.

Gum bumelia's half-inch-long, single-seeded, purple or black fruits attract birds, and hobbyists use its fine-grained wood to make small specialty items and cabinets.

LEAVES: Evergreen
HEIGHT: To 15 feet
GROWTH: Slow
VALUE: Dye, heritage, landscape, medicinal, wildlife
FAMILY: Rose (Rosaceae)
REGION(S): 7, 8, 10

*T*HE NAVAJO PEOPLE have employed mountain mahogany extensively throughout their long history: its hard, heavy wood found many uses as implements and makes excellent firewood. They also brewed the twigs into a laxative tea; utilized the roots, called *tse'e'sdaazii*, to produce a reddish dye for their ceremonial baskets; and placed branches under beds to repel insects.

You can easily recognize mountain mahogany by its little pointed fruits with silvery, featherlike tails, which become showy in late summer and fall. The evergreen foliage, too, creates an attractive effect and adds to mountain mahogany's striking landscape potential. It offers important browse for deer and antelope.

This small tree occurs in several varieties across the American West, in far West Texas, the South Texas Plains, the Big Bend, and in a few counties in the western Edwards Plateau. It usually grows at elevations of 4,000 feet or more.

Despite its common name, mountain mahogany is not related to the big tropical mahogany tree (*Swietenia macrophylla*) of commerce.

MAYHAW

Crataegus opaca

LEAVES: Deciduous
HEIGHT: To 30 feet
GROWTH: Slow
VALUE: Edible parts, landscape, wildlife
FAMILY: Rose (Rosaceae)
REGION(S): 1

THIS HAWTHORN IS the source of one of the tastiest of all preserves, the renowned mayhaw jelly, which connoisseurs across the South rightfully regard in the same manner as a fine wine. Mayhaws grow in low areas called "flats," which remain flooded for much of the year. People often cull the fruits directly from the surface of the water and even use minnow seines for this purpose. Mayhaws can adapt to the relatively dry terrain of home landscapes, though, and reward growers with showy flowers and then fruits that attract wildlife. To enjoy the fruits yourself, refer to the recipe for mayhaw jelly in appendix G.

In Texas, all the trees of this species occur naturally only east of the Trinity River, except for an isolated colony in Montgomery County. The fragrant white flowers bloom as early as February, before the leaves appear, and most of the fruits ripen in April. They look like little apples about three quarters of an inch in diameter.

LITTLE HIP HAWTHORN

THE STORIES OF HOW this little tree got its name vary. Some say that the name refers to the two small matching "hips" on the sides of its leaves. Others say that "hip" refers to the fruits, which resemble miniature rose hips. Either way, its white spring flowers and bright red fall and winter "berries" charm everyone who sees them. The fruits are actually pomes, which persist all winter on the twigs, providing food for a number of birds. Most true hawthorn fruits are also edible to humans, but, with a few exceptions, taste dry and seedy.

The tree's species name means "spoon-shaped" and refers to the leaves, which look like small spatulas. Little hip hawthorn somewhat resembles parsley hawthorn (p. 140), although the leaf edges of the latter appear more torn and irregular. They share the same range across East Texas, but little hip predominates and may represent the most populous "haw" in the state. The flaking bark of old specimens reveals a knobby, gnarled trunk, and the exceptionally tough wood once found use for tool handles that needed to withstand stress. Little hip hawthorn grows slowly but lives for a long time.

LEAVES: Deciduous
HEIGHT: To 25 feet
GROWTH: Slow
VALUE: Landscape, wildlife
FAMILY: Rose (Rosaceae)
REGION(S): 1–4

PAWPAW

LEAVES: Deciduous
HEIGHT: To 30 feet
GROWTH: Fast
VALUE: Edible parts, heritage, landscape, medicinal, wildlife
FAMILY: Custard Apple (Annonaceae)
REGION(S): 1

THIS MEMBER of the custard apple family, with its large, drooping leaves and banana-like fruit, resembles its tropical cousins. Pawpaw, however, may have far more to offer the world than good looks and soft, sweet fruit with a taste reminiscent of egg custard. In recent studies done at Purdue University, researchers isolated a compound from pawpaw called asimicin, which yields promising results in inhibiting certain leukemia and ovarian cancer cells. The twigs and bark also contain a natural insecticide.

While fossils resembling this species date to the Eocene epoch (54–38 million years ago), the earliest historical reference to pawpaw appears in the writings of Hernando de Soto's expedition along the Mississippi Valley in 1541. Native Americans throughout the southeastern United States considered pawpaws a favorite food and served them to de Soto's conquistadors. Pawpaws also sustained the Lewis and Clark expedition during their return trip in 1810, when their food supplies ran low.

While a few people today still enjoy the highly nutritious fruits—the largest borne by any native North American tree—attempts to grow pawpaws commercially meet with mixed results. Growers produce some promising strains, but big seeds, inconsistent taste, and less-than-forgiving shipping characteristics still pose obstacles, and some people respond with allergic reactions. Foxes, raccoons, opossums, and squirrels eagerly eat the fruits, and birds like to peck at them.

Although pawpaw grows as far north as New York and Michigan, in Texas it appears only in eastern and northeastern parts of the state. Some nurseries offer it for its ornamental value. However, you will need at least two specimens to cross-pollinate if you want to harvest the fruit. Pawpaw prefers a moist, semi-shaded habitat and shows some vulnerability to drought, especially in its early years.

SOUTHERN WAXMYRTLE

Myrica cerifera

LEAVES: Semi-evergreen
HEIGHT: To 30 feet
GROWTH: Fast
VALUE: Culinary, heritage, landscape, wildlife
FAMILY: Waxmyrtle (Myrtaceae)
REGION(S): 1–3

S EMI-EVERGREEN leaves and a crooked trunk characterize this small tree, which thrives around ponds, streams, and lakes in East Texas. Also known as southern bayberry, it possesses many attractive qualities that make it popular in landscapes.

A waxy coating surrounds its tiny blue fruits, important in the past for candle making. We still enjoy the delightful fragrance of bayberry candles during the Christmas holidays, but today these are scented with New England bayberries (*Myrica pennsylvanica*), a related species that occurs very rarely in Texas. Only female trees produce the fruits. However, more than forty species of birds relish these berries, which persist on the twigs until consumed. The bushy branches also offer good nesting sites.

Bronze-green leaves reveal small oil dots when held to the light and exude a subtle aroma when crushed. They make a good spice for seafood and gumbos and enhance almost all crab boil and shrimp boil seasonings.

$\mathcal{D}$ECIDUOUS HOLLY REVEALS its ultimate beauty in winter when the brilliant orange-red berries of female trees ornament its bare branches throughout the dormant woods of Central and East Texas. Its deciduous nature serves to underscore its striking good looks. This tree prefers wood edges and fencerows where it can get sun, but one of these trees can also create an outstanding focal point in any yard or landscape.

Although sometimes called possumhaw, this tree is not a hawthorn, but opossums do enjoy the fruits. So do a number of bird species. Since the berries remain on the branches all winter, they provide food throughout the season.

As with almost all hollies, the berries prove purgative to humans. But birds can digest many things that people cannot.

LEAVES: Deciduous
HEIGHT: To 20 feet
GROWTH: Slow
VALUE: Landscape, wildlife
FAMILY: Holly (Aquifoliaceae)
REGION(S): 1–5, 7

See color illustration, p. xvii

TEXAS HAWTHORN

Crataegus texana

OTANISTS ARGUE unendingly about classification of these little trees in the *Crataegus* genus. The three dozen or so species, subspecies, varieties, and hybrids remain in constant dispute. Texas hawthorn, however, causes little argument. Its limited range covers only nine or ten counties of the coastal plain and south-central Texas, but its name and its beauty provide ample justification for including it among the hawthorns here.

The mealy-apple taste of Texas hawthorn "berries" surpasses the dry, seedy nature of other hawthorn fruits, with the obvious exception of mayhaw (p. 20). Some people cook Texas hawthorn fruits—which are really pomes—into jams and jellies. Wine aficionados occasionally distill them into exotic liquors. Mostly, however, birds depend on hawthorn fruits for survival through the winter months, and some mammals, such as squirrels, opossums, and raccoons, also savor them.

Nearly all "haws" exhibit pretty spring flowers, and their dense and often thorny crowns provide attractive nesting sites. Texas hawthorn grows slowly but proves worth waiting for in home landscapes.

LEAVES: Deciduous
HEIGHT: To 25 feet
GROWTH: Slow
VALUE: Edible parts, landscape, wildlife
FAMILY: Rose (Rosaceae)
REGION(S): 2, 3

BIG TREE HAWTHORN

ELL NAMED, this hawthorn grows to the relatively large size of 35 or 40 feet and develops a trunk of nearly a foot in diameter. It thrives in rich, moist soil and makes its habitat from East Texas into the Post Oak Savannah and Blackland Prairies.

Big tree hawthorn distinguishes itself from its closest relative, cockspur hawthorn (p. 29), by its larger size, but it wields less impressive thorns than its smaller cousin.

Big tree hawthorn produces a prolific crop of orange-red fruits in fall, and the pretty spring flowers earn it serious consideration for its landscape potential. Its species name refers to its leaves, which resemble those of barberry (*Berberis vulgaris*).

Like other hawthorns, this tree provides food and nest sites for many birds. Woodworkers and craftspeople employ the tough wood of this and other "haws" for tool handles and wheel hubs.

LEAVES: Deciduous
HEIGHT: To 35 feet
GROWTH: Slow
VALUE: Landscape, wildlife
FAMILY: Rose (Rosaceae)
REGION(S): 1, 3, 4

WINTERBERRY HOLLY

Ilex verticillata

*T*EXAS TREE GUIDES did not list this small tree until recent years, after botanists discovered it growing along the Sabine River north of Orange, in the far southeastern reaches of the state. There, this swamp-loving species finds a home among water tupelos (p. 45), Carolina ash (p. 194), and bald cypress (p. 221). But it is fairly common elsewhere in the South, its natural habitat extending from Texas east to Florida and north to Nova Scotia and Quebec.

The species name *verticillata* means "arranged in whorls" and refers to the pseudowhorl configuration of the flowers and fruits around the stems. Winterberry develops relatively long leaves and pretty and persistent bright red fruits, which look particularly striking set against a snowy winter backdrop. At least twenty species of birds eat the berries, and people have planted the tree for ornament for more than 200 years. Recently researchers suggested that this species could present a source of biodegradable detergent because of its high saponin content.

LEAVES: Deciduous
HEIGHT: To 20 feet
GROWTH: Fast
VALUE: Landscape, wildlife
FAMILY: Holly (Aquifoliaceae)
REGION(S): 1, 2

Crataegus crus-galli # COCKSPUR HAWTHORN

$\mathcal{B}$OTH THE COMMON and generic names of this species pay tribute to its long, impressive thorns, which resemble a rooster's spurs. These small trees, with their protective spines, make ideal nesting sites.

The thin, dry fruits of cockspur hawthorn persist all winter, providing food for birds. As with most hawthorn fruits, their attractive red color enhances the tree's landscape value. The spring flowers mimic little clusters of apple blossoms, and the highly glossy leaves look as if just polished. Because of these features, both Europeans and Americans often plant these trees for ornament. In colonial times, people groomed them into impenetrable hedges.

Cockspur hawthorn grows north and east to Michigan and southern Canada and, in Texas, occurs widely through north, east, and central parts of the state to beyond the Edwards Plateau. The tree differs from its closest relative, big tree hawthorn (p. 27), in its smaller size but larger thorns.

LEAVES: Deciduous
HEIGHT: To 25 feet
GROWTH: Slow
VALUE: Landscape, wildlife
FAMILY: Rose (Rosaceae)
REGION(S): 1–5, 7

FRINGE TREE

Chionanthus virginica

LEAVES: Semi-evergreen
HEIGHT: To 25 feet
GROWTH: Moderate/fast
VALUE: Landscape, medicinal, wildlife
FAMILY: Olive (Oleaceae)
REGION(S): 1, 2

FRINGE TREE BLOOMS with delicate, lacelike clusters of white flowers in early to midspring, making this one of the loveliest species of the Texas Piney Woods, with occasional specimens appearing as far west as Navasota. A relatively rare tree, this member of the olive family makes a dramatic show from wood edges, clearings, and an occasional front yard.

The genus name combines two Greek words, *chion,* which means "snow," and *anthos,* which means "flower." A host of common names, including old man's beard, flowering ash, and snowflower tree, attempt to capture this species' whimsical aura when in full bloom. This unique native tree deserves to be showcased more often in landscapes.

Birds and small mammals eat the dark blue fruits that follow the gleaming, gossamer blossoms. In the past, people used the bark of fringe tree for many medicinal purposes, such as concocting diuretics and fever remedies. The wood exhibits a beautiful grain, but the tree seldom reaches a size suitable for commercial use.

Celtis reticulata

NET LEAF HACKBERRY

LEAVES: Deciduous
HEIGHT: To 30 feet
GROWTH: Moderate/fast
VALUE: Shade, wildlife
FAMILY: Elm (Ulmaceae)
REGION(S): 2–5, 7–10

*T*HIS SMALL HACKBERRY, with its corky, gray trunk, adapts to drier conditions than do most of the other hackberry species. It dots the sandy coastal plain and grows from parts of Central Texas up into the Panhandle and in scattered West Texas locales. Known populations in Burleson County near Clay and in Grimes County just northeast of Navasota subsist on calcareous limestone.

Net leaf hackberry's name derives from the conspicuous netlike veins on the undersides of the leaves, and its species name, *reticulata,* further reflects this characteristic. The tree is also distinguished from sugar hackberry (p. 33) by the relative thickness of its leaves, the upper surface of which feels like sandpaper, and by its more westerly distribution.

The wood has little use except as posts and fuel, and the disheveled and sprawling aspect of young specimens belies the attractive appearance of the mature trees. The pea-sized, orange fruits persist on the tree throughout the winter, offering nourishment to a variety of bird species that depend on them for food.

LINDHEIMER HACKBERRY

Celtis lindheimeri

 *T*HIS TEXAS NATIVE, like several others, borrows its name from naturalist and newspaper editor Ferdinand Jacob Lindheimer (1801–79), who scouted the region in the mid-1800s. Born in Frankfurt, Germany, Lindheimer settled in New Braunfels, becoming Texas' first permanent resident plant collector and thereby earning a reputation as the father of Texas botany. He discovered several hundred species of plants and gave his name to forty-eight of them. Various museums around the world, including the British Museum in London, the Durand Herbarium in Paris, the Komarov Botanic Institute in St. Petersburg, and the Gray Herbarium at Harvard, house his extensive collections.

Most hackberries look alike. You can differentiate this one from the others by the downy, hairlike texture on the undersurfaces of the leaves. This hoary growth lends the tree a grayish cast.

Lindheimer hackberry occurs exclusively in Texas, except for a population in the Mexican state of Coahuila. In Texas, it flourishes only in a small area that includes Austin and San Antonio. Like other hackberries, it produces small, reddish fruits that provide important winter forage for birds.

LEAVES: Deciduous
HEIGHT: To 40 feet
GROWTH: Fast
VALUE: Shade, wildlife
FAMILY: Elm (Ulmaceae)
REGION(S): 7

Celtis laevigata

SUGAR HACKBERRY

LEAVES: Deciduous
HEIGHT: To 60 feet
GROWTH: Fast
VALUE: Shade, wildlife
FAMILY: Elm (Ulmaceae)
REGION(S): 1–8, 10

Sugar hackberry, or sugarberry, while not highly regarded as a landscape tree, does possess some very positive qualities. First, it attracts wildlife. Numerous bird species and squirrels avidly eat the small orange to red to black fruits, just as the Caesars valued European hackberry fruits as snacks. Unfortunately ours taste rather too dry and seedy for human consumption.

Second, it grows rapidly to make an excellent shade tree. If all hackberries suddenly vanished from Texas, many yards would be left entirely without shade.

Finally, this hardy tree thrives in virtually anything from flood plains to relatively arid conditions and remains almost disease-free. Only a harmless nipple gall disfigures its leaves, but this occurs so frequently as to offer a clue in the tree's identification.

Even without the prolific galls, sugar hackberry remains one of the most recognizable trees in Texas. Although *laevigata* means "smooth," hackberries protect their thin, easily damaged bark with a mass of warty bumps covering their trunks. These warts discourage large mammals from scratching themselves or deer from rubbing their antlers on the tree.

CAMPHOR TREE

Cinnamomum camphora

*T*HIS OUTWARDLY ordinary tree is the commercial source of the camphor used extensively in chest rubs and inhalants for coughs and colds. When crushed, the leaves smell strongly of camphor, a characteristic that will help you distinguish the species from the similar red bay (p. 6) and cherry laurel (p. 36) trees.

A member of the laurel family, which includes red bay and sassafras (p. 102), the camphor tree originates in East Asia. It was introduced into the United States in the nineteenth century because its shiny evergreen leaves and dense, rounded form make it an attractive landscape specimen. When the occasional hard freeze extends into South Texas, killing the branches and causing the trunks to suffer, the tree usually resprouts. More ominously, this tree has no predators or diseases outside its native habitat. Prolific, black, pea-sized fruits attract numerous birds, which aid the tree in naturalizing along the Texas coast and across the lower South to Florida. There the tree invades woodlands so aggressively that it often outnumbers native species. It has made itself a pest in Australia, taking over aboriginal forests there as well. Because of its propensity to displace local flora, we cannot recommend that you plant this tree.

Warning: Invasive species

LEAVES: Evergreen
HEIGHT: To 60 feet
GROWTH: Fast
VALUE: Landscape, medicinal
FAMILY: Laurel (Lauraceae)
REGION(S): non-native

Citharexylum berlandieri **TAMAULIPAN FIDDLEWOOD**

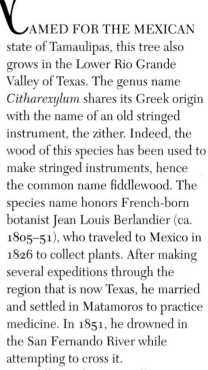

NAMED FOR THE MEXICAN state of Tamaulipas, this tree also grows in the Lower Rio Grande Valley of Texas. The genus name *Citharexylum* shares its Greek origin with the name of an old stringed instrument, the zither. Indeed, the wood of this species has been used to make stringed instruments, hence the common name fiddlewood. The species name honors French-born botanist Jean Louis Berlandier (ca. 1805–51), who traveled to Mexico in 1826 to collect plants. After making several expeditions through the region that is now Texas, he married and settled in Matamoros to practice medicine. In 1851, he drowned in the San Fernando River while attempting to cross it.

Fiddlewood occasionally grows to 25 feet or more but usually remains much smaller. The tree develops crowded leaves, usually 2 to 3 inches long, mottled gray bark, and small tubular white flowers. The blossoms occur frequently in warm weather and mature into an array of small yellow-to-red berries that eventually turn black. These fruits attract a number of birds.

Curanderos in Mexico concoct a cold remedy from this plant.

LEAVES: Deciduous
HEIGHT: To 25 feet
GROWTH: Fast
VALUE: Landscape, medicinal, wildlife
FAMILY: Verbena (Verbenaceae)
REGION(S): 6

CHERRY LAUREL

Prunus caroliniana

$\mathcal{T}$HE LEAVES AND BARK of this tree contain prussic acid, or cyanide, and, while a number of birds eat the small black fruits, all parts of the tree are toxic to humans and livestock. This holds true for most members of the *Prunus* genus, since prussic acid is present in peach, plum, and cherry trees, except in the pulp of the fruits.

To the novice, cherry laurel may resemble red bay (p. 6), which shares much of its habitat. Cherry laurel's dark green, somewhat leathery leaves appear less elongated, however, and exude a mild aroma when crushed. Their scent resembles that of almonds, maraschino cherries, or cherry cough drops.

Warning:
Known poisonous properties

Native to the southeastern part of Texas, cherry laurel owes its popularity as an ornamental to its evergreen foliage and thick shade. This tree takes a handsome pyramidal form when it receives full sun. It can be trimmed into a thick hedge and has been used in forming mazes. Nurseries also sell a horticultural dwarf variety.

LEAVES: Evergreen
HEIGHT: To 30 feet
GROWTH: Moderate/fast
VALUE: Landscape, wildlife
FAMILY: Rose (Rosaceae)
REGION(S): 1–3

JAPANESE AND WAX LEAF LIGUSTRUM

Ligustrum japonicum and *Ligustrum lucidum*

LEAVES: Evergreen
HEIGHT: To 30 feet
GROWTH: Fast
VALUE: Landscape, wildlife
FAMILY: Olive (Oleaceae)
REGION(S): Non-native

For A CENTURY OR MORE, people have cultivated these two similar plants in Texas and across the South. The large panicles of showy white flowers in late spring and early summer and the bluish black fruits that follow combine with dark green leaves to seduce homeowners into planting this tree in their yards. Mockingbirds, robins, waxwings, and other birds avidly eat the winter fruits and disperse the seeds. As a result, Japanese ligustrum increasingly escapes into the woods, naturalizing in clearings and edges, where its evergreen foliage shows up especially well in winter.

A native of Asia, this foreigner seems to have found a happy home in Texas, especially in the eastern half of the state. But botanists express concern that this species, and to a lesser extent wax leaf ligustrum, displace native plants. Homeowners should also take note of the highly toxic properties of the fruits, which may be fatal to humans if eaten.

Warning: Invasive species, known poisonous properties

FLOWERING DOGWOOD

Cornus florida

A NUMBER OF *CORNUS* species grow scattered around the northern hemisphere, and naturalists vigorously debate how these trees got their name. Some say that the bark of a European form was made into a wash for treating mangy dogs. Others insist that "dogwood" is a corruption of "dagwood," referring to the wood's former use for dagger handles. Still others explain that the branches were utilized as "dogs," an old term meaning spits on which to roast meat. Whatever the case, when the early colonists found our tree in the eastern forests, they immediately recognized it as a *Cornus* and gave it the name flowering dogwood.

The tree's delicate form, attractive red berries, and good autumn color add to its landscape potential, but it needs fairly acidic soil and almost perfect drainage to thrive.

A variety of birds eat the berries, as do squirrels and deer. The genus name *Cornus* comes from the Latin word for horn and refers to the hard wood, which Native Americans favored for arrow shafts. It also became a preferred wood for shuttles, tool handles, mallets, and golf clubs.

LEAVES: Deciduous
HEIGHT: To 40 feet
GROWTH: Moderate/slow
VALUE: Heritage, landscape, wildlife
FAMILY: Dogwood (Cornaceae)
REGION(S): 1, 3

When its white bracts shine through the still bare woods of early spring, this graceful tree warms the hearts of all its admirers and inspires the seemingly ubiquitous dogwood festivals. All throughout the East Texas Piney Woods it emerges in clearings and along forest edges.

Cornus drummondii   **ROUGH LEAF DOGWOOD**

LEAVES: Deciduous
HEIGHT: To 20 feet
GROWTH: Moderate/fast
VALUE: Landscape, wildlife
FAMILY: Dogwood (Cornaceae)
REGION(S): 1, 3–5, 7

THE ROUGH LEAF DOGWOOD lives in the shadow of its popular cousin the flowering dogwood (p. 38), and it deserves more attention in its own right. It is pretty enough as a landscape specimen to inspire people to ask, "What is that tree?"

Named for the rough surfaces of the leaves, this dogwood flowers in late spring with small white blossoms in charming clusters about 3 inches across. Bunches of pretty white fruits, each berry about a quarter inch in diameter, attract at least forty species of birds. This feature alone makes the tree worth including in a landscape. While commonly a wood-edge dweller in nature, it can succeed well in full sun. Rough leaf dogwood usually develops a rather thick, shrubby form, making it ideal for shelterbelt plantings and large hedges. It occupies a wide range in Texas, growing in eastern, central, and southern parts of the state.

Like a number of other Texas plants, it borrows its species name from Thomas Drummond (ca. 1790–1835), a Scottish naturalist who made two voyages to America, one to the arctic region and one to the western and southern United States. In all, he collected an amazing 750 species of plants and 150 species of birds. He died in Havana, Cuba, while on a collecting expedition there.

OSAGE ORANGE

Maclura pomifera

LEAVES: Deciduous
HEIGHT: To 40 feet
GROWTH: Fast
VALUE: Heritage, landscape, wildlife
FAMILY: Mulberry (Moraceae)
REGION(S): 3, 4

**Warning:
Known poisonous
properties**

HE NAME *BOIS D'ARC* used by the French—pronounced "bodark" by Texans—means "wood of the bow." Early French explorers found that Native Americans, especially the Osage Indians of Arkansas and Oklahoma, greatly valued the wood of this tree for making bows. They traded it far and wide, and bodark wood has been found in archeological sites as far away as New York.

This unique member of the mulberry family once had a limited original range, primarily in Oklahoma, southwestern Arkansas, northwestern Louisiana, and in the Red River Valley of Texas. Stephen F. Austin's colonists spread the tree across his original grant, which was located near the western fringe of the Piney Woods. Today it grows throughout most of eastern and Central Texas, often as dense hedgerows, earning it the name hedge apple. Some people also call it horse apple.

The huge fruits borne by the female trees are inedible, even toxic, to humans, but squirrels and gallinaceous birds, such as quail, eat the seeds. The fruits have limited use as a cockroach repellent.

LEAVES: Deciduous

HEIGHT: To 50 feet

GROWTH: Moderate/fast

VALUE: Edible parts, heritage, shade, wildlife

FAMILY: Ebony (Ebenaceae)

REGION(S): 1, 3, 5, 7, 8

COUNTRY KIDS once played "ridin' 'simmon saplin's" by climbing to the top of a young persimmon and bending it so as to reach and switch over to another tree. Done right, this enabled them to swing like Tarzan from tree to tree without ever touching the ground.

This tough, supple species grows throughout East Texas and westward in scattered patches as far as the Panhandle. Along the western edge of the Piney Woods it poses a problem for farmers because it root-sprouts in large colonies.

Diospyros means "fruit of the gods" in Greek, and early Texas settlers once considered persimmons as good as manna from heaven. Today people leave the fruits for the wildlife. Until they ripen fully, persimmons are extremely astringent and pucker the mouth, but when mature, especially after the first frost, they taste wonderfully sugary. Much sweeter than the large oriental persimmons sold in grocery stores, these little morsels can be consumed right off the tree or added to puddings, cookies (appendix G), and cakes.

The trees are either male or female; female, fruiting specimens comprise the minority. Fortunately, persimmons are borne on relatively young trees. Birds, raccoons, opossums, deer, foxes, and squirrels eagerly devour them. People once valued the strong, fine-grained wood for shuttles, golf clubs, billiard cues, and spools.

BUTTON BUSH

Cephalanthus occidentalis

LEAVES: Deciduous
HEIGHT: To 15 feet
GROWTH: Fast
VALUE: Erosion control, heritage, medicinal, wildlife
FAMILY: Madder (Rubiaceae)
REGION(S): 1–10

Warning:
Known poisonous properties

THE RUBIACEAE FAMILY to which button bush belongs includes important crops such as coffee, quinine, and ipecac and popular ornamentals such as gardenia. Button bush's value lies in its ability to hold soil banks against erosion and in its crop of seed heads, which provide nourishment for at least twenty-five species of birds, especially mallards. The plant produces a substance called cephalanthin, formerly used to treat bronchial, skin, and venereal diseases and as a laxative and fever remedy. Used incorrectly, cephalanthin causes vomiting, convulsions, paralysis, and death.

This plant's ball-like bunches of nutlets develop from globular flower clusters that look like one-inch-diameter pincushions and that attract butterflies. The flowers bloom throughout the summer and inspire this plant's other common name, Spanish pincushion.

Button bush grows over major parts of North America. In Texas it thrives along shallow pond edges and sunny stream margins. It often forms small colonies in its wet habitat, and submerged parts of the plant provide shelter for the tiny invertebrates at the bottom of the food chain.

As its name implies, button bush is small, and some botanists would debate whether it warrants tree status. But its widespread occurrence, its value, its beauty, and its occasional 15 feet of woody trunk tipped the balance in favor of including it in this book.

Solanum erianthum

POTATO TREE

LEAVES: Evergreen
HEIGHT: To 30 feet
GROWTH: Fast
VALUE: Landscape, medicinal
FAMILY: Nightshade (Solanaceae)
REGION(S): 6

SOME PAGAN GROUPS promote potato tree, also called mullein, as a magical remedy supplying powerful protection against any "unwanted influences."

We cannot confirm this assertion, but potato tree, like potatoes and tomatoes, belongs to the nightshade family, which carries with it a host of mystical associations.

In Latin America, women find a more mundane use for the large, fuzzy leaves—as dish cloths. Others apply them as poultices for skin ulcers, boils, and headaches.

This little flat-topped resident of the Lower Rio Grande Valley, and of many tropical areas around the world, can grow to 30 feet with a 6-inch trunk. Its half-inch fruits, resembling the berries of its cousin the horse nettle (*Solanum carolinense*), might appear during any warm part of the year.

BLACK GUM

Nyssa sylvatica

LEAVES: Deciduous
HEIGHT: To 100 feet
GROWTH: Slow
VALUE: Heritage, landscape, wildlife
FAMILY: Tupelo (Nyssaceae)
REGION(S): 1–3

See color illustration, p. xiii

*O*LD BLACK GUMS often become hollow and sometimes host a wild honeybee hive and all its sweets. Pioneers took their cue from nature, cutting two-foot lengths of the trunks to construct their own beehives, which they called "gums." The cavities also offer valuable homes to tree-dwelling mammals, owls, and other birds.

The tree served Native Americans in two ways: it provided their favorite wood for making corn-pounding tools, since the wood imparts a sweet taste to the cornmeal when used in this way. Additionally, the tree supplied their best drums. Besides the trees often being hollow, the wood has good resonance.

Slow to grow, black gum, sometimes called black tupelo, nevertheless deserves a place in the landscape. The leaves, if they survive summer droughts, turn a brilliant red in early fall—probably the deepest red of any Texas tree. The branches, no matter what the size of the tree, tend to be thin, short, and crookedly horizontal. The half-inch-long, blue-black fruits make a litter under the tree in early fall, but more than thirty species of birds and other wildlife soon carry them away.

Though less common than many of the other hardwoods and pines of East Texas, black gum regularly appears scattered among them, usually in moist areas or bottomlands.

Nyssa aquatica

LEAVES: Deciduous
HEIGHT: To 100 feet
GROWTH: Fast
VALUE: Honey, wildlife, wood uses
FAMILY: Tupelo (Nyssaceae)
REGION(S): 1

FUNCTIONING SOMETHING like a tumbler doll, this tree's swollen, bulbous base keeps it upright in the soft mud and helps it to withstand the force of floodwaters. The root system also spreads widely, adding to the tree's stability.

Intense competition for sunlight limits water tupelo to a wet habitat where few other trees can survive; it grows in swamps and ponds across the South alongside bald cypress (p. 221) and a handful of other water-tolerant species. In Texas, this native inhabits only about eight counties of the state's southeastern corner.

Birds and other wildlife value the inch-long fruits, which look like miniature eggplants. The light but tough wood is useful for boxes, crates, and woodenware, and the small flowers provide a good honey source.

MOHR OAK

LEAVES: Evergreen
HEIGHT: To 20 feet
GROWTH: Slow
VALUE: Wildlife
FAMILY: Beech (Fagaceae)
REGION(S): 7, 8, 10

*A*RID LIMESTONE SOIL in the Trans-Pecos, South Plains, and western Edwards Plateau plays host to this variable little West Texas oak. Mohr oak hybridizes with several other oaks of the region, particularly with its close relative the gray oak (p. 87). Examine the leaves to distinguish the two: Mohr oak leaves appear leathery, blue-green, and shiny on top with wooly undersurfaces, although there is variation in its hybrids. The leaves of gray oak, which sport a fuzzy coat on both surfaces, look dusty.

Most often a thicketing, shrubby species, Mohr oak occasionally reaches 20 feet in height. Because of its diminutive size, it shares the names scrub oak and shin oak with several other trees. Its common and generic names commemorate pharmacist and botanist Dr. Karl "Charles" Theodor Mohr (1824–1901), who emigrated from Germany to become one of the foremost botanists in the United States. At the request of the U.S. Forest Service, he compiled the *Plant Life of Alabama*, one of fifty-five scientific works he published in his lifetime.

The wood of Mohr oak supplies good posts and firewood, and the tree is prolific enough to provide a significant boon to wildlife, offering cover, nest sites, and food

BLACK CHERRY

LEAVES: Deciduous
HEIGHT: To 50 feet
GROWTH: Fast
VALUE: Edible parts, heritage, landscape, wildlife, wood uses
FAMILY: Rose (Rosaceae)
REGION(S): 1, 3, 7, 10

**Warning:
Known poisonous properties**

$\mathcal{B}$LACK CHERRY and its varieties, escarpment black cherry (var. *eximia*) and southwestern choke cherry (var. *rufula*), enjoy a wide distribution across North America east of the Rockies, westward to Arizona, and southward into Mexico. Escarpment black cherry thrives in the heart of the Edwards Plateau. Choke cherry usually grows in mountainous areas above 4,000 feet, clinging to canyons, streamsides, and moist banks in the Trans-Pecos. Wherever it appears, black cherry typically takes the form of a fairly short-trunked tree with an open crown. Its gray bark displays distinctive horizontal striations and rings of lichen.

The spring flowers of this species, borne in delicate white racemes, give the tree an airy look as the new leaves emerge. The little black fruits are edible and sweet and attract numerous species of birds and small mammals. In the past, cooks converted these little cherries to wines, jellies, and pies, and they still provide flavoring in the form of extract. Despite the presence of cyanide in most parts of the tree, the bark is renowned for its historical use as an ingredient in cough medicines.

Black cherry wood, valued for furniture, cabinets, and fine woodwork, takes a beautiful polish.

SOUTHERN CRABAPPLE

Malus angustifolia

*R*ARE IN TEXAS, southern crabapple grows in Newton County and possibly in a few other locations in East Texas. This small tree's abundant deep pink buds burst forth into pale pink flowers in early spring and gradually fade to white. George Washington planted some of these trees at Mount Vernon and commented in his diary about their blossoms' delightful fragrance.

Pioneer orchardists employed this species as an understock for grafting cultivated varieties of apples imported from Europe, and settlers used the small, tart fruits to make cider and preserves. A number of birds, including quail, blue jays, cardinals, and prairie chickens eat them. Skunks, opossums, raccoons, rabbits, and foxes also relish them.

LEAVES: Deciduous
HEIGHT: To 30 feet
GROWTH: Moderate
VALUE: Edible parts, heritage, landscape, wildlife
FAMILY: Rose (Rosaceae)
REGION(S): 1

LEAVES: Deciduous
HEIGHT: To 25 feet
GROWTH: Moderate/fast
VALUE: Edible parts, landscape, wildlife
FAMILY: Rose (Rosaceae)
REGION(S): 1–5, 7

*C*LUSTERS OF CHERRY blossom–like flowers, initially white, then fading to pink, lend a storybook effect to the still-dormant woods of late winter. The blooms of Mexican plum compete for attention with those of eastern redbud (p. 127) and attract butterflies and swarms of hungry bees with their fragrance.

The tree also produces a plum, which you can eat raw, although it tastes better cooked or made into jelly. Native Americans sun-dried the fruits for winter consumption. Several species of birds and small mammals also enjoy them. Ripening in mid- to late summer, the pinkish red plums are relatively free from pests and blights and add to the tree's appeal as a landscape choice.

Though called Mexican plum, this tree probably occurs more often in Texas than in Mexico. It grows solitary in clearings, along fencerows, and at woodland edges from the eastern and central parts of the state to as far north as South Dakota. Though small, Mexican plum achieves tree status more often than most indigenous American plums, which usually remain dense shrubs.

GREEN HAWTHORN

Crataegus viridis

LEAVES: Deciduous
HEIGHT: To 35 feet
GROWTH: Slow
VALUE: Landscape, wildlife
FAMILY: Rose (Rosaceae)
REGION(S): 1–5, 7

*T*HIS TREE'S PROFUSION of delicate spring flowers qualifies it as one of the more handsome "haws." Bright red or orange pomes resembling tiny apples follow the dainty blossoms and add to this species' charm. The fruits of green hawthorn provide winter food for a number of birds, and the thick branches offer good cover and protection for nests. Its striking gray bark exfoliates to reveal a cinnamon underbark, and in fall the foliage turns a vivid scarlet.

Although it grows slowly, this tree's abundant good looks make it a worthwhile addition to any landscape. Winter King, a cultivar introduced on the market in recent years, has met with accolades. Its larger, shiny fruits put on an especially spectacu-lar show in northerly climates, where they persist well into winter to twinkle, bright red, beneath crisp caps of snow.

Green hawthorn is native to the eastern half of Texas as well as much of the eastern half of the United States. It can vary from a shrubby form to a tree of 35 feet in height and thrives in either acid or alkaline soil.

See color illustration, p. iv

S LIPPERY ELM OWES its name to a white, mucilaginous inner bark used for centuries by Native American healers to treat urinary tract infections, cold sores, and skin irritations. From 1820 to 1960, the *U.S. Pharmacopeia* listed it as a cough suppressant, pain reliever, and skin ointment. Today, it forms one of four ingredients in the herbal cancer remedy *Essiac.*

Pitchers also chewed this inner bark to apply the resulting slippery substance to their baseballs. But spitballs are no longer legal in the game.

The long, thin twigs of slippery elm once served as primitive tooth-brushes. By chewing the ends, you can get them to fray and flare out into little brushes. Today, people value its wood, like that of American elm (p. 52), for posts, ties, veneer, boats, furniture, and tool handles.

This species grows rapidly and makes a fine shade tree throughout the northeast quadrant of the state and into Central Texas. It develops a broad, open crown. A number of herbivorous mammals browse the rough, sandpapery foliage, and some birds eat the tiny seeds, known as samaras.

LEAVES: Deciduous
HEIGHT: To 70 feet
GROWTH: Fast
VALUE: Heritage, medicinal, shade, wildlife, wood uses
FAMILY: Elm (Ulmaceae)
REGION(S): 1, 3–5, 7

LEAVES: Deciduous
HEIGHT: To 100 feet
GROWTH: Fast
VALUE: Heritage, shade, wildlife
FAMILY: Elm (Ulmaceae)
REGION(S): 1–8

*A*MERICAN ELM grows over the eastern half of the United States from the Gulf states north into Canada. Always beloved as a street tree in the Northeast, it has been decimated there by Dutch Elm disease. In Texas, the disease does not pose a major problem, and the tree thrives in North, Central, East, and parts of South Texas.

This species develops a classical vase form when it grows in the open. In the woods, it may take a leaning shape as it seeks the sunlight. Both its vase form and the absence of corky "wings" on its twigs help to distinguish this tree from winged elm (p. 54). The asymmetrical bases of the leaves differentiate elms from similar looking trees, such as American hornbeam (p. 56) and wooly hop hornbeam. American elm prefers moist sites and commonly makes its home in stream bottoms and on other flat terrain.

Elm wood once boasted multiple uses, such as for barrel staves, wheel hubs, yokes, boats, toys, agricultural implements, and baskets. Native Americans employed the inner bark to make strong cordage. Anyone who tries to break an elm branch will be impressed with its toughness and resilience.

Deer, opossums, and rabbits browse the twigs and foliage, and squirrels also nibble on them. Numerous birds eat the tiny fruits, or samaras, which the tree bears in early spring. The leaves turn a lively, clear yellow in autumn.

LEAVES: Deciduous
HEIGHT: To 100 feet
GROWTH: Fast
VALUE: Edible parts, lumber, shade, wildlife
FAMILY: Beech (Fagaceae)
REGION(S): 1

*B*EECH TREES HAVE A lengthy historical relationship with the written word. The German term Buchstabe literally translates as "beech stave," dates back at least eighteen centuries to runic times, and means "letter of the alphabet." Beech also features prominently in the poet Virgil's *Eclogues* as a symbol of protection. Still today, the tree's smooth, gray bark invites the sentimental and harmful carvings of thoughtless people.

The beautiful, big American beech, with its lustrous, dense foliage, puts on a good show of orange-yellow color in autumn. It bears copious quantities of tasty little beechnuts that are gathered commercially in the Northeast. These lent both their name and their flavor to the once-famous Beechnut gum. Deer, raccoons, opossums, and other mammals relish them, as do many birds. Wood uses include charcoal, handles, furniture, musical instruments, toys, and crates.

American beech grows over much of the eastern United States and reaches its southwestern-most natural occurrence in East Texas. This tree defines the Upper Thicket portion of the Big Thicket National Preserve.

WINGED ELM

Ulmus alata

WIDE, CORKY "WINGS" on its twigs give winged elm its moniker. Some individuals display this feature conspicuously while others show little or none of it. Where the wings are obscure or absent, people have difficulty distinguishing the tree from American elm (p. 52). But whereas American elm tends toward a classical vase shape, with open, spreading limbs, winged elm presents a disheveled tangle of twigs and minor branches. The leaves of winged elm also look somewhat smaller and narrower than those of its more majestic cousin.

People sometimes confuse winged elm with cedar elm (p. 86) as well. But winged elm has smooth, pointed leaves and bears flowers and fruits in the spring. Cedar elm has rough, blunt leaves and blooms and bears fruit in the fall. Winged elm is an upland plant, while cedar elm prefers wetter sites.

The fast-growing winged elm makes a good street or shade tree, but it seldom attains more than 40 feet in height. The fruits are typical samaras: tiny kernels surrounded by small flat wings. Squirrels and a number of birds eat them.

The hard wood of winged elm proves useful for tool handles and furniture. People once employed the bark to make baling twine.

LEAVES: Deciduous
HEIGHT: To 40 feet
GROWTH: Fast
VALUE: Shade, wildlife, wood uses
FAMILY: Elm (Ulmaceae)
REGION(S): 1–5

CHINESE ELM

LEAVES: Deciduous
HEIGHT: To 40 feet
GROWTH: Fast
VALUE: Landscape, shade
FAMILY: Elm (Ulmacea)
REGION(S): Non-native

*T*HIS GRACEFUL ASIAN TREE, planted widely across Texas for its delicate good looks, escapes cultivation in many places. It develops a slightly pendulous form and attractive gray-brown bark, which exfoliates to reveal a peachy inner bark. This gives it an intricate, mottled appearance and earns it the nickname lace bark elm. These features, together with its petite leaves and supple roots, also place Chinese elm among the recommended species for bonsai.

The tree produces small, winged fruits called samaras by the thousands when the leaves begin to fall, and together with the leaves, these create considerable litter in a landscape setting. The seeds, like those of other elms, sprout readily in flowerbeds and gardens.

While it can grow to 40 feet or more, Chinese elm usually tops out at about 30 feet. Its spreading branches offer pleasant shade.

AMERICAN HORNBEAM *Carpinus caroliniana*

LEAVES: Deciduous
HEIGHT: To 30 feet
GROWTH: Slow
VALUE: Landscape, wildlife, wood uses
FAMILY: Birch (Betulaceae)
REGION(S): 1–3

*T*HIS COMPACT, muscular looking tree holds its own in the floodplains and moist woods throughout East Texas. Readily recognizable by its fluted, sinewy trunk, it often takes a leaning, angular form as it strains to reach for light through the dense forest undergrowth.

Another common name, ironwood, pays tribute to the tree's hard, heavy wood, valued for implements that must withstand stress. Also called blue beech, it is neither blue nor a beech, but perhaps this name refers to the gray tint of its smooth bark, which resembles that of American beech (p. 53). In this regard, American hornbeam differs from wooly hop hornbeam (p. 57), which has a darker, rough-textured trunk.

American hornbeam displays good fall color in the amber-to-orange range, and though it grows slowly, it supplies an appealing landscape feature where a small tree is desired. The leaves, while they resemble those of elms (pp. 51, 52, 54, 55), appear more elongated, and unlike elm leaves, they commonly have symmetrical bases. Several species of birds eat the fruits, borne in pendulous clusters of bracts.

Ostrya virginiana

WOOLY HOP HORNBEAM

THIS UNDERSTORY TREE of East Texas forests gets the name "wooly" from its bark, which breaks into small, shredded scales up and down the trunk as the tree matures; the bark of young hop hornbeam looks very different, appearing smooth and gray with horizontal striations like the bark of black cherry (p. 47). "Hop" refers to the fruiting structures, the clusters of papery sacs resembling the hops used in brewing beer. "Hornbeam" alludes to the wood's former service in ox yokes.

Like American hornbeam (p.56), this tree belongs to the birch family. Both trees answer to the name ironwood because of their hard wood, which served as wagon wheel spokes, axles, tool handles, posts, and mallets.

Wooly hop hornbeam can be distinguished from American hornbeam by its brownish, textured bark; the bark of American hornbeam looks smooth and gray. People also tend to confuse hop hornbeam with American elm (p. 52) and winged elm (p. 54) because of the similarity of their leaves. Elm leaves, however, commonly have asymmetrical bases.

Hop hornbeam's rather small stature and lightly drooping branches lend it an attractive aspect, but it grows slowly, and people rarely plant it in landscapes. A number of birds eat the seeds, and the cover this tree provides makes it a good nesting place.

LEAVES: Deciduous
HEIGHT: To 30 feet
GROWTH: Slow
VALUE: Wildlife, wood uses
FAMILY: Birch (Betulaceae)
REGION(S): 1, 3

TWO WING SILVER BELL

Halesia diptera

LEAVES: Deciduous
HEIGHT: To 20 feet
GROWTH: Moderate/fast
VALUE: Landscape, wildlife
FAMILY: Storax (Styracaceae)
REGION(S): 1, 2

*T*HE BLOSSOMS of silver bell, borne in March, develop in small, loose clusters, each flower a perfect white bell about the size of a quarter across its mouth. The stamens form petite yellow clappers.

Dangling fruits, about one inch long with two thin "wings," form after the flowers fade. Squirrels eat these fruits, and travelers once rolled them in their mouths as an acidic thirst quencher.

Silver bell, also called American silverbell and snowdrop tree, enjoys popularity in European landscapes, but perhaps because of its lamentably short, two-week bloom period, people rarely plant it in the United States. In nature, it occurs as an understory or wood-edge species of the East Texas Piney Woods and across the American South.

CAROLINA SILVER BELL

LEAVES: Deciduous
HEIGHT: To 30 feet
GROWTH: Fast
VALUE: Landscape
FAMILY: Storax (Styracaceae)
REGION(S): 1, 2

A close relative of the much more common two wing silver bell, Carolina silver bell occurs only rarely in East Texas. From there, however, its habitat cuts a wide swath all the way to the Atlantic Coast and as far north as Illinois. It thrives in rich, well-drained soil and sheltered locations, such as wood edges, where it can grow to 30 feet or more, usually with an irregular crown.

Carolina silver bell's flowers appear more closed than those of its cousin. The four distinct wings on its fruits further distinguish it. This beautiful flowering tree's more regular form, larger range, and longer bloom period have earned it a place in landscapes: since the mid-1700s, people in both the United States and Europe have cultivated it for its beauty.

SWAMP PRIVET

Forestiera acuminata

AMED IN HONOR of the seventeenth-century French physician and botanist Charles Le Forestier, this unassuming tree grows sparsely scattered throughout swamps and wet places in East Texas and along the central coast. It also occurs north to Illinois and across the southeastern United States, and presents some landscape potential in wet areas.

Swamp privet, which is unrelated to Chinese privet (p. 66), can grow to 25 feet or more and usually develops several trunks. The opposite leaves look yellowish green and grow 2 to 4 inches long. This otherwise obscure little tree becomes showy in spring when male and female blossoms appear on separate individuals before the leaves emerge. The yellow male flowers grow in frilly clusters, and the female blooms develop into 1-inch blue-black fruits. Wild ducks, which eat these fruits, probably serve as the tree's main distributor.

LEAVES: Deciduous
HEIGHT: To 25 feet
GROWTH: Fast
VALUE: Landscape, wildlife
FAMILY: Olive (Oleaceae)
REGION(S): 1-3

LEAVES: Evergreen
HEIGHT: To 15 feet
GROWTH: Fast
VALUE: Landscape, wildlife
FAMILY: Flacourtia (Flacourtiaceae)
REGION(S): 6

*C*ALLED *CORONILLO* and *manzanillo* in its native Mexico, *Xylosma flexuosa* (right), originally occupied a single county in Texas— Cameron County in the Lower Rio Grande Valley. People have also planted it in South Texas landscapes for many years.

Florists across Texas and elsewhere once valued *Xylosma congestum,* a species native to China, for cuttings to use in bouquets, since the dark green leaves last well and lend a good contrast to flowers. Its popularity for this purpose has waned in recent years, but the plant apparently escaped cultivation and now emerges here and there in woods as far north as Houston (left).

This evergreen tree may attain a shrubby form to 15 feet. The twigs and branches sport slender spines at the leaf nodes, and some trunks come armed with long, impressive thorns. Xylosma provides good nesting sites and winter cover for birds.

CHINKAPIN OAK

Quercus muhlenbergii

LEAVES: Deciduous
HEIGHT: To 50 feet
GROWTH: Fast
VALUE: Heritage, shade, wildlife
FAMILY: Beech (Fagaceae)
REGION(S): 3–5, 7

*T*HIS TREE IS NOT A chinquapin (p. 63), but it sure looks like one. Both trees belong to the beech family, their leaves resemble each other, and even their common names sound alike. Fortunately the fruits differ vastly, the chinkapin oak bearing acorns and the Allegheny chinquapin producing small chestnuts. They also do not share the same range, and confusion is therefore unlikely.

The rapidly growing chinkapin oak, with oblong leaves notched in a saw-edged manner, belongs to the white oak group. Uncommon in this state, it appears only in scattered spots from northeast to Central Texas and in a few places in the Trans-Pecos. This tree usually grows in well-drained soil and more upland locations than its cousin the swamp chestnut oak (p. 92).

The durable wood of the chinkapin oak supplies fence posts, railroad ties, paneling, and lumber. The fairly large acorns comprised a staple of the Native American diet, and deer, small mammals, and even some birds eat them.

This tree's species name memorializes Pennsylvania-German minister and pioneer botanist Gotthilf Heinrich Ernst Muhlenberg (1753–1815). Publisher of books and member of numerous scientific societies, Muhlenberg received the honor of having numerous plant species and even a genus named for him.

Castanea pumila

ALLEGHENY CHINQUAPIN

THE TASTY NUTS OF THIS TREE are enclosed in spiny burs, which discourage people from gathering them. Children once used them to play "hully-gull," a game in which they would try to guess how many kernels were held in another child's closed hand. Guessing right would earn a fistful of nuts, but a wrong guess meant losing your own hard-won supply.

A tree of deep East Texas, Allegheny chinquapin occurs no farther west than about Montgomery County. It can grow to 50 feet but usually remains much smaller in stature, with heavy branches forming low on the trunk. The pretty, bright green leaves, up to 6 inches long, are noteworthy for their saw-toothed edges. Unfortunately, the blight that eradicated the related American chestnut (*Castanea dentata*) is slowly diminishing the chinquapin as well.

Chinquapin wood, with its attractive white and brown contrasts, proves ideal for small woodworking projects. Many birds and mammals relish the nuts, and the tree possesses ornamental possibilities.

LEAVES: Deciduous
HEIGHT: To 50 feet
GROWTH: Fast
VALUE: Edible parts, heritage, wildlife, wood uses
FAMILY: Beech (Fagaceae)
REGION(S): 1

CRAPEMYRTLE

Lagerstroemia indica

LEAVES: Deciduous
HEIGHT: To 35 feet
GROWTH: Slow
VALUE: Heritage, landscape
FAMILY: Loosestrife (Lythraceae)
REGION(S): Non-native

SOMETIMES CALLED THE lilac of the South, the crapemyrtle originated in Asia, where gardeners have cultivated it since time immemorial. During the T'ang Dynasty (A.D. 618–906), it graced the palace gardens of the Chinese emperors. Sometime around the middle of the seventeenth century, sailors of the Dutch East India Company introduced it to Europe when they carried specimens back on merchant ships. By 1759, crapemyrtle was featured at what are now the Royal Botanic Gardens at Kew, west of London, and soon afterward it found its way to colonial America.

Beautiful both for its flowers and for smooth, exfoliating trunks in shades of pink, gray, and green, it is available in many colorful horticultural forms and dwarf varieties.

Crapemyrtle does not naturalize in Texas, but it persists for generations of human lives. Even when the trunks die back, it often sprouts again from the roots. For this reason, it makes a great indicator tree: if you come across a crapemyrtle in the woods or in a field, you can be sure someone planted it there. Most likely you have stumbled upon an old homestead, the crapemyrtle being the only obvious sign that someone once lived there.

In sun or shade, good years and bad, this old "live forever tree" has managed to survive to tell tales of someone else's admiration for its beauty.

Ehretia anacua

ANAQUA

A NICE, ROUNDED SHADE tree, anaqua ("ah*nah*kwah") exhibits some unique features: it blooms in late fall or in winter as well as in early spring. The fragrant white flower clusters precede multitudes of quarter-inch yellow-to-red fruits that prompted German settlers in the area to dub the tree *Vogelbeerbaum*— literally "bird berry tree"—after the similar but unrelated European native rowan (*Sorbus aucuparia*). The copious red fruits of both attract vast numbers of birds and small mammals.

The leaves' distinctive rough texture led to another common name: sandpaper tree. The tough wood formerly provided yokes, spokes, wheels, and tool handles.

"Knockaway" is native in this country only in Texas, but its range extends into northern and eastern Mexico. In this state, it grows southward from around Austin, over to Victoria, and down the coast to the Rio Grande Valley.

LEAVES: Semi-evergreen
HEIGHT: To 50 feet
GROWTH: Fast
VALUE: Landscape, shade, wildlife
FAMILY: Borage (Boraginaceae)
REGION(S): 2–4, 6

CHINESE PRIVET

Ligustrum sinense

*T*HE SPECIES name *sinense* confirms the Chinese origin of this plant; however, privet was introduced to the United States via England, where it has been cultivated for centuries for its rich, dense foliage. No English manor house could be considered suitable without a neatly trimmed privet hedge to invite the occasional caller to stroll its gardens or explore its extensive grounds. Trimmed into various shapes sometimes geometric, sometimes whimsical—the English privet hedge properly earns admiration as a living sculpture.

In the United States, we plant privet for its ornamental foliage and its clusters of white spring flowers. The blue berries, which prove purgative to humans, are popular with birds, and the thick growth invites nesting in it. Privet naturalized readily in the South and now appears as a common feature in East Texas. The plant grows as a bushy shrub in the open, but in the woods it can become a single-trunked tree to about 20 feet. Unfortunately, it has become invasive, displacing native species and posing a serious threat to biodiversity in many places. We do not recommend planting this tree.

LEAVES: Semi-evergreen
HEIGHT: To 20 feet
GROWTH: Fast
VALUE: Landscape, wildlife
FAMILY: Olive (Oleaceae)
REGION(S): Non-native

**Warning:
Invasive species, known
poisonous properties**

LEAVES: Semi-evergreen
HEIGHT: To 25 feet
GROWTH: Slow
VALUE: Landscape, wildlife
FAMILY: Heath (Ericaceae)
REGION(S): 1–3

*M*OST HUCKLEBERRIES are small bushes, but this one, as the name *arboreum* implies, grows into a handsome tree with a crooked, gnarled trunk and shiny leaves. Sometimes called sparkleberry, this slow-growing species produces its small, urn-shaped, white flowers and dark fruits at a fairly young age.

Farkleberry somewhat resembles yaupon (p. 82); however, you can distinguish yaupon by the serrations on its leaf edges and by its red berries. The leaf edges of the farkleberry are smooth. Its blue-black fruits, though edible, taste dry and seedy.

Native Americans once concocted a diarrhea remedy using an extract from the root bark. The bark also yields tannic acid for tanning leather.

From near Corpus Christi to Bastrop, farkleberry grows eastward across most of East Texas. Native plant lovers cultivate it in increasing numbers for its own beauty and because so many birds relish the little fruits.

TOBACCO TREE

Nicotiana glauca

LEAVES: Evergreen
HEIGHT: To 20 feet
GROWTH: Fast
VALUE: Landscape
FAMILY: Nightshade (Solanaceae)
REGION(S): Non-native

*T*HE FRENCH AMBASSADOR to Portugal, Jean Nicot (1530–1600), sent tobacco seeds to Paris in 1561 and received the dubious honor of having the genus and the addictive substance *nicotine* named for him. Tobacco tree belongs to the same genus as the cultivated tobacco plant, *Nicotiana tabacum.* Both form part of the nightshade family, which includes tomatoes, potatoes, peppers, and belladonna.

This interesting little tree, with its slender, weak stems and tubular yellow flowers, can be grown from seed, and people in warm countries the world over plant this Argentine native as an ornamental. In the United States, gardeners cultivate tobacco tree from Florida across southern Texas to California. It frequently naturalizes throughout that range, often appearing on gravel bars in watercourses.

The large leaves serve as poultices for headaches, but they prove toxic if ingested. Do not smoke them!

Warning:
Known poisonous properties

Arbutus xalapensis

TEXAS MADRONE

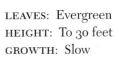

LEAVES: Evergreen
HEIGHT: To 30 feet
GROWTH: Slow
VALUE: Dye, edible parts, medicinal, landscape, wildlife
FAMILY: Heath (Ericaceae)
REGION(S): 7, 9, 10

CONSIDERED BY MANY people to be one of the state's most beautiful trees, the Texas madrone's main distinction lies in its peeling bark, which reveals a smooth trunk in colors of tan, salmon pink, or reddish brown. This fleshy display led to the tree's other aliases, lady's legs and naked Indian. Its leaning habit and dramatically crooked branches serve to enhance the striking feature of evoking a human figure.

Found in nature in some western areas of the Edwards Plateau as well as in the Big Bend region and other parts of the Trans-Pecos, this madrone has a range extending into southeastern New Mexico and southward as far as Guatemala.

Clusters of small white flowers appear in early spring and fade to leave behind pretty orange or bright red berries that rival the pomes of the best hawthorn. A number of birds consume these berries, which are also edible to humans. Madrone's hard, tough wood has been employed for tool handles and charcoal. The bark and leaves produce orange and yellow dyes, and settlers once used the tree medicinally to treat diseases of the urinary tract organs.

AMERICAN SMOKE TREE

Cotinus obovatus

LEAVES: Deciduous
HEIGHT: To 25 feet
GROWTH: Slow
VALUE: Dye, landscape, wildlife
FAMILY: Sumac (Anacardiaceae)
REGION(S): 7

AMERICAN Smoke Tree obtained its name not from its airy greenish spring blossoms but from the hazy-appearing "hairs" attached to the flower stalks of spent blooms. These combine to form pink or hot-pink puffs of "smoke" rising from the tree. Squirrels nibble at the tiny purple drupes that follow. Spring leaves emerge bronze to amethyst and turn an interesting shade of blue-green. But American smoke tree displays its most brilliant colors in fall, when the leaves change to vibrant shades of yellow, orange, red, and maroon, often on the same tree. This species could provide an interesting addition to home landscapes, and some nurseries now offer it for sale.

Also called chittamwood, this rather rare species consists of only scattered populations in Missouri, Arkansas, Alabama, Tennessee, Oklahoma, and Texas. In Texas, it occurs in just five counties—Uvalde, Bandera, Kerr, Kendall, and Blanco—a separation of more than 500 miles from the nearest sister population in Oklahoma. Another member of the genus *Cotinus* is the European smoke tree, *Cotinus coggygria,* which homeowners often plant in the northern states.

A yellow dye was an important past product of this small tree, and its durable wood was used for fence posts.

CAROLINA BUCKTHORN

LEAVES: Deciduous
HEIGHT: To 25 feet
GROWTH: Fast
VALUE: Landscape, wildlife
FAMILY: Buckthorn (Rhamnaceae)
REGION(S): 1–5, 7

*T*HE DARK GREEN LEAVES of this tree, with their distinctive pinnate veins showing on the upper surfaces, accompany fruits about one third of an inch in diameter, which turn pink, then red, and then black in the maturing process. These inspired the tree's other nickname, Indian cherry. The berries stay on the tree until October and attract many species of birds. This plant deserves cultivating both for its ornamental values and for its importance to wildlife.

Carolina buckthorn grows across most of the eastern United States, including East Texas, the Dallas–North Texas area, and here and there around the Edwards Plateau. This versatile small tree with interesting foliage and fruits adapts to many soil types.

ANACAHUITA

Cordia boissieri

LEAVES: Evergreen
HEIGHT: To 25 feet
GROWTH: Fast
VALUE: Edible parts, landscape, wildlife
FAMILY: Borage (Boraginaceae)
REGION(S): 6

ANACAHUITA ("ahnahcah*wee*tah") explodes into bloom in late spring, sporting crisp white hibiscus-like flowers with yellow throats. Somewhat reminiscent of the twirling skirts of Mexican *folklorico* dance costumes, they enliven the landscape intermittently throughout the long South Texas summer, especially after rain showers. The off-white, olive-shaped fruits grow to about 1 inch long and are edible, although eating more than one or two may cause dizziness. Birds, mammals, and livestock relish these fruits, and goats even climb up the tree limbs to reach them. Although sometimes called Texas olive or wild olive, anacahuita is not an olive at all; rather it belongs to the borage family, which includes forget-me-not (*Myosotis asiatica*).

This showy small tree of the Lower Rio Grande Valley and Mexico can survive northward to San Antonio and Houston but will freeze back in cold winters. Because it can endure heat and drought, it makes an excellent landscape object on a protected patio or against a south-facing wall.

Anacahuita takes its species name from noted French botanist Pierre-Edmond Boissier (1810–85).

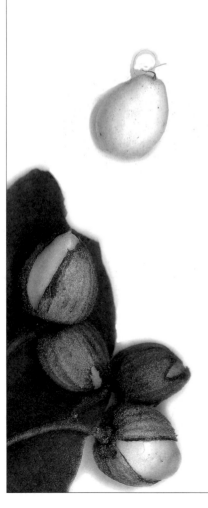

LEAVES: Semi-evergreen
HEIGHT: To 80 feet
GROWTH: Fast
VALUE: Culinary, landscape, perfume
FAMILY: Magnolia (Magnoliaceae)
REGION(S): 1

*T*HE GENUS NAME *Magnolia* honors Pierre Magnol (1638–1715), professor of botany and medicine and director of the botanic garden at Montpellier, France. This species' common names are too numerous to list here, but one of its more popular designations, white bay, pays tribute to the bright white undersides of its baylike leaves, which aid identification. Its moisture-loving character earned it another common title: swamp bay.

The flowers of sweet bay magnolia, though much smaller than those of southern magnolia (pp. 74–75), exude such a pleasant fragrance that manufacturers sometimes use them as an ingredient in making perfumes. The leaves have been used to flavor meats, but because some botanists suspect them of being somewhat toxic, we recommend the use of red bay (p. 6) instead.

Sweet bay magnolia grows from Long Island south to Florida and west to Texas, where it inhabits the Big Thicket and most of southeast Texas. It has a slender trunk and erect habit and usually attains 40 or 50 feet in height, though it can achieve 80 feet in special situations.

SOUTHERN MAGNOLIA

SOUTHERN MAGNOLIA

LEAVES: Evergreen
HEIGHT: To 100 feet
GROWTH: Slow
VALUE: Landscape, wildlife
FAMILY: Magnolia (Magnoliaceae)
REGION(S): 1

A PARAMOUNT SYMBOL of the South, this magnolia extends its native habitat into the southern two thirds of East Texas. But because of its beauty, people often plant it elsewhere, including in Europe, and some consider it the world's most beautiful flowering tree.

Its leathery, evergreen leaves appear glossy and dark green on top with rusty velvet undersides. In May, huge, fragrant blossoms with creamy white petals give way to russet colored cones. These expel bright red seeds, dangling precariously on tiny crimson threads. Squirrels and several species of birds eat the seeds.

Magnolias grown in an open area take a pyramidal form with low branches that may hide the trunk entirely. In the woods, however, the tree twists and leans to reach the light, and nothing rivals the character of an ancient magnolia. Many old magnolias become hollow, providing homes for raccoons, opossums, and squirrels.

In winter, when other trees go bare, southern magnolia reveals itself to be common in southeast Texas forests, usually inhabiting rich floodplain soil.

LEAVES: Evergreen
HEIGHT: To 50 feet
GROWTH: Slow
VALUE: Heritage, lumber, shade, wildlife
FAMILY: Beech (Fagaceae)
REGION(S): 2–7

*P*LATEAU LIVE OAK has rooted itself as deeply in the history and culture of Central Texas as it has in the dry limestone soil of the region. More than 100 years ago, German settlers in the area built sturdy houses from alternating layers of square-hewn live oak beams and limestone blocks. You can still see many of those homes today in Fredericksburg and neighboring towns. The walls, often two or three feet thick, were made to last, to fend off Comanche raids, and to insulate the inhabitants from heat and cold.

Botanists once considered plateau live oak a varietal form of the better known live oak (p. 77). Today science assigns it a classification of its own. Together with Ashe juniper (p. 213), it rules the Hill Country, and these two species form more than half of the large vegetation seen in parts of the area. This vital tree slowly develops its dark, furrowed trunks into pillars of the plateau.

Plateau live oaks often bear masses of ball moss on their horizontal branches. Ball moss is an epiphyte, not a parasite, and does not take its nutrients from the tree. However, it does some damage to the bark where it attaches itself.

Quercus virginiana

LIVE OAK

LEAVES: Evergreen
HEIGHT: To 50 feet
GROWTH: Slow
VALUE: Heritage, shade, wildlife
FAMILY: Beech (Fagaceae)
REGION(S): 2–4, 6, 7

WHAT IMAGE OF THE OLD South would be complete without a plantation house at the end of an avenue lined with majestic live oaks draped in Spanish moss? A great character tree of the Gulf and South Atlantic coasts, live oak succeeds in the open coastal plain and thrives in rather salty soil. It is not adapted to forests, because it cannot compete with fast-growing pines and hardwoods for light. Early settlers recognized its ability to withstand storms, however, and planted it around many homesteads. Today, live oak trees surround almost every courthouse in the milder

parts of Texas. When you find a live oak tree in the Piney Woods or far beyond the coastal region, you will know that a person probably planted it there.

This tree seldom grows to more than 50 feet in height, but it can have a crown spread twice that wide. Its massive limbs branch out low and sometimes even rest on the ground. Live oak also reaches a great age. The oldest tree in Texas is reputed to be a coastal live oak growing near Fulton. Botanists estimate it at more than 1,000 years old. Think how many hurricanes a tree like that has endured.

In the past, shipbuilders frequently used the stout wood of live oak for their vessels. The oldest war ship of the United States Navy, the historic USS *Constitution,* was built of live oak timbers. A boon to wildlife, this tree bears a profuse crop of acorns that feeds many birds and mammals.

The Spanish moss that makes its home in live oak branches is neither Spanish nor moss, and it is an epiphyte, not a parasite; it does not take nutrients from the tree. Spanish moss is a bromeliad, a close relative of the pineapple.

SMOOTH ALDER

Alnus serrulata

LEAVES: Deciduous
HEIGHT: To 20 feet
GROWTH: Fast
VALUE: Erosion control, heritage, landscape, wildlife
FAMILY: Birch (Betulaceae)
REGION(S): 1

SMOOTH ALDER, also called hazel alder, grows over most of East Texas, usually in thicketing clumps along streams and lakesides. Its native habitat extends north to Minnesota and east to the Atlantic states. This attractive species could be planted more often in landscapes, along ponds or pool margins.

Pretty, glossy leaves, multiple trunks, and little seed structures resembling tiny pine cones characterize this tree. Hobby shops often sell the "cones" as craft items, and jewelry stores occasionally offer them, gold-plated, as pendants or earrings. Some birds eat the alder seeds.

Historically, various parts of the plant have found medicinal uses for anything from syphilis to eye irritations. The plant also serves as a great erosion control species, and the roots host nitrogen-fixing bacteria, a characteristic usually associated with legumes.

Betula nigra

LEAVES: Deciduous
HEIGHT: To 90 feet
GROWTH: Moderate/fast
VALUE: Erosion control, heritage, landscape, wildlife
FAMILY: Birch (Betulaceae)
REGION(S): 1, 3

*P*IONEERS ONCE TAPPED this birch in spring for its sweet sap, just as maple farmers in the North tap sugar maple (*Acer saccharum*) today. Birch beer also quenched the thirst of early settlers, and nothing kept discipline more efficiently in the old one-room schoolhouse than the sting of a fresh birch "rod."

In recent years, river birch has gained popularity in both home and commercial landscapes because of its papery, dramatically peeling bark and graceful form. Although it can grow as high as 90 feet, it normally reaches a modest 20 to 40 feet.

Most birches are northern trees. This southern birch is the only one found in Texas. Common in the Piney Woods region along creeks and rivers, it usually grows just up the bank from black willow (p. 11). River birch provides excellent erosion control, spreading its fine rootlets along the sandy banks.

A number of birds eat the tiny seeds, and campers should know that the bark makes good tinder, wet or dry.

TEXAS CRABAPPLE

Malus ioensis var. *texana*

LEAVES: Deciduous
HEIGHT: To 30 feet
GROWTH: Moderate/fast
VALUE: Edible parts, landscape, wildlife
FAMILY: Rose (Rosaceae)
REGION(S): 7

ONLY FIVE COUNTIES in Central Texas can claim Texas crabapple as a resident. A variety of the prairie crabapple that grows from Texas northward to Minnesota, Texas crabapple is restricted to Blanco, Gillespie, Kendall, Bexar, and Comal Counties.

This highly ornamental tree should be planted more often for both aesthetic and ecological reasons. Its soft, pale pink spring flowers resemble those of southern crabapple (p. 48) and exude a wonderful fragrance. Though the little apples taste so sour as to "crab up" the mouth, they present a boon to wildlife. Foxes, squirrels, skunks, rabbits, deer, opossums, raccoons, and even some birds eat them. People, too, can enjoy them in the form of jellies and vinegars.

Viburnum rufidulum **RUSTY BLACKHAW VIBURNUM**

LEAVES: Deciduous
HEIGHT: To 25 feet
GROWTH: Slow
VALUE: Heritage, landscape, wildlife
FAMILY: Honeysuckle (Caprifoliaceae)
REGION(S): 1–5, 7, 10

RUSTY BLACKHAW viburnum's high-gloss leaves, creamy flower clusters in spring, and blue-black fruits, so abundant that the branches sometimes droop under their weight, make it distinctive and worthy of a place in the landscape. Rusty red fuzz covers the leaf buds and young shoots and appears in patches on the leaf stems and along the major veins on the undersides of the leaves. The foliage turns dark red in fall.

This small tree grows throughout East and most of Central Texas. Nurseries cultivate many viburnums from the Orient and several that are Texas natives, including arrowwood viburnum (*Viburnum dentatum*) and mapleleaf viburnum (*Viburnum acerifolium*). However, rusty blackhaw viburnum represents the only Texas native regularly attaining tree status.

Foxes, deer, and a number of birds eat the fruits. Records show that the bark was once used medicinally for "female problems" and as an anti-spasmodic, but its value in that regard is now in doubt.

YAUPON HOLLY

Ilex vomitoria

LEAVES: Evergreen
HEIGHT: To 25 feet
GROWTH: Fast
VALUE: Edible parts, heritage, landscape, wildlife
FAMILY: Holly (Aquifoliaceae)
REGION(S): 1–4

CABEZA DE VACA lived among the Karankawa Indians of East Texas for nearly six years (1528–34) and observed their *mitotes*, or ritual cleansing ceremonies. After returning to Spain, he wrote *La Relación*, a lengthy account translated as *Adventures in the Unknown Interior of America*, in which he describes how the Indians made a "black drink" of the leaves of the yaupon ("*yoh*pon") tree. For three days and nights, the Indians sang and danced around their campfire, consuming nothing but about five gallons of the tea each day. This made them high, and sick, which was their intent; it was after all a purging ceremony. Their use of yaupon leaves resulted in the species name *vomitoria*.

Actually, the leaves of yaupon contain nothing worse than caffeine and can be made into a pleasant, mildly stimulating drink without adverse side effects. (Ordinary commercial teas used the same way would bring about similar results.) In making yaupon tea (appendix G), however, do not mistake Chinese privet (p. 66) for yaupon, or the effect will be far worse than "cleansing!"

Yaupon is the most common understory tree of East Texas and grows westward to the Edwards Plateau and southward along the coast to Matagorda Bay. In the open, it becomes a thick bush, but in the woods it grows into a small tree, often with several trunks.

Its evergreen leaves and the bright red berries on female trees make yaupon a popular landscape plant that can be pruned and shaped into various forms. Nurseries also offer horticultural dwarf and weeping varieties. In fields, cattle browse yaupon as high as they can reach, sculpting the plants into whimsical mushroom shapes. The berries provide important winter food for birds.

See color illustration, p. xvii

LEAVES: Evergreen
HEIGHT: To 20 feet
GROWTH: Slow
VALUE: Edible parts, heritage, honey, wildlife
FAMILY: Elm (Ulmaceae)
REGION(S): 6, 7, 10

*T*HIS DEMURE CITIZEN of the South Texas brush country extends its range west to Arizona and south through much of Mexico. Its spiny branches zigzag up to attain a height of barely 20 feet. It occurs frequently in the Lower Rio Grande Valley, and the small town of Granjeno ("grahn*hay*no") in Hidalgo County is named for this little tree.

Numerous bird species, including the green jay, pyrrhuloxia, cactus wren, and scaled quail, eagerly eat the sweet, bright orange drupes of granjeno. Raccoons, deer, and rabbits also relish them, and though the fruits are too small to provide us much nutrition, they make a tasty treat for people as well. Indians once ground them with parched corn to sweeten the flour.

The blooms of granjeno are inconspicuous except to bees, which treat them as a good source of honey. The tree also serves as a larval host plant for various species of butterflies. Sometimes called spiny hackberry, granjeno provides wood for fuel and fence posts in its range.

DOWNY HAWTHORN

Crataegus mollis

LEAVES: Deciduous
HEIGHT: To 40 feet
GROWTH: Slow
VALUE: Landscape, wildlife
FAMILY: Rose (Rosaceae)
REGION(S): 1–5, 7

*T*HE SOFT FUZZINESS of the leaves gives the downy hawthorn its name. Its clusters of apple blossom–like flowers, shiny red autumn fruits, and amber fall foliage make it a good ornamental. It sports big leaves for a "haw," and its pomes, too, grow larger than average. The tree's dense branches form good protection for nesting sites, and the fruits provide food for birds. As with other hawthorns, beware of the thorns.

Downy hawthorn occupies a wide but scattered range in North, East, and Central Texas and the more northerly parts of South Texas. Occasionally it grows to a height of 40 feet, but it usually tops out at less than 25 feet tall. Easy to grow, it adapts to many kinds of soil conditions and resists the ill effects of pollution.

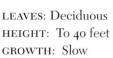

Crataegus tracyi

MOUNTAIN HAWTHORN

LEAVES: Deciduous
HEIGHT: To 20 feet
GROWTH: Slow
VALUE: Landscape, wildlife
FAMILY: Rose (Rosaceae)
REGION(S): 7, 10

*T*EXAS BOASTS MORE than thirty species of hawthorns, but only this one is widespread throughout the West. It occurs in the Big Bend, the Davis Mountains, the far western wedge of Texas, and in parts of the Edwards Plateau. Mountain hawthorn, also called Tracy hawthorn, most commonly grows along rocky streamsides in its range.

This tree bears the name of naturalist, botanist, and agronomist Samuel Mills Tracy (1847–1920), who discovered the species in the Davis Mountains in 1902. Typical of the *Crataegus* genus, the tree has five-petaled flowers with pink anthers, which develop into red fruits in the fall. The autumn foliage turns a beautiful russet, and the tree's scaly silver-gray bark becomes dark and fissured with age.

As with most hawthorns, its hard wood is useful for tool handles that must take a lot of stress, and the red pomes provide a food supply for wintering birds. Mountain hawthorn presents great landscape potential for the western parts of the state.

85

CEDAR ELM

Ulmus crassifolia

LEAVES: Deciduous
HEIGHT: To 60 feet
GROWTH: Fast
VALUE: Shade, wildlife
FAMILY: Elm (Ulmaceae)
REGION(S): 1–7

*F*EW TREES RIVAL CEDAR elm for scruffiness. Its leaves feel rough as sandpaper; its bark splits and scales in ridges. The hard, heavy wood is knotty, with little commercial value beyond that of hubs and fence posts.

Don't let the occasional corky wings on this species' twigs and branches fool you. This is not winged elm (p. 54). Cedar elm's leaves are smaller and more rounded than those of winged elm, and while the latter bears its fruits in spring, cedar elm's samaras form in the fall. Some gallinaceous birds such as quail, wild turkeys, and prairie chickens eat the seeds, and deer and rabbits browse the foliage.

Cedar elm grows over most of South, Central, and North Texas and over large parts of the eastern United States. It can reach 60 feet or more but often ends up as a smaller tree. Cedar elm prefers limestone soil and moist locations but adapts to a wide range of conditions. In acid or alkaline soil, drought or flood, cedar elm makes a pleasant shade tree.

LEAVES: Deciduous
HEIGHT: To 60 feet
GROWTH: Slow
VALUE: Wildlife
FAMILY: Beech (Fagaceae)
REGION(S): 10

ABOUT 48 to 35 million years ago, during a time known as the Tertiary period, the region we now call the Davis and Chinati mountains of West Texas boiled with volcanic action. Eons of wind and water have ground the exploded debris into gravelly layers of igneous soil, the preferred foundation for this little oak.

Gray oak most often takes a shrubby form but can become a significant tree under ideal conditions of water and light. Prominent in the mountains of West Texas, the tree also occurs in New Mexico and in the desert states of Mexico. Both the common and the scientific name refer to the gray-green leaves of this tree. Gray oak bears a strong resemblance to its cousin Mohr oak (p. 46), and the two hybridize on occasion, but the leaves of gray oak look fuzzy on both sides, whereas those of Mohr oak appear green and shiny on top.

Gray oak acorns offer important food for ground squirrels, javelinas, and some birds. Deer and porcupines browse the foliage, and people use the wood for fuel and posts.

HAVARD SHIN OAK

Quercus havardii

LEAVES: Deciduous
HEIGHT: To 25 feet
GROWTH: Slow
VALUE: Erosion control, wildlife
FAMILY: Beech (Fagaceae)
REGION(S): 8, 9

*L*OCALLY CALLED SHINNERY, this little oak with its highly variable leaves plays an important role as a stabilizer of shifting sands in the lower Panhandle. Despite the diminutive aboveground tree, its roots can go down an amazing 90 feet in search of water. It also produces rather large acorns, which provide nourishment for quail, prairie chickens, deer, and other wildlife.

French immigrant Valery Havard (1846–1927), for whom this and several other Texas plants are named, was a botanist and surgeon with the United States Army medical corps. While stationed at various frontier posts, he began taking an interest in the food and drink plants of the Indians, Mexicans, and settlers. In addition to his *Manual of Military Hygiene*, he published a number of articles on the flora of the American West.

Havard shin oak grows over most of the Panhandle and into New Mexico. This usually dwarfed species develops a shrubby form about 3 feet tall, but under the right conditions it can become a tree to 25 feet or more. It forms thickets by means of underground rhizomes.

Quercus laceyi

LACEY OAK

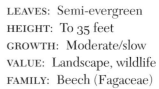

LEAVES: Semi-evergreen
HEIGHT: To 35 feet
GROWTH: Moderate/slow
VALUE: Landscape, wildlife
FAMILY: Beech (Fagaceae)
REGION(S): 7, 10

*T*HIS SLEEPER LANDSCAPE tree flaunts foliage bound to attract attention and admiration. It certainly attracted the attention of Kerrville rancher and naturalist Howard George Lacey (1856–1929), a British aristocrat who immigrated to Kerr County and introduced Angora goat farming to the Texas Hill Country. He discovered the tree growing on his property and was the first to recognize it as a distinct species. The tree now bears his name, as do several other kinds of Texas plants and animals. Shortly before his death, Lacey donated his collection of specimens to the Witte Museum in San Antonio.

The peculiar bluish tint of the leaves of this tree gives rise to another common name: blue oak. Although the species is deciduous, leaves persist late into winter. Lacey oak grows in limited areas of the Edwards Plateau and in northern Mexico. It can thrive under very dry conditions and on hard limestone surfaces. A medium-sized tree with low branches and a rounded form, Lacey oak is earning increasing appreciation as a landscape item beyond its natural range.

WHITE SHIN OAK

Quercus sinuata var. breviloba

*C*ALLED SHIN OAK OR "shinnery" because of its diminutive size, this plant does grow to somewhat more than shin-high. It reaches a minimum of about 3 feet and can form impenetrable hedges or even cover acres of ground. But although it often appears as a thicket-forming shrub, white shin oak can develop into a tree topping out at about 40 feet.

Often called Bigelow oak, this variety's range extends from the Red River in North Texas in a broad band across the central part of the state. It grows mainly over hard limestone. The light gray, shaggy bark of mature trees, responsible for the moniker scalybark oak, distinguishes it from the similarly configured Lacey oak (p. 89), which shares a portion of its habitat.

Because the white shin oak sheds its leaves relatively late in the season, it provides good shelter for wildlife, and its acorns offer them a valuable source of food. The highly variable leaves often resemble those of Havard shin oak (p. 88).

LEAVES: Deciduous
HEIGHT: To 40 feet
GROWTH: Slow
VALUE: Wildlife
FAMILY: Beech (Fagaceae)
REGION(S): 4, 5, 7, 8

LEAVES: Deciduous
HEIGHT: To 50 feet
GROWTH: Fast
VALUE: Landscape, shade, wildlife
FAMILY: Beech (Fagaceae)
REGION(S): 10

𝒰NTIL THE STATE'S 1988 acquisition of the Big Bend Ranch—more than 280,000 acres of Chihuahuan Desert wilderness—botanists did not think Mexican oak grew in the United States. During a survey of that huge tract, however, they found it thriving along the Devil's River.

The tree is also known as the Coahuila oak or Monterrey oak and, as these designations imply, is most at home in northern Mexico. In growing trials in Houston and elsewhere in Texas, however, this oak proved adaptable, and some nurseries now offer it for sale.

The tree develops upright at first, attaining a height of about 50 feet, but later spreads its crown in live oak fashion. The attractive foliage and pinkish new growth make this a very promising shade and landscape tree for much of Texas.

The acorns of Mexican oak resemble those of Shumard oak (p. 113) and will present a valuable food source for wildlife wherever people may plant this tree.

LEAVES: Deciduous
HEIGHT: To 100 feet
GROWTH: Fast
VALUE: Heritage, landscape, shade, wildlife
FAMILY: Beech (Fagaceae)
REGION(S): 1, 2

*F*RENCH BOTANIST André Michaux (1747–1802) traveled through Persia and Afghanistan collecting plant specimens and enduring many perilous adventures. Upon his return to France, he was sent by the director of the Royal Gardens of Versailles to America to do the same. He dined with Benjamin Franklin and George Washington and came to know the flora of the American wilderness better than any other white man ever had. In 1793 he proposed to Thomas Jefferson the mission that eventually resulted in the expedition of Lewis and Clark. Only his loyalty to his French assignment prevented him from undertaking the journey himself. In the interim, he discovered myriad plants, many of which bear his name today.

The handsome swamp chestnut oak named for the bold adventurer grows in moist woods and bottomlands from extreme eastern Pennsylvania south to Florida and west through East Texas. People also call it basket oak for the baskets made from its wood and cow oak because cows eat the acorns.

These large acorns, up to 1½ inches long, contain relatively small amounts of tannic acid, and Native Americans harvested them for food. Deer, hogs, wild turkeys, and doves seek them out. Aside from baskets, the wood of this tree also provided barrels and buckets. It splits along growth rings, making it ideal for splints and staves.

Swamp chestnut oak differs from chinkapin oak (p. 62) in that its leaf margins look undulating rather than saw-toothed.

LEAVES: Deciduous
HEIGHT: To 100 feet
GROWTH: Slow
VALUE: Heritage, lumber, wildlife
FAMILY: Beech (Fagaceae)
REGION(S): 1, 3

*H*AILED AS THE CLASSIC king of the American oaks, white oak occupies much of the eastern United States, attains great size, and lives a long life. It constitutes the most valuable lumber oak, and people everywhere prize it for its stately form, its pale, shredding bark, and its neatly lobed foliage.

The large acorns of white oak contain less tannic acid than those of most other oaks and provided an important item of diet for many Native Americans. The acorns can be shelled and then leached of tannin by repeated boiling and draining or by immersing them overnight in a swiftly flowing stream, as the Indians did.

They can then be ground and baked into breads or added to soups and stews as a nutritious thickening agent.

Deer, squirrels, and other mammals as well as turkeys and quail eagerly seek these nuts. Farmers once ran their hogs into the woods to fatten them on the acorns, hence the expression: "They ran hog wild!" People once called acorns of the white oak group "sweet mast" because they actually flavor the pork.

People have long prized white oak wood for baskets and barrels, flooring and furniture, tools, boat building, and more.

BLACKJACK OAK

LEAVES: Deciduous
HEIGHT: To 30 feet
GROWTH: Slow
VALUE: Shade, wildlife
FAMILY: Beech (Fagaceae)
REGION(S): 1–5, 7

*J*ACK IS AN OLD TERM meaning "fellow," as in "jack of all trades." That personification, together with the dark, rough bark of the tree, may have resulted in the common name blackjack oak. Another theory holds that the name refers to the wide-at-the-top, narrow-at-the-bottom shape of the tree, resembling the club or truncheon called a blackjack.

A small, slow-growing oak with big leaves, blackjack thrives in well-drained gravelly or sandy locations over parts of East Texas, most of Central Texas, and north all the way to Minnesota. The tree adapts to poor conditions and occurs in Texas in association with black hickory (p. 188), farkleberry (p. 67), and post oak (p. 96). Blackjack oak may be the dominant tree in some rocky, dry places, particularly in north-central Texas. In a few areas it provides the only shade.

Blackjack leaves appear dark green, tough, and somewhat scaly on the undersides and can be 7 inches long or more, in a broad wedge shape. The acorns take two years to develop, and deer and wild turkeys eat the mature nuts.

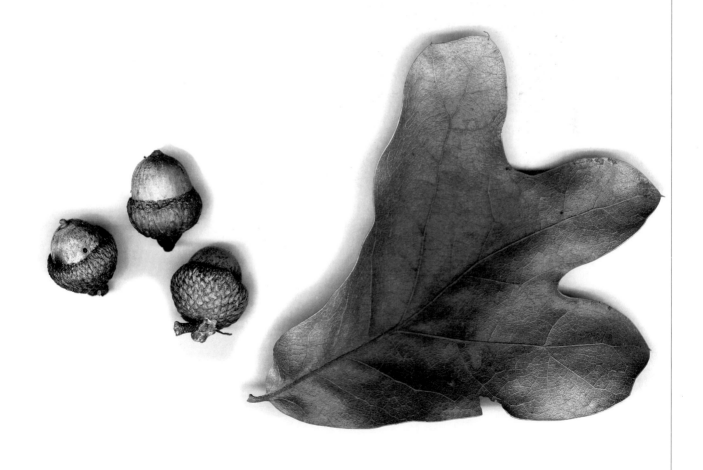

POST OAK

LEAVES: Deciduous
HEIGHT: To 50 feet
GROWTH: Slow
VALUE: Shade, wildlife, wood uses
FAMILY: Beech (Fagaceae)
REGION(S): 1–8

*P*OST OAK RANKS AMONG the slowest growing of our native oaks; a tree 2 feet in diameter can be upwards of 100 years old. Its slow growth discourages people from planting it in landscapes, but where post oak already exists, it proves highly desirable.

It often contorts into a leaning form with gnarled branches. Its leaves, which typically appear in the shape of a cross, inspired the nickname cross oak. Its rugged, antique character enhances any yard and lends a sense of permanence and value. But be careful with home construction: even minor root damage can cause a tree to die.

Post oak most frequently inhabits higher, dryer slopes or elevations and makes itself at home where it does not have to compete for light with faster-growing trees. When it does appear among other trees in a forest, post oak tends to develop a straighter trunk with higher branches to reach the all-important sunshine.

As its name implies, post oak has been widely used for fence posts. Other uses include furniture and railroad crossties. The wood is durable, heavy, hard, and close-grained.

If you have post oaks on your property, think a long time before cutting them down. You won't be able to replace them in your lifetime.

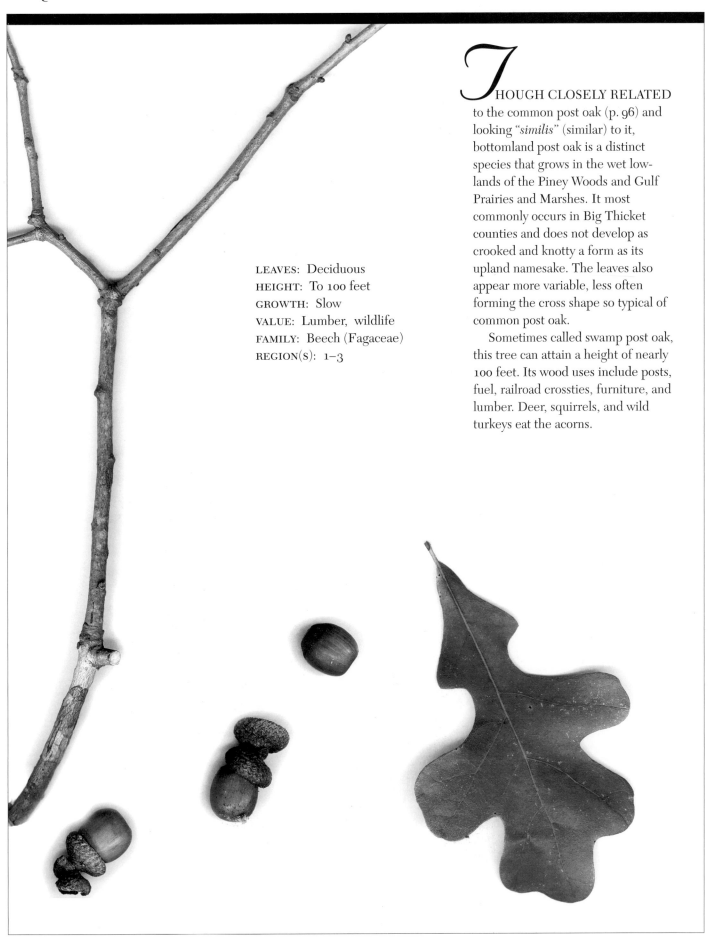

Quercus similis

BOTTOMLAND POST OAK

LEAVES: Deciduous
HEIGHT: To 100 feet
GROWTH: Slow
VALUE: Lumber, wildlife
FAMILY: Beech (Fagaceae)
REGION(S): 1–3

*T*HOUGH CLOSELY RELATED to the common post oak (p. 96) and looking *"similis"* (similar) to it, bottomland post oak is a distinct species that grows in the wet lowlands of the Piney Woods and Gulf Prairies and Marshes. It most commonly occurs in Big Thicket counties and does not develop as crooked and knotty a form as its upland namesake. The leaves also appear more variable, less often forming the cross shape so typical of common post oak.

Sometimes called swamp post oak, this tree can attain a height of nearly 100 feet. Its wood uses include posts, fuel, railroad crossties, furniture, and lumber. Deer, squirrels, and wild turkeys eat the acorns.

OVERCUP OAK

Quercus lyrata

LEAVES: Deciduous
HEIGHT: To 60 feet
GROWTH: Slow
VALUE: Wildlife, wood uses
FAMILY: Beech (Fagaceae)
REGION(S): 1–3

*T*HE COMMON NAME of this oak seems apropos: gray, warty cups almost completely swallow up the plump acorns inside. The species name refers to the lyre-shaped leaves. This slow-growing member of the white oak group prefers swampy locations throughout East Texas, toward the coast, and outside the western verge of the Piney Woods.

Its wood was once utilized for barrels, buckets, railroad ties, posts, tools, and fuel. Some ducks eat the acorns in flooded winter swamps, and several mammals, such as deer and squirrels, also feed on them. Because of the tree's slow growth and irregular form, few people ever plant it.

Quercus gambelii

GAMBEL OAK

LEAVES: Deciduous
HEIGHT: To 40 feet
GROWTH: Moderate
VALUE: Wildlife, wood
FAMILY: Beech (Fagaceae)
REGION(S): 10

THE NAME OF THIS TREE honors Dr. William Gambel (1823–49), a physician and ornithologist who began his career under the tutelage of Thomas Nuttall (see the oak named for him, p. 111). Gambel was the first trained naturalist ever to explore the flora and fauna of California's interior, a mission he began at the youthful age of eighteen. During the California gold rush, he was among the survivors of an ill-fated party traveling across the Sierra Nevada after the first snows of winter. However, upon reaching the famed Rose's bar on the Yuba River, he contracted typhoid fever and died at the age of twenty-six. During his short lifetime, he discovered several species of birds, a genus of lizard, and this oak, all of which bear his name.

This small member of the white oak group grows at some of Texas' highest elevations: 7,000–8,000 feet in the Davis, Chisos, Chinati, and Guadalupe mountains. Gambel oak occurs across the West as far north as Wyoming and south into the Mexican states of Coahuila and Chihuahua.

It can attain a height of 40 feet and up but more typically reaches only about 15 to 25 feet. The fine, rounded lobes of the leaves closely resemble those of the great white oak (p. 93) of East Texas.

Like most acorns of the white oak group, those of Gambel oak are sweet, and pigs, squirrels, and deer eagerly seek them out. Deer and porcupines also browse the foliage. The wood makes good posts and firewood.

LEAVES: Deciduous
HEIGHT: To 100 feet
GROWTH: Slow
VALUE: Edible parts, lumber, wildlife
FAMILY: Beech (Fagaceae)
REGION(S): 2–5, 7

*M*ACROCARPA MEANS "big fruit," and that is precisely what this tree has. Huge acorns with fringed cups earn it the designation mossy cup oak. These nuts, up to 2 inches in both length and diameter, may be enclosed halfway or more in the big caps. Crafters weave these impressive acorns into wreaths and other decorations and make miniature "baskets" and "bird nests" from the caps.

Since the tree belongs to the white oak group, its acorns contain less tannic acid than those of many other oaks. Deer and squirrels prize them as food, and people can eat or cook with them after leaching out the tannins. Acorn bread (appendix G) has a rich nutty flavor, especially when served warm from the oven.

Bur oak grows too slowly to compete with faster-growing trees for light. As a result it does not adapt to woodlands. It does, however, thrive in stream bottoms and open areas, eventually attaining a great height of 100 feet or more. In Texas you will find it near the Brazos, Colorado, Guadalupe, and Nueces rivers. Its range runs from north-central Texas southward to the Edwards Plateau and almost to the central coast. Beyond Texas it grows scattered here and there across the eastern two thirds of the United States and into southern Canada.

People use bur oak lumber in the same ways as that of white oak, namely for baskets, railroad ties, fences, cabinets, and flooring.

SASSAFRAS

Sassafras albidum

IN THE SEVENTEENTH century, Native Americans so touted the medicinal values of sassafras that it was literally worth its weight in gold as an export to England. Sir Walter Raleigh tried to corner the market when he unsuccessfully petitioned Queen Elizabeth to grant him a monopoly on sassafras trade. However, modern research has not confirmed any real health benefits from the tree, and today no one considers it a commodity.

The name Sassafras comes from the Latin *saxifragus*, which means "stone breaker" and possibly refers to an archaic application of sassafras in the treatment of kidney stones. Its historical use in concocting healing herbal teas evolved into the beverage we call root beer. If you smell sassafras root, you will definitely sense the root beer aroma. In 1960, scientists determined that safrole, a chemical compound in the plant, is a weak carcinogen. Subsequently, the FDA banned the use of sassafras oil as an ingredient in commercial root beer, and today the drink is flavored artificially.

Sassafras leaves are highly variable, yet readily recognizable. They come in right-handed and left-handed "mittens" and mittens with two thumbs or no thumbs. Whatever their shape, they turn attractive shades of amber and yellow in autumn. Choctaw Indians were the first to dry the leaves and grind them up to make the filé seasoning used in gumbo. In fact, the very name gumbo derives from the Choctaw word *kombo* for sassafras, which in turn came from the East African term *ochinggombo,* meaning okra.

Greenish yellow flowers herald little blue pear-shaped fruits, which sit neatly on red stalks and feed many species of birds. In sunny fields, sassafras roots sprout to form large colonies that often present a problem for farmers in East Texas and along the edge of the Post Oak belt.

LEAVES: Deciduous
HEIGHT: To 50 feet
GROWTH: Moderate/fast
VALUE: Culinary, heritage, wildlife
FAMILY: Laurel (Lauraceae)
REGION(S): 1, 3

LEAVES: Evergreen
HEIGHT: To 40 feet
GROWTH: Slow
VALUE: Heritage, landscape, wildlife
FAMILY: Holly (Aquifoliaceae)
REGION(S): 1–3

AMERICAN HOLLY TAKES its aura from centuries of reverence for the English holly, *Ilex aquifolium*. From the time of the Druids, worshipers have used that tree in religious rites, and Christians adopted it as a symbol of their faith. The words *holly* and *holy* stem from the same ancient term.

Usually an understory tree of the East Texas Piney Woods, American holly is best known for its use in Christmas decorations. The rather large berries shine bright red among bristly, dark green leaves.

These berries persist through the winter and present a favorite food of about twenty species of birds. But, as with most hollies, female fruiting trees constitute only a small minority of the population. Whether male or female, however, the thick evergreen foliage of this tree provides good winter protection for wildlife.

Nurseries have developed a number of horticultural forms of American holly and usually offer a selection of these for sale. The native form and its varieties all prove highly ornamental.

EMORY OAK

LEAVES: Evergreen
HEIGHT: To 60 feet
GROWTH: Slow
VALUE: Heritage, wildlife
FAMILY: Beech (Fagaceae)
REGION(S): 10

ILLIAM HEMSLEY EMORY (1811–87), a cartographer for the United States Army, surveyed the U.S.-Mexican border and created maps of Texas and the American Southwest so accurate as to render all previous maps of these regions obsolete. Emory married the great-granddaughter of Benjamin Franklin and served as brigadier general for the Union Army during the Civil War.

The oak that bears his name occurs as a small tree in the Davis and Chisos mountains of the Trans-Pecos at elevations above 4,500 feet, but in moist canyons and bottomlands it can reach a solid 60 feet in height. The tree remains virtually evergreen, merely changing its foliage in spring. Its dark green leaves display pretty, hollylike toothed margins and differ markedly from the paler, grayish leaves of scrub oak (p. 107). Its dark, almost black trunk provides another distinguishing feature, setting it apart from the somewhat similar Vasey oak (p. 106) with its silvery trunk.

Although a member of the black oak group, which usually produces bitter acorns, Emory oak yields acorns that are edible and sweet. In the past, they served as a significant food source for southwestern and Mexican Indians. Deer, chipmunks, squirrels, and quail also relish them, and people make use of the wood for fuel and posts.

WAVY LEAF OAK

LEAVES: Semi-evergreen
HEIGHT: To 15 feet
GROWTH: Slow
VALUE: Wildlife
FAMILY: Beech (Fagaceae)
REGION(S): 10

*B*OTANISTS CLASSIFY THIS little oak in various ways, sometimes identifying it as a subspecies of sandpaper oak (p. 108). Its leaves appear highly variable but usually have undulate, or wavy, margins, and both the common name and the species name refer to this trait. These mostly evergreen leaves are larger and more elongated than those of either sandpaper oak or scrub oak (p. 107) and more deeply cut than the leaves of those two species or of Vasey oak (p. 106).

Wavy leaf oak grows widely in the Trans-Pecos, over much of the Southwest, and in the Mexican state of Coahuila. It flourishes mainly in the mountains, between 3,000 and 6,000 feet, where it sometimes forms thickets.

This small tree provides valuable cover for birds and mammals, and the acorns, borne annually, constitute important wildlife food.

VASEY OAK

Quercus vaseyana

LEADS: Semi-evergreen
HEIGHT: To 40 feet
GROWTH: Slow
VALUE: Landscape, wildlife
FAMILY: Beech (Fagaceae)
REGION(S): 7, 10

$\mathcal{B}$OTANISTS, WHO OFTEN classify Vasey oak as a variety of sandpaper oak (p. 108), describe it as a premier landscape tree for arid country. It can reach up to 40 feet in height or be groomed into a thicketing shrub. Other special features include its glossy leaves, which persist through most of the year, and its adaptability to various soil types. Like other small oaks, it provides important wildlife cover and food.

Dr. George Vasey (1822–93) was a physician and author of articles, books, and treatises on natural history. He also served as first botanist for the Department of Agriculture and as director of the Smithsonian's National Herbarium. In 1868 he explored the Rocky Mountains and Grand Canyon, collecting various new plants.

This tree bearing his name resembles plateau live oak (p. 76), except that its leaves look narrower and toothier. It somewhat approximates Emory oak (p. 104), a tree that shares portions of its range, but its silvery trunk contrasts sharply with the dark, furrowed bark of both live oak and Emory oak. Vasey oak leaves are also less serrated than those of Emory oak or wavy leaf oak (p. 105) and generally appear larger than the leaves of scrub oak (p. 107) and sandpaper oak (p. 108).

Vasey oak occurs naturally in the western part of the Edwards Plateau, throughout the Big Bend area, and in the Davis Mountains. It ranks among the several small oaks commonly referred to as shinnery.

SCRUB OAK

LEAVES: Evergreen
HEIGHT: To 15 feet
GROWTH: Slow
VALUE: Wildlife
FAMILY: Beech (Fagaceae)
REGION(S): 10

A SMALL OAK OF THE DESERT mountains of West Texas, scrub oak frequently goes by the names of *encino* and shrub live oak. It grows in El Paso, Hudspeth, and Brewster counties, usually at about 4,000- to 5,000-foot elevations. This tree extends its range over most of the other southwestern states as well.

Its stiff, spiny leaves, which remain evergreen, look very similar to those of sandpaper oak (p. 108) but feel smoother. They are generally smaller than the leaves of Vasey oak (p. 106), lighter and grayer than the leaves of Emory oak (p. 104), and less deeply cut than the leaves of wavy leaf oak (p. 105).

Scrub oak acorns, which develop to about half an inch in both length and width, ripen much earlier than those of other oaks, providing a much-needed source of wildlife forage. The species name *turbinella* means "little top" and refers to the whimsical shape of these little acorns.

This tree can withstand substantial drought, and with its persistent leaves, it offers vital cover, protection, and nest sites for wildlife.

SANDPAPER OAK

Quercus pungens

LEAVES: Evergreen
HEIGHT: To 20 feet
GROWTH: Slow
VALUE: Wildlife
FAMILY: Beech (Fagaceae)
REGION(S): 10

*T*HE FRANKLIN, QUITMAN, Guadalupe, and Chinati mountains and the Sierra Diablo claim this little Trans-Pecos tree as a native. There it resides at lower elevations, where it often forms thickets.

Its common name refers to the rough upper surface of the leaves, which remain on the tree throughout the year. This sandpapery character-istic sets this species apart from the very similar scrub oak (p. 107). The leaves feel stiff and develop sharply toothed margins, though they appear less deeply lobed than those of wavy leaf oak (p. 105). The leaves are also generally smaller than those of Vasey oak (p. 106).

This tree's acorns offer good wildlife food, and the groves provide cover and nesting sites for birds and small mammals. Although it is sometimes called scrub oak, that term applies to a number of other species of small oaks as well.

LEAVES: Deciduous
HEIGHT: To 70 feet
GROWTH: Slow
VALUE: Dye, shade, wildlife
FAMILY: Beech (Fagaceae)
REGION(S): 1, 3

A FAIRLY UNCOMMON species of the Texas Piney Woods, black oak nevertheless ranks as a significant member of the red oak group. This tree does not dominate anywhere, but it thrives across a wide range covering East Texas and most of the eastern United States, north as far as Ontario. Black oak prefers well-drained locations such as sandy hilltops and survives in rather poor soil.

The name *velutina* refers to the fuzzy, gray-white undersides of its otherwise dark green, glossy leaves.

The bark of this tree contains high amounts of tannins and settlers used it to produce a yellow dye or to tan leather. It also yields a compound formerly used medicinally as mild astringent.

The acorns of black oak, too, are laced with tannic acid and taste bitter compared with acorns in the white oak group. Deer, squirrels, and wild turkeys will eat them, although more reluctantly than they eat white oak acorns.

SOUTHERN RED OAK

Quercus falcata

LEAVES: Deciduous
HEIGHT: To 80 feet
GROWTH: Moderate/fast
VALUE: Lumber, shade, tannin, wildlife
FAMILY: Beech (Fagaceae)
REGION(S): 1–3

THE COMMON RED OAKS found in East Texas include many varietal forms, but typically red oak grows straight upward with slightly ascending branches. The leaves appear quite variable, usually broad and three-lobed on the lower limbs and slender with five to seven irregular lobes on the upper branches. Bands of gray lichen, similar to those on black cherry (p. 47), often ring their trunks, inspiring the name cherry-bark oak. Other common names include swamp red oak and pagoda oak.

This tree grows moderately fast and makes a desirable landscape, shade, or street tree, its direct, upright posture adding a handsome natural feature almost anywhere.

Red oak is rich in tannic acid, and because of the bitterness of the acid, animals do not seek its acorns as eagerly as they do those of the white oak group. The bark of these trees provides much of the world's supply of tannin for tanning leather. It is also a valuable lumber tree.

The branches of oak trees often develop ruffles of blue-green lichen. Lichen is not a single organism; rather it represents a fine example of mutuality. Lichen consists of fungi and algae locked in a symbiotic relationship: the fungi retain moisture, while the algae conduct photosynthesis.

LEAVES: Deciduous
HEIGHT: To 100 feet
GROWTH: Fast
VALUE: Landscape, wildlife, wood uses
FAMILY: Beech (Fagaceae)
REGION(S): 1

*U*NCOMMON IN TEXAS, this tree grows only in the eastern part of the state. It bears the name of Thomas Nuttall (1786–1859), a botanist and ornithologist who explored the American frontier from the Great Lakes to New Orleans and from Massachusetts to Oregon, California, and even Hawaii. In 1822 he was appointed lecturer of natural history and curator of the botanic gardens at Harvard. He published a number of books about nature, including one on North American trees not covered in the works of André Michaux (p. 92).

Nuttall oak resembles southern red oak (p. 110) and Shumard oak (p. 113) in some ways but adapts more readily to areas where water stands for extended periods. Its lobes are more symmetrical than those of red oak and fewer in number than those of Shumard oak, but both the leaves and acorns vary somewhat.

Because of its finely cut foliage and the handsome form of the tree, a number of nurseries now offer Nuttall oak. It grows fairly rapidly in moist situations.

The wood can be utilized for boxes, crates, furniture, and firewood. Several birds eat the acorns, as do deer, squirrels, and other mammals.

TEXAS OAK

Quercus buckleyi

*T*EXAS OAK RESEMBLES Shumard oak (p. 113) in form and foliage and crosses with it along the interface of the Balcones Escarpment. The Texas oak tops out at a substantially smaller size, however, and adapts to a more western, arid habitat. Texas oak commonly occupies a range from the Red River north of Dallas down through the Hill Country.

Also called Buckley oak, it memorializes Samuel Botsford Buckley (1809–84), a member of the Shumard Geological Survey. Buckley became state geologist of Texas and later served as president and co-founder of the Academy of Science of Texas.

The tree that carries his name usually attains about 40 feet in height and, with its finely lobed leaves and rounded form, makes a pleasant sight from the roadway, especially in autumn, when it turns bright shades of red and orange.

The acorns of Texas oak provide important food for deer, squirrels, turkeys, jays, and other wildlife.

LEAVES: Deciduous
HEIGHT: To 40 feet
GROWTH: Fast
VALUE: Landscape, wildlife,
FAMILY: Beech (Fagaceae)
REGION(S): 3–5, 7

SHUMARD OAK

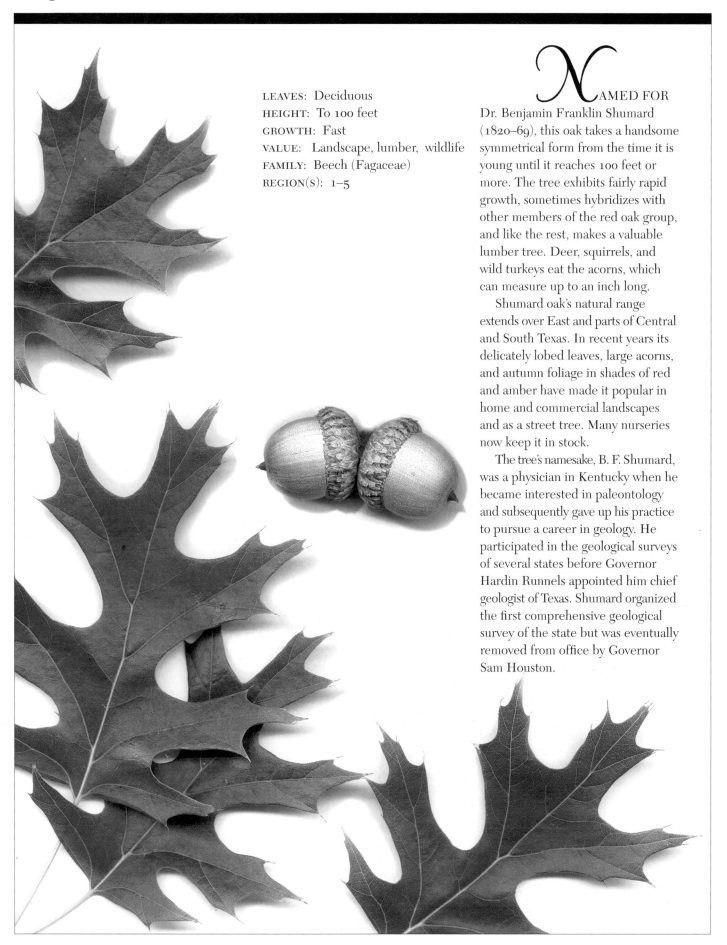

LEAVES: Deciduous
HEIGHT: To 100 feet
GROWTH: Fast
VALUE: Landscape, lumber, wildlife
FAMILY: Beech (Fagaceae)
REGION(S): 1–5

NAMED FOR Dr. Benjamin Franklin Shumard (1820–69), this oak takes a handsome symmetrical form from the time it is young until it reaches 100 feet or more. The tree exhibits fairly rapid growth, sometimes hybridizes with other members of the red oak group, and like the rest, makes a valuable lumber tree. Deer, squirrels, and wild turkeys eat the acorns, which can measure up to an inch long.

Shumard oak's natural range extends over East and parts of Central and South Texas. In recent years its delicately lobed leaves, large acorns, and autumn foliage in shades of red and amber have made it popular in home and commercial landscapes and as a street tree. Many nurseries now keep it in stock.

The tree's namesake, B. F. Shumard, was a physician in Kentucky when he became interested in paleontology and subsequently gave up his practice to pursue a career in geology. He participated in the geological surveys of several states before Governor Hardin Runnels appointed him chief geologist of Texas. Shumard organized the first comprehensive geological survey of the state but was eventually removed from office by Governor Sam Houston.

CHISOS RED OAK

Quercus gravesii

LEAVES: Deciduous
HEIGHT: To 40 feet
GROWTH: Moderate
VALUE: Heritage, landscape, wildlife
FAMILY: Beech (Fagaceae)
REGION(S): 10

CHISOS RED OAK ADORNS the rugged elevations of the Chisos, Davis, and Glass mountains of the Trans-Pecos and mountains in the state of Coahuila, Mexico, clustering mainly on north-facing slopes above 5,000 feet. Also called Graves oak, Texas red oak, and mountain oak, it has sharply lobed leaves that turn brilliant shades of red and gold in autumn, delivering the most spectacular display of color of any oak in that region.

Like most West Texas trees, this oak reaches only a modest size, attaining an ultimate height of about 40 feet. It has proven itself hardy in growing trials in the San Antonio and Dallas areas, withstanding prolonged periods of freezing temperatures. However, it does not appear to produce its vivid fall colors outside its native range.

Squirrels, quail, and wild turkeys eat the half-inch-long acorns, which Indians formerly collected and ground into meal. Deer often browse the foliage.

The tree's namesake, Henry Solon Graves (1871–1950), became chief of the five-year-old U.S. Forest Service in 1910. During his ten-year no-nonsense stint at the helm, this professional forester gained the respect of his staff, acquired new national forests in the East, and launched the national forest policy that has preserved our timberlands for generations.

Acer saccharinum

SILVER MAPLE

LEAVES: Deciduous
HEIGHT: To 50 feet
GROWTH: Fast
VALUE: Landscape, shade, wood uses
FAMILY: Maple (Aceraceae)
REGION(S): Non-native

*P*EOPLE OFTEN PLANT silver maple in Texas because of its pretty five-lobed leaves, the silvery undersurfaces of which make the tree appear to shimmer and dance at the slightest breeze. It grows rapidly, offers quick shade, and even naturalizes in some areas. Its wood proves useful for fuel and furniture, and squirrels eat the little maple keys.

Despite its positive points and popularity as a yard tree, we cannot recommend silver maple for Texas landscapes. This short-lived species suffers during dry periods, easily succumbs to wind damage, and is susceptible to borers and other insects.

Indigenous to the Northeast, silver maple enjoys far more success in northerly climates and thrives well into Canada.

LEAVES: Deciduous

HEIGHT: To 100 feet

GROWTH: Fast

VALUE: Heritage, landscape, shade, wildlife, wood uses

FAMILY: Witch Hazel (Hamamelidaceae)

REGION(S): 1–3

*P*IONEER CHILDREN quickly learned that the sap of this tree makes a sweet-tasting, mildly stimulating chewing gum; hence the name sweetgum. In 1869, a Dr. William Cook touted it in his *Physiomedical Dispensatory* as an ingredient in ointments for "scaly forms of skin disease" and in tinctures of "aralia" (p. 143) or "prunus" (p. 47) for the treatment of "coughs and pulmonary debility." In Europe and Latin America people still use it to flavor medicines, and in Mexico and Central America it serves as a source of incense.

This vigorous, fast-growing tree thrives from the eastern half of the United States all the way south to Honduras, although in its more southerly reaches it occurs only at elevations above 1,000 feet.

Sweetgum is among the dominant climax species of East Texas forests. Because of its abundance, it provides more fall color than any other native tree within its range. The leaves turn countless subtle shades of yellow, orange, red, maroon, and purple.

Aside from its brilliant autumn hues, sweetgum supplies thick shade and significant wildlife food. It would gain more popularity as a yard tree were it not for the spiny seed balls it drops during much of the year. But crafters employ those in wreaths and Christmas decorations.

Gray squirrels, flying squirrels, and at least twenty-five species of birds eat the seeds. The wood offers a wide variety of uses for musical instruments, veneers, cabinets, furniture, boxes, and more.

See color illustration, p. 1

Acer rubrum

See color illustrations, pp. i, x

LEAVES: Deciduous
HEIGHT: To 100 feet
GROWTH: Fast
VALUE: Landscape, wildlife, wood uses
FAMILY: Maple (Aceraceae)
REGION(S): 1–3

*L*ATIN SPEAKERS TOOK the term *Acer* from the old Celtic name for maple, and *rubrum,* of course, means "red." The tree's name suits it well, since it exhibits some red in virtually every season. In spring, the scarlet flowers precede pairs of winged, crimson fruits called keys. The twigs are red, and in fall, vermilion leaves highlight the tree's impressive ornamental qualities. Even in winter, the buds shine like ruby-colored beads through the woods.

Red maple grows from eastern Texas to Florida and northward into Canada. In southeast Texas, the variety called Drummond red maple dominates. It has larger keys and prefers damp, even swampy areas. Drummond red maple gathers increasing numbers of admirers and continues to grow in popularity as a landscape tree.

Carpenters and crafters employ the wood of this tree for furniture, gunstocks, and hobby woodenware. The tree's sap could be tapped like that of sugar maple (*Acer saccharum*), but it yields inferior syrup. Squirrels and chipmunks eat the seeds, and deer browse the foliage.

BIGTOOTH MAPLE

Acer grandidentatum

*T*O APPRECIATE THE spectacular beauty of this tree fully, visit Lost Maples State Natural Area near Vanderpool, Texas, during the last two weeks in October or the first two weeks of November. But don't expect to be alone in your reverie. The park's bigtooth maples, which also occur in scattered locations throughout the Edwards Plateau and in Central Texas, draw crowds of admirers. In the Trans-Pecos, the tree's presence is particularly marked in the Guadalupe Mountains.

Both the common name and the species name derive from the large "teeth" on the leaf margins. Uvalde bigtooth maple, an especially attractive variety of this tree, has leaves with three longer and more smooth-margined lobes.

This maple seems to do well in dry locations, and Uvalde bigtooth maple even grows over limestone, particularly in Real, Kendall, and Bandera counties. The twinned fruits or maple keys are designed to flutter in the wind for dispersal. The pleasing rounded form of the tree and the attractive leaves, which turn brilliant shades of red and yellow in autumn, make it a highly desirable landscape feature.

LEAVES: Deciduous
HEIGHT: To 50 feet
GROWTH: Fast
VALUE: Landscape, shade
FAMILY: Maple (Aceraceae)
REGION(S): 7, 10

TRIDENT MAPLE

LEAVES: Deciduous
HEIGHT: To 60 feet
GROWTH: Fast
VALUE: Landscape, wildlife, wood uses
FAMILY: Maple (Aceraceae)
REGION(S): 1

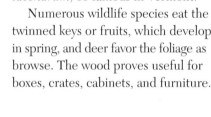

MONG THE CONFUSING varieties of red maple (p. 117), this one deserves special recognition because of its prevalence in northeast Texas, because of its trident-shaped, three-lobed leaves, and because of its unusual fall color. Most maples in the *Acer rubrum* complex turn varied shades of red in the fall, but this one turns gold. As a result, many nurseries in Texas now offer trident maple.

Like other red maples, this tree can be tapped for syrup, but it yields less in both quantity and quality than the common sugar maple (*Acer saccharum*) so famous in Vermont.

Numerous wildlife species eat the twinned keys or fruits, which develop in spring, and deer favor the foliage as browse. The wood proves useful for boxes, crates, cabinets, and furniture.

CHALK MAPLE

Acer leucoderme

LEAVES: Deciduous
HEIGHT: To 20 feet
GROWTH: Fast
VALUE: Landscape, shade
FAMILY: Maple (Aceraceae)
REGION(S): 1

*C*HALK MAPLE, considered by some to be the loveliest of all Texas maples, grows natively in this state only in a few counties near the Sabine River. However, it constitutes the most common maple in Sabine National Forest. A small tree, often with several trunks, it usually achieves less than 20 feet in height. Chalk maple somewhat resembles southern sugar maple (p. 121), but distinguishes itself by its smaller stature and by the fuzzy, gray-green undersides of its leaves.

Both the species name and the common names chalk maple and whitebark maple refer to its light gray, chalky appearing trunk. Despite its limited range in Texas, chalk maple can be cultivated in rich, moist soil and makes an attractive landscape item. The leaves turn a lovely scarlet in autumn.

Acer barbatum

SOUTHERN SUGAR MAPLE

LEAVES: Deciduous
HEIGHT: To 50 feet
GROWTH: Fast
VALUE: Heritage, landscape, shade, wood uses
FAMILY: Maple (Aceraceae)
REGION(S): 1

*C*ONSIDERED THE SMALLER cousin of the true sugar maple (*Acer saccharum*), which probably does not occur natively in Texas, southern sugar maple is limited in the state to a small tier of counties in deep East Texas. From there it grows eastward all the way to Florida, earning it the common name Florida maple. Like its more noted relative, it has been tapped for syrup and sugar, but remains less productive since the seasonal rise in sap is less pronounced.

Nurseries sometimes cultivate southern sugar maple for its beautiful red, orange, and yellow fall colors, and manufacturers employ the wood for furniture, veneer, and flooring. This attractive, fast-growing shade tree succeeds in Texas well outside its native range.

CHINESE PARASOL TREE

LEAVES: Deciduous
HEIGHT: To 50 feet
GROWTH: Fast
VALUE: Landscape, shade
FAMILY: Chocolate (Sterculiaceae)
REGION(S): Non-native

WHAT AN UNUSUAL TREE! The huge leaves of Chinese parasol can measure up to a foot across, and the large panicles of off-white flowers, borne in midsummer, prove equally impressive. But this tree's most interesting feature by far is its seed structures, which look something like beige tulips composed of five papery, petal-like bodies that support the seeds aligned along their margins. Stiff and brittle, these strange constructions make a dramatic addition to dried flower arrangements.

North Americans have cultivated this native of China and Japan since before the Revolutionary War. Also called bottle tree and Japanese varnish tree, this species belongs to the family that produces chocolate, cocoa butter, and cola nuts. It naturalizes in many places across the South, including Texas, and grows rapidly and easily from seed.

AMERICAN SYCAMORE

Platanus occidentalis

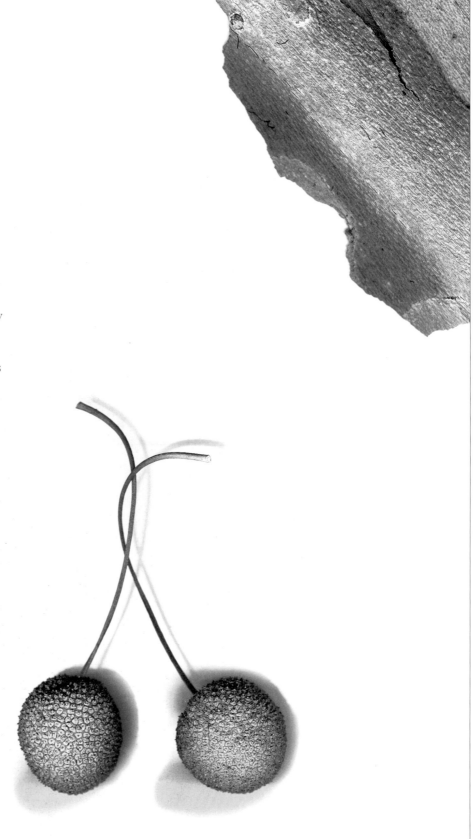

LEAVES: Deciduous
HEIGHT: To 100 feet
GROWTH: Moderate/slow
VALUE: Shade, wildlife
FAMILY: Sycamore (Platanaceae)
REGION(S): 1–5, 7

AMERICAN SYCAMORE ranks among the most massive of any deciduous tree in the United States. A striking species, it develops large leaves and mottled bark, which peels off to reveal a smooth, white trunk. The flaking bark becomes increasingly pronounced with age.

This elephantine tree produces copious, flea-sized seeds, borne in round balls about 1 inch across, which dangle by slender stems from the twigs. A number of bird species eat these seeds, and old sycamores often become hollow, providing homes for raccoons, opossums, squirrels, and other wildlife.

Sycamore grows widely across Texas, from the Sabine River to near Big Bend. It finds its favorite habitat along streams and in other moist locations. Although people often plant sycamore as a shade tree, it does not do well in dry soil and may succumb to anthracnose, a blight caused by a fungus.

TEXAS REDBUD

Cercis canadensis var. *texensis*

LEAVES: Deciduous
HEIGHT: To 50 feet
GROWTH: Moderate/fast
VALUE: Edible parts, landscape
FAMILY: Legume (Fabaceae)
REGION(S): 4, 5, 7, 8

*B*OTANISTS OFFICIALLY classify Texas redbud as a varietal form of eastern redbud (p. 127), but it merits separate treatment in our book of Texas trees because of its characteristics and regional uniqueness. The tough, leathery leaves of this variety fall in line along its branches in a regular, almost martial arrangement, and the flowers exhibit an even deeper pink-rose than the blossoms of the classic redbud. Like those of the eastern redbud, the flowers and new seedpods of the Texas redbud are edible.

The tree prevails in a band from the north-central part of the state across Central Texas and to the southwest. It thrives in dry limestone soil but can adapt to most landscapes. A heavily flowering tree, Texas redbud earns a place in the home landscape, particularly where dry, calcareous conditions prove inhospitable to its eastern counterpart.

LEAVES: Deciduous
HEIGHT: To 30 feet
GROWTH: Moderate
VALUE: Edible parts, heritage, landscape
FAMILY: Legume (Fabaceae)
REGION(S): 1–5

*T*HIS BEAUTIFUL NATIVE tree attracted the attention of the first European settlers with its romantic flowers and heart-shaped leaves, and these immigrants planted it for ornament from early colonial times. Redbud grows naturally over most of the eastern United States and into parts of southern Canada.

It provides the earliest spring color over much of its range, since the fuchsia blossoms appear before the leaves emerge. Almost fluorescent, these vibrant flowers cover every branch and twig of the tree.

Native Americans, such as the Lipan Apaches in Texas, were also aware of its beauty but valued it for another reason: redbud blossoms prove edible and tasty. You can eat them raw or add them to salads. Gather a quart or two of the flowers from even a small tree; they will never be missed, so thickly do they form on the trunk and limbs. The young, pealike pods, too, can be stir-fried and eaten like snow peas.

Redbud makes its home along wood edges. It prefers morning sun and afternoon shade.

See color illustration, p. ii

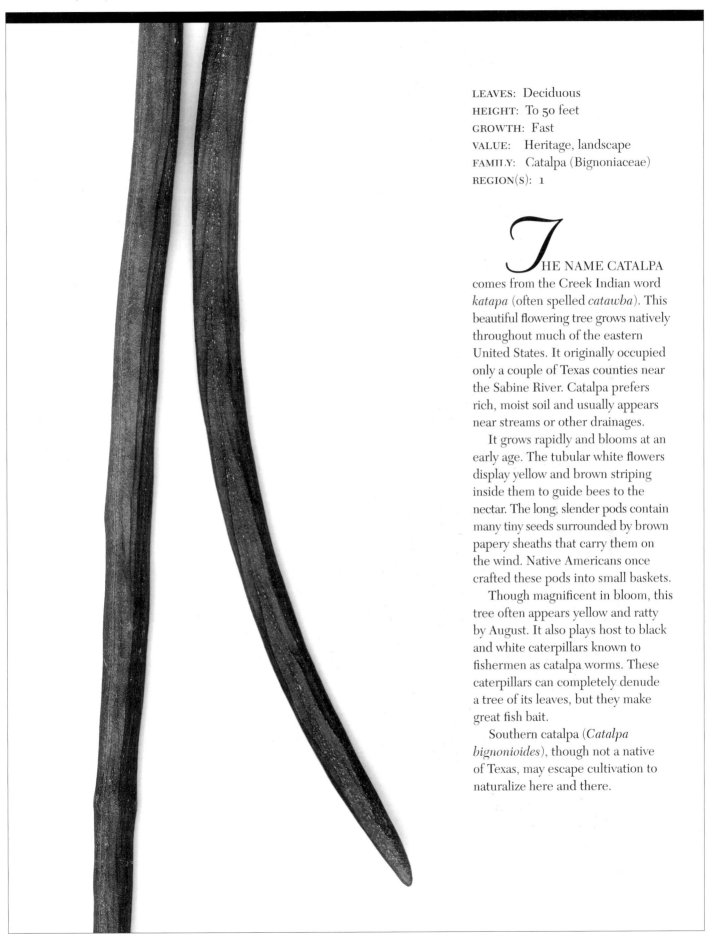

Catalpa speciosa

LEAVES: Deciduous
HEIGHT: To 50 feet
GROWTH: Fast
VALUE: Heritage, landscape
FAMILY: Catalpa (Bignoniaceae)
REGION(S): 1

*T*HE NAME CATALPA comes from the Creek Indian word *katapa* (often spelled *catawba*). This beautiful flowering tree grows natively throughout much of the eastern United States. It originally occupied only a couple of Texas counties near the Sabine River. Catalpa prefers rich, moist soil and usually appears near streams or other drainages.

It grows rapidly and blooms at an early age. The tubular white flowers display yellow and brown striping inside them to guide bees to the nectar. The long, slender pods contain many tiny seeds surrounded by brown papery sheaths that carry them on the wind. Native Americans once crafted these pods into small baskets.

Though magnificent in bloom, this tree often appears yellow and ratty by August. It also plays host to black and white caterpillars known to fishermen as catalpa worms. These caterpillars can completely denude a tree of its leaves, but they make great fish bait.

Southern catalpa (*Catalpa bignonioides*), though not a native of Texas, may escape cultivation to naturalize here and there.

TUNG OIL TREE

Aleurites fordii

*C*OMMERCIAL GROWERS cultivate this native of Central Asia and China across the Gulf States. The poisonous nuts, which begin to develop on five-year-old trees, produce tung oil, an important ingredient in paints, varnishes, soaps, wood finishes, thinners, and linoleum. In Asia, manufacturers press the oil from the nuts for fuel, lamp oil, and for treating cloth.

The large eye-catching leaves, flowers, and nuts of this unusual tree attract attention wherever people plant it. Tung oil tree grows rapidly and makes a good shade or landscape feature as long as homeowners keep in mind the poisonous properties of the nuts. This stout, spreading tree, which attains a height of 30 feet or more, sometimes escapes cultivation to naturalize around parent trees.

The species name *fordii* honors Charles Ford, who was appointed in 1871 as the first superintendent of the Hong Kong Zoological and Botanical Gardens.

LEAVES: Deciduous
HEIGHT: To 30 feet
GROWTH: Fast
VALUE: Landscape, paint products, shade
FAMILY: Spurge (Euphorbiaceae)
REGION(S): Non-native

Warning:
Known poisonous properties

CHINESE TALLOW TREE

Sapium sebiferum

LEAVES: Deciduous
HEIGHT: To 40 feet
GROWTH: Fast
VALUE: Shade, wildlife
FAMILY: Spurge (Euphorbiaceae)
REGION(S): Non-native

**Warning:
Invasive species,
known poisonous
properties**

*L*IKE GUESTS WHO have worn out their welcome, Chinese tallows have been imposing on our landscape for nearly a century. In its native China, people valued this tree for the waxy coating of its seeds. They made candles, cloth dressings, and soaps from the wax. Americans introduced Chinese tallow to the United States in the early 1900s with a possible candle industry and the expectation of fast shade and fall color in mind. The candle industry never materialized. And while the tree does produce a seductive array of vivid autumn color, it aggressively displaces large patches of our native species in some areas of Texas.

Chinese tallow grows extremely fast. A rice field left fallow for just two or three years can transform into a forest of tallow trees. This invader grows where trees have never grown before. It can endure long periods of standing water and readily resprouts when cut.

Robins, waxwings, and grackles eat the white seeds, which are toxic to humans. Grackles in particular, wintering in Texas by the millions and also considered to be something of a pest, spread this tree across the coastal plain and into southeastern parts of the state. Arguably, Chinese tallow represents the most troublesome tree ever introduced to Texas.

QUAKING ASPEN

LEAVES: Deciduous
HEIGHT: To 40 feet
GROWTH: Fast
VALUE: Landscape, wildlife, wood uses
FAMILY: Willow (Salicaceae)
REGION(S): 10

2UAKING ASPEN GROWS not only in the Rockies but also across the entire northern tier of states all the way to Pennsylvania, making it one of the most widespread trees of North America. It succeeds in several scattered locations in Texas, high in the Davis, Chisos, and Guadalupe mountains.

At those altitudes it reaches a height of about 40 feet. The leaves of quaking aspen hang at right angles to their leaf stems, or petioles, which accounts for their trembling movement at the slightest breeze. The slender, white trunks resemble those of white birch (*Betula papyrifera*).

Manufacturers fabricate clothespins, matchsticks, tubs, pails, and boxes from its soft wood. Many mammals, such as squirrels, porcupines, beavers, black bears, and deer browse the twigs, buds, and bark, and grouse and other birds eat the seeds. But the shimmering autumn gold of this tree and the pleasant rustling of its leaves earn it a special place in human appreciation. leaveslispecial place in human appreciation.

ARIZONA COTTONWOOD

Populus fremontii var. mesetae

JOHN C. FREMONT (1813–90) was an army surveyor who started life as the illegitimate son of a Virginia socialite and a penniless French immigrant. A vigorous social climber, Fremont married the daughter of Missouri senator Thomas Hart Benton, who employed his ambitious son-in-law to promote his expansionist movement known as Manifest Destiny. With Benton's patronage, Fremont led surveys of the Oregon Trail, Oregon Territory, Great Basin, and Sierra Nevada and became known as the "Pathfinder," publishing wildly popular accounts of the western frontier. During the Civil War, however, President Lincoln stripped him of his command, and he eventually died in obscurity.

This relatively small cottonwood memorializes Fremont while providing green relief along streams and arroyos in the Big Bend region. Residents of the area plant it for shade around their homes and small towns. This attractive, useful tree represents the most common cottonwood along the Rio Grande below Presidio.

Arizona cottonwood grows westward to its namesake state and southward through the central plateau of Mexico, where people call it *meseta* cottonwood, *meseta* being a Spanish word for plateau.

As with other *Populus* species, Indians ate the catkins and wove with the twigs. The soft wood yields fuel and fence posts in a region where few sizable trees grow. This tree also provides important shelter and shade for wildlife.

LEAVES: Deciduous
HEIGHT: To 50 feet
GROWTH: Fast
VALUE: Heritage, shade, wildlife, wood uses
FAMILY: Willow (Salicaceae)
REGION(S): 10

RIO GRANDE COTTONWOOD

DRY CONDITIONS in West Texas ensure that most trees there reach only modest proportions at best. Rio Grande cottonwood stands out as a glaring exception. This massive tree with deeply furrowed bark often branches low to the ground, and its impressive bulk places it among the giants of Texas trees. It rapidly achieves its gargantuan size but proves relatively short-lived.

Named for German-born botanist and physician Friedrich Adolph Wislizenus (1810–89), this cottonwood flourishes along the Rio Grande, particularly from Presidio to El Paso. It also grows in the Davis Mountains along creeks and arroyos.

The soft wood of this tree, like that of most cottonwoods, finds use as rough lumber, posts, and fuel. Indians ate the spring catkins and wove baskets and mats with the twigs. They also ate the inner bark in times of necessity and used it for women's skirts. Birds and small mammals use the tree for shelter and deer and cattle browse the leaves.

The fast growth and stately beauty of Rio Grande cottonwood have made it a popular shade tree in the arid West, where it flourishes. But the fuzzy spring seeds can rapidly clog window screens and create a nuisance on washdays for those who hang their clothes outdoors to dry.

LEAVES: Deciduous
HEIGHT: To 100 feet
GROWTH: Fast
VALUE: Heritage, shade, wildlife
FAMILY: Willow (Salicaceae)
REGION(S): 10

EASTERN AND PLAINS COTTONWOOD

Populus deltoides and *Populus sargentii*

$\mathcal{I}$NDIANS ONCE USED the soft wood of these trees as the bases of fire drills, which are primitive tools for starting campfires. To use a fire drill, rapidly turn a stick back and forth inside a hole in a piece of cottonwood until you produce enough friction to create a spark. Make sure you have good tinder, such as the bark of river birch (p. 79), and serviceable firewood, such as the resinous stump of an old loblolly pine (p. 226). But never build a campfire where it is illegal or in violation of park rules!

Today, the soft wood of cotton-wood trees serves to make paper pulp and crating material.

Eastern cottonwood is a signature tree of river bottoms and wet places across the United States, almost to the Rockies. The Spanish word for cottonwood is *alamo*, and legend holds that a grove of cottonwoods growing along the San Antonio River inspired the nickname for Texas' most famous historical landmark.

The species name *deltoides* refers to the triangular shape of the leaves, similar to the Greek letter delta. The scientific name of the western species, plains cottonwood, honors Charles Sprague Sargent (1841–1927), the founding director and co-designer of Harvard's Arnold Arboretum. Plains cottonwood grows from the Panhandle and plains of north-central Texas north-ward all the way to Saskatchewan. It too serves as a reliable indicator of the presence of a stream or water source in its range. Both trees provide important cover for wildlife.

Eastern cottonwood rapidly attains a size up to 100 feet tall, with a trunk eight feet in diameter. The leaves of the somewhat smaller plains cottonwood have only about half as many teeth on their margins as those of eastern cottonwood. Both trees develop shallow roots and live relatively short lives. The cottony, air-borne seeds make a mess, but these species create shade faster than any other tree within their range.

LEAVES: Deciduous
HEIGHT: To 100 feet
(Plains Cottonwood: 80 feet)
GROWTH: Fast
VALUE: Heritage, shade, wildlife
FAMILY: Willow (Salicaceae)
REGION(S): 1–5, 7
(Plains Cottonwood: 3–5, 8)

Tilia caroliniana

CAROLINA LINDEN

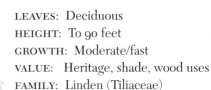

LEAVES: Deciduous
HEIGHT: To 90 feet
GROWTH: Moderate/fast
VALUE: Heritage, shade, wood uses
FAMILY: Linden (Tiliaceae)
REGION(S): 1, 3, 7

*T*HIS UNIQUE TREE'S relatives live in dispersed communities all around the northern hemisphere. The British call the European linden a lime, and Berlin's famed avenue *Unter den Linden* honors the presence of these well-loved trees. In the United States, Carolina linden grows in scattered populations in the southern forests from Texas to the Atlantic.

Linden wood, used for carving and whittling, also has specialty applications in beehives, piano keys, and furniture core stock. Some people call the tree basswood, because Native Americans and settlers once took "bast," or fiber, from the wood for weaving and making cordage. Europeans brew the dried blossoms of a species of linden into a tea that serves as a cold remedy.

This tree exhibits moderately rapid growth and makes a handsome landscape feature. It develops well in partial shade or on wood edges. The fairly large leaves differ from mulberry (p. 138) leaves in having asymmetrical bases; and unlike the leaves of redbud (p. 127), linden leaf margins are serrated. Carolina linden also develops a unique, adapted leaf from which its fruits hang suspended. This special leaf whirls in the wind when released, widely distributing the seeds.

RED MULBERRY

Morus rubra

LEAVES: Deciduous
HEIGHT: To 40 feet
GROWTH: Fast
VALUE: Edible parts, heritage, landscape, wildlife
FAMILY: Mulberry (Moraceae)
REGION(S): 1–5, 7

*R*ED MULBERRY seldom grows into a big tree in Texas, but it attracts notice because of its large leaves and edible fruit. Housewives once valued it for the berries, which they made into jams and jellies and baked into pies. Tree-climbing children enjoyed them raw. Today, people seldom eat mulberries, perhaps because they usually contain a little extra protein in the form of tiny insects. Many species of birds eagerly devour them though, as do squirrels and other mammals. If you sit in a mulberry tree at fruiting time, you may be joined by a northward-migrating flock of cedar waxwings or goldfinches.

Mulberry bark is soft and fibrous, and Native Americans sometimes made cloth from it. Bark skirts were popular with Indian women of several tribes.

This tree grows over almost all of the eastern half of the United States. In Texas, it thrives from the Louisiana border south to Corpus Christi, west across much of the Edwards Plateau, and north to the Red River. Its highly variable foliage sometimes resembles that of Carolina linden (p. 137) except that mulberry leaves have symmetrical bases. Unlike those of redbud (p. 127), mulberry leaves exhibit serrated margins. They may also appear similar to those of white mulberry (p. 139), but the undersides of red mulberry leaves feel fuzzy all over, whereas those of white mulberry have hairs only on the veins.

The tree's attractive foliage and spreading habit make red mulberry a good landscape choice, but don't plant fruiting trees over sidewalks or driveways. Mulberry juice will stain, and both the berries and the birds that process them can make quite a mess. In response, many nurseries now offer fruitless, male trees.

WHITE MULBERRY

*T*HE SILK INDUSTRY of China depends upon this tree, the leaves of which constitute the primary food source of silkworms. Though native to the Orient, white mulberry has spread widely around the globe and now commonly appears in many parts of Texas. Here, people plant it mostly for shade and for windbreaks.

As the name suggests, white mulberry often produces white fruits, although it can also bear fruits in shades of pink or red. Like those of red mulberry (p. 138), they constitute a favorite food of many species of birds. Opossums and raccoons also relish them, although people, if they eat mulberry fruits at all, seem to prefer those of red mulberry. The irregular leaves of the two species often resemble each other, but you can tell them apart by the hairs on their undersides: red mulberry leaves feel fuzzy all over their undersurfaces, whereas white mulberry leaves sprout hairs primarily on the veins.

The trunk of this tree can attain a diameter of up to three feet, and manufacturers value its wood for furniture, utensils, and boat building. The tree tolerates drought well.

LEAVES: Deciduous
HEIGHT: To 40 feet
GROWTH: Fast
VALUE: Shade, wildlife, wood uses
FAMILY: Mulberry (Moraceae)
REGION(S): Non-native

PARSLEY HAWTHORN

Crataegus marshallii

ONE OF THE MOST delicate and attractive of our native hawthorns, this one gets its common name from its parsley-like leaves. The species name memorializes Humphrey Marshall (1722–1801), an eminent Pennsylvania botanist, considered the father of American dendrology, and the first person to describe Parsley hawthorn.

All through East Texas this tree peers from wood edges and openings. The pretty, white spring flowers incorporate red anthers and develop into crimson "berries"—technically they are pomes—that adorn the tree throughout the winter months. The trunk sports gray bark that peels off to reveal a contrasting reddish layer beneath, and the leaves display an array of vivid gold, orange, and red hues in autumn.

Because of these attributes, home-owners sometimes plant parsley hawthorn for ornament. It grows slowly but enjoys a long life. A variety of birds utilize the fruits as winter food, and the thorny crowns offer good, protected nesting sites.

LEAVES: Deciduous
HEIGHT: To 20 feet
GROWTH: Slow
VALUE: Landscape, wildlife
FAMILY: Rose (Rosaceae)
REGION(S): 1–3

See color illustration, p. xv

140

LEAVES: Deciduous
HEIGHT: To 100 feet
GROWTH: Slow
VALUE: Edible parts, landscape, medicinal
FAMILY: Ginkgo (Ginkgoaceae)
REGION(S): Non-native

*T*HE ORDER GINKGOALES reached its peak as a dominant group of trees during the Jurassic epoch—the great age of the dinosaurs, about 180 million to 135 million years ago. By the Cretaceous period, it had begun to decline. Today, only *Ginkgo biloba* remains to represent this ancient group of plants. Its survival may be credited in part to Buddhist monks, who considered the tree sacred and brought it from China to Japan to plant around their temples. Ginkgo no longer occurs in the wild in China; however, its admirers plant it worldwide. It especially enjoys success in the northeastern United States, where people have cultivated it since the 1780s. It also does well in North Texas and persists around old plantings.

The medicinal uses of this tree are legendary, and today you can purchase ginkgo extract as a popular over-the-counter herbal remedy. Holistic practitioners use it to treat depression, and researchers are testing it for its effects on dementia and Alzheimer's disease. Even convenience stores offer it, but some experts express concerns about possible interaction with drugs.

Only female trees bear the small ginkgo fruits, and many Asians enjoy eating the kernels. But because the pulp exudes a somewhat offensive odor, Americans mostly plant male trees. Ginkgo's ability to endure exhaust fumes and other pollutants makes it an excellent street tree.

The species name *biloba* refers to the attractive two-lobed leaves, which turn yellow in autumn and which ginkgo has the unusual habit of shedding all at once.

ANACACHO BAUHINIA

Bauhinia lunarioides

LEAVES: Deciduous
HEIGHT: To 20 feet
GROWTH: Moderate/fast
VALUE: Landscape
FAMILY: Legume (Fabaceae)
REGION(S): 7

*B*AUHINIAS GROW in widely diverse areas of the world —in southern Asia, Mexico, South America, and Australia. The United States can claim only Anacacho bauhinia ("ahnah*kah*cho bow*hee*nia") as a native, and this species grows in the wild only in the Anacacho Hills west of Uvalde, Texas.

Trees of this genus are also called orchid trees because of their delicate flower forms, and the genus name honors sixteenth-century Swiss herbalists John and Caspar Bauhin. Like its cousins, Anacacho bauhinia is highly ornamental with its showy white flowers, which develop in March and April. The tree's dark green, deeply divided leaves measure only 1 inch across, tiny for a member of this genus.

Some people cultivate bauhinias in the southern half of Texas, but they often freeze back in extreme cold weather. Various Texas arboretums display Anacacho bauhinia among their arid-country natives.

Aralia spinosa

DEVIL'S WALKING STICK

ONE LOOK AT THIS TREE leaves little doubt as to the source of its name: the trunk often appears as a single, slim pole with multitudes of sharp, prickly spines covering its length to protect the bark. At the upper end of this "walking stick," a few branches with huge doubly or triply compound leaves—up to 4 feet long, with numerous leaflets— form a flattened crown. Tiny off-white blossoms appear in big clusters at the very top of the tree and develop into bunches of purple-black, mildly toxic berries. Perhaps the blooms are responsible for one of the plant's many other common names: angelica tree. Various species of birds eagerly eat the berries, and both Indians and early settlers once used the bark and berries medicinally for a wide variety of problems from boils to snakebite to venereal disease.

Although some people call it Hercules' club, don't confuse this tree with the real thing. A member of the citrus family, true Hercules' club (p. 197) is a larger tree with singly compound leaves. It has fatter corky prickles, which on older specimens appear far more knobby than prickly. The spines of devil's walking stick are very thin and sharp.

With its unusual configuration, lush, tropical-looking leaves, and crown of flower clusters and berries, this native of East Texas possesses real ornamental possibilities. Still, devil's walking stick seems to garner more appreciation in Europe than in its homeland.

LEAVES: Deciduous
HEIGHT: To 30 feet
GROWTH: Fast
VALUE: Landscape, medicinal, wildlife
FAMILY: Ginseng (Araliaceae)
REGION(S): 1–3

EST TEXAS LOCALS refer to several species of acacia as catclaw because they have in common the insidious little curved spines that inevitably reach out in ambush to snag passers-by. More often than not, catclaw means Gregg acacia. A common tree in both South Texas and much of the western part of the state, it sometimes forms impenetrable thickets that provide shelter for small wildlife. This plant most readily attracts notice in spring when its profuse white or pale yellow blossoms shine across the alkaline flats.

The species is named for Josiah Gregg (1806–50), a sometime teacher, sometime surveyor, who traveled the Santa Fe Trail on the advice of his physician in order to recover from a bout of consumption. The journey resulted in a successful career as a merchant and in his much-lauded book *Commerce on the Prairies.* While on an expedition to California in 1850, Gregg, apparently weakened and near starvation, fell from his horse and died.

Some botanists support merging Gregg and Wright acacias (p. 145) into a single species, since intermediate populations exist. The leaflets of Wright acacia normally develop to about twice the size of those of Gregg acacia.

Catclaw furnishes a fine honey, and Indians once ground the beans into a *pinole,* or mush, for bread. The hard wood serves to make fence posts and fire wood, and home-owners should consider this tree as a potential landscape plant for dry areas.

LEAVES: Deciduous
HEIGHT: To 30 feet
GROWTH: Slow
VALUE: Edible parts, heritage, honey, landscape, wildlife
FAMILY: Legume (Fabaceae)
REGION(S): 6, 7, 10

LEATES: Deciduous
HEIGHT: To 25 feet
GROWTH: Moderate/fast
VALUE: Honey, landscape
FAMILY: Legume (Fabaceae)
REGION(S): 5–8, 10

WRIGHT ACACIA OWES its name to one of the best known of U.S. botanists, Charles Wright (1811–85), who spent much of his life as an educator. In 1844 he began a lifelong correspondence and association with famed Harvard botanist Asa Gray, who secured him a botanical expedition along the Rio Grande Valley. Wright walked the 673 miles to El Paso, enduring many hardships and collecting some 1,400 plant specimens to send back to Gray. During his lifetime, he also befriended Dr. Ferdinand Lindheimer (p. 32), joined a survey of the U.S.-Mexican border, and became a member of the North Pacific Exploring Expedition, which traveled to points of interest all around the world.

This small, native tree is one of many plants that bear his name. It grows on the Edwards Plateau and in west-central, Trans-Pecos, and South Texas. The tree forms an irregular crown of spiny, bare-barked branches and thrives in dry, rocky places.

Its white or pale yellow blossoms erupt in spring and at other times of the year after a rain. They emit a delightful fragrance and attract swarms of honeybees. This and several other acacias provide the source of fine, clear "Uvalde honey." People use the hard, heavy wood for posts and fuel. Other features of this plant include its resistance to drought and its ferny leaves, with leaflets about twice the size of those of Gregg acacia (p. 144). Wright acacia's positive characteristics make it an excellent plant for arid country landscapes or for any well-drained location.

ROEMER ACACIA

Acacia roemeriana

LEAVES: Deciduous
HEIGHT: To 15 feet
GROWTH: Moderate/slow
VALUE: Honey, landscape
FAMILY: Legume (Fabaceae)
REGION(S): 7, 8, 10

*T*HE NAME OF THIS ACACIA commemorates German paleontologist Dr. Ferdinand von Roemer (1818–91), who explored the flora, fauna, and geology of a slice of Texas from Galveston to Fredricksburg during the mid-1840s. Author of *Texas* (1849) and *The Cretaceous Formations of Texas and Their Organic Inclusions* (1852), he later became a professor at the University of Breslau. He was elected to the scientific societies of London and Berlin, to the Imperial Academy of Science in St. Petersburg, and to the Royal Bavarian Academy of Science in Munich.

Sometimes called catclaw because of its small, curved spines, Roemer acacia grows from Travis County northwest into the Rolling Plains and southwest into the Big Bend area. Like other acacias, this attractive plant requires little care to produce pretty blossoms amid ferny, compound foliage. The spring flowers of Roemer acacia, borne in airy round white balls, constitute an important source of sweet, clear Texas honey. The plant develops into a small tree where it has access to deep soil and sufficient moisture.

Parkinsonia texana var. *macra*   **PALOVERDE**

LEAVES: Deciduous
HEIGHT: To 20 feet
GROWTH: Fast
VALUE: Landscape
FAMILY: Legume (Fabaceae)
REGION(S): 2, 6, 7

*P*ALOVERDE MEANS "green stick," an apt name for this small tree of the Lower Rio Grande Valley and Mexico. This subtropical species certainly has green bark and twigs. In extreme drought conditions, it can even shed its leaves to conserve water and continue photosynthesis through the stems alone.

The bright yellow, pealike flowers may appear at any time of year after rains but most often emerge during the warm season. Though the crooked branches produce many spines, this attractive plant deserves serious consideration as a landscape item in dry locations.

The genus *Parkinsonia* is named for John Parkinson (1567–1650), apothecary to King James I and botanist to King Charles I of England. It includes another Texas native, retama (p. 160), a species often confused with paloverde.

HUISACHE

Acacia farnesiana (A. smallii)

LEAVES: Deciduous
HEIGHT: To 30 feet
GROWTH: Fast
VALUE: Landscape, medicinal, perfume, wildlife
FAMILY: Legume (Fabaceae)
REGION(S): 2, 3, 6, 7, 10

*T*HE HUISACHE— correctly pronounced "wee*saht*chay" but widely called "*wee*satch" by gringos—gets its name from an Aztec term meaning "many thorns." Technically this tree does not have any thorns; it has spines (see glossary). But you won't care about the difference if you get tangled up in one. Deer and cattle ignore the armor and browse the foliage anyway.

While this plant boasts many medicinal uses, for everything from curing headaches to dressing wounds, the true glory of huisache lies in its flowers, which emerge as early as February. The profuse blossoms develop in little globular clusters that gild the tree. Perfume manufacturers in France cultivate huisache especially for its delicate fragrance, and honeybees swarm over its flowers, collecting the sweet nectar. The graceful, ferny foliage provides an added attraction for landscapes, and the tree's dark pods, about 1 to 2 inches long, envelop a multitude of tiny brown seeds.

Despite our lengthy and intimate relationship with this plant, botanists can't seem to agree on its correct classification or natural origin. Some give it the species name *farnesiana*, after Roman Catholic Cardinal Odoardo Farnese (1573–1626), while others insist upon *smallii*, after John

Warning: Invasive species

Kunkel Small (1869–1938), the first curator of museums at the New York Botanic Gardens. Various sources hold that the tree originates in Africa; others trace it to tropical America, while yet others describe it as a native of the American Southwest. Whatever the case, it certainly makes itself at home in Texas.

Our most populous acacia, huisache covers the southern third of the state with vast colonies from Houston to Austin and up the Rio Grande to Big Bend National Park. In the prairies around Victoria it constitutes the dominant large vegetation.

HUISACHILLO

LEAVES: Deciduous
HEIGHT: To 20 feet
GROWTH: Slow
VALUE: Honey, landscape, wildlife
FAMILY: Legume (Fabaceae)
REGION(S): 2, 6, 7

*H*UISACHILLO ("weesat*chee*yoh") or "little huisache" develops as a small, gnarled, and leaning tree with foliage similar to that of its bigger cousin, huisache (p. 148), but with longer and narrower seed-pods. It borrows its species name from Whilhelm Schaffner, a German dentist and botanist who settled in Mexico City in 1856. Huisachillo thrives throughout much of South Texas, particularly on the Rio Grande Plains.

The globular deep yellow flower clusters burst forth in early spring and provide an excellent honey source for bees. These flowers emit a sweet fragrance and develop into the pods, which can grow up to 5 inches long. Although slow to mature, huisachillo makes an attractive character tree and provides good nesting and wildlife protection.

Warning: Invasive species

TENAZA

Pithecellobium pallens

OFTEN A SHRUB but sometimes a tree of up to 30 feet tall, tenaza resides in deep South Texas. In contrast to its dark, almost glossy cousin, Texas ebony (p. 151), this plant's compound leaves appear light green and ferny. Pairs of slender spines flank the twigs.

The white or pale yellow flowers of tenaza form in semirounded heads on small panicles that lightly scent the air when the tree is in full bloom. The straight seedpods that follow end in pointed tips. The flowers provide a good source of nectar for honey, the foliage offers cover and browse, and the plant presents definite ornamental possibilities.

LEAVES: Deciduous
HEIGHT: To 30 feet
GROWTH: Fast
VALUE: Honey, landscape
FAMILY: Legume (Fabaceae)
REGION(S): 2, 6

LEAVES: Evergreen
HEIGHT: To 40 feet
GROWTH: Moderate/fast
VALUE: Edible parts, landscape, wildlife, wood uses
FAMILY: Legume (Fabaceae)
REGION(S): 2, 6

*E*BONY'S CREAMY YELLOW flowers bloom through much of the summer, giving way to thick, curved pods up to 5 inches long. These highly distinctive fruits inspire the tree's more whimsical common name: ape's earring. Some people in Mexico cook and eat the unripe beanlike seeds or pop them like popcorn once they have ripened. Finely ground, they make a substitute for coffee. The seeds' high protein content also renders them popular with deer, javelinas, and other mammals. The dark red to purple-brown wood serves as fuel and posts, and carpenters utilize it for cabinet-work and small woodenware.

Texas ebony's spiny, almost evergreen crown can reach a substantial 40 feet or more in height. Common to coastal South Texas and the Lower Rio Grande Valley, its sturdy presence causes many residents to consider it the Lower Valley's most valuable tree. The border community of Los Ebanos, site of the only hand-pulled ferry on the U.S.-Mexican border, takes its name from the many ebony trees lining the riverbank there.

CHAPARRO PRIETO

Acacia rigidula

LEAVES: Deciduous
HEIGHT: To 15 feet
GROWTH: Fast
VALUE: Honey, landscape
FAMILY: Legume (Fabaceae)
REGION(S): 7, 10

*T*HE SPANISH WORD *chaparro* ("shah*pah*rro") derives from a Basque term meaning "a small, evergreen oak." In the United States the expression came to be associated with thorny brush country, or chaparral, and led to the word *chaps* for the protective leg wear donned by cowboys for riding through such terrain. *Prieto* ("pri*ay*toh") is a Mexican term meaning "dark" and refers to the tree's rich, deep green foliage. Also called blackbrush acacia, this small shrubby tree of Texan and Mexican chaparrals has rigid branches, twigs, and leaves—hence the species name *rigidula*.

Fragrant spring flowers, borne in white to light yellow spikes, precede the slender, dramatically curved pods, which, together with sharp spines along the twigs, accent the dark green leaves. Chaparro prieto grows over much of Central, South, and West Texas and sometimes forms dense thickets.

Like most native acacias, it provides good nectar for honey. This tree also makes an exceptionally attractive ornamental. Able to thrive in hot, dry places, the dark foliage gives a lush and healthy appearance to otherwise arid looking landscapes.

Caesalpinia mexicana

MEXICAN POINCIANA

LEAVES: Deciduous
HEIGHT: To 30 feet
GROWTH: Fast
VALUE: Landscape
FAMILY: Legume (Fabaceae)
REGION(S): 6

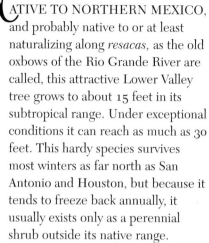

NATIVE TO NORTHERN MEXICO, and probably native to or at least naturalizing along *resacas,* as the old oxbows of the Rio Grande River are called, this attractive Lower Valley tree grows to about 15 feet in its subtropical range. Under exceptional conditions it can reach as much as 30 feet. This hardy species survives most winters as far north as San Antonio and Houston, but because it tends to freeze back annually, it usually exists only as a perennial shrub outside its native range.

The fragrant, bright yellow flowers are probably responsible for the nickname Mexican bird of paradise. Delicate compound foliage adds to Mexican poinciana's desirability as a landscape plant for patios and other sunny places. Its seedpods occasionally burst open with an unexpected popping sound, sometimes startling or perplexing the uninitiated. Also called Mexican caesalpinia, this tree tolerates poor soil, heat, and considerable drought.

The genus name *Caesalpinia* recalls Andrea Caesalpini, chief physician to Pope Clement VIII and author of one of the first Renaissance era books on botany (published in 1583) with a taxonomic system based strictly on reproductive structures. The genus that bears his name encompasses over 200 species of trees and shrubs.

MIMOSA

LEAVES: Deciduous
HEIGHT: To 30 feet
GROWTH: Fast
VALUE: Landscape
FAMILY: Legume (Fabaceae)
REGION(S): Non-native

*A*LSO CALLED SILK TREE, this native of Asia has long enjoyed popularity as an ornamental and naturalizes here and there across the eastern part of Texas. Usually a modest tree of about 20 feet in height, it can reach 30 feet or more, but its sparse limbs and compound leaves give little shade. In late spring, pink powder puffs adorn the long, arching branches. These otherworldly flowers and the delicate ferny foliage produce an ethereal effect that belies the tree's tough nature: it often resprouts from the ground if cut down or frost-killed.

When not deliberately planted, mimosa appears at wood edges or over roadside ditches, but it has never developed into a troublesome invader like many other introduced trees.

The genus name honors the eighteenth-century Italian naturalist Fillipo degli Albizzi.

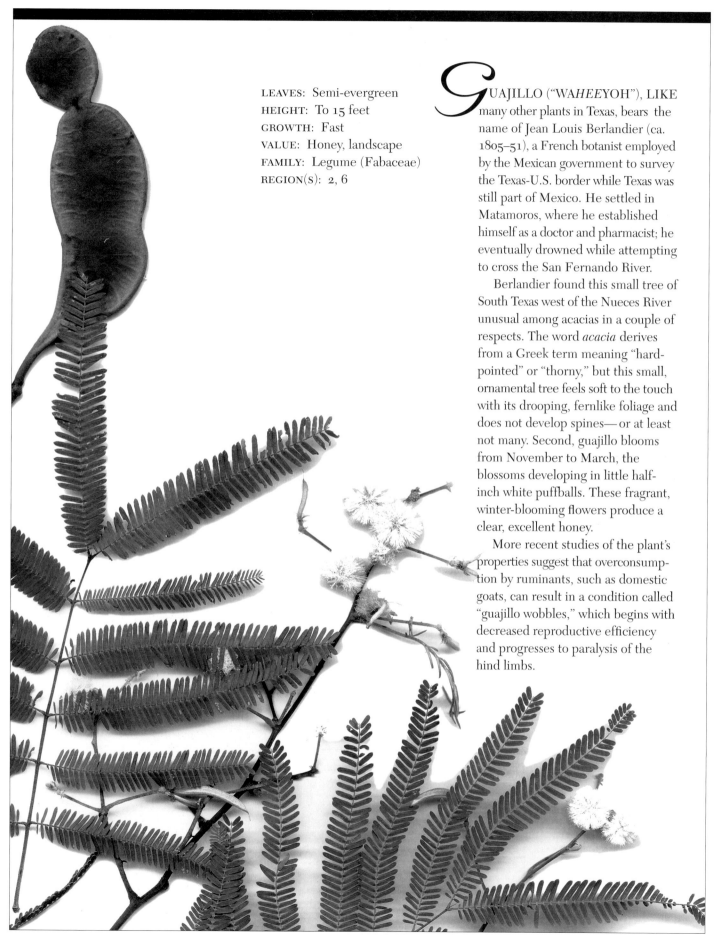

GUAJILLO

LEAVES: Semi-evergreen
HEIGHT: To 15 feet
GROWTH: Fast
VALUE: Honey, landscape
FAMILY: Legume (Fabaceae)
REGION(S): 2, 6

GUAJILLO ("WA*HEEY*OH"), LIKE many other plants in Texas, bears the name of Jean Louis Berlandier (ca. 1805–51), a French botanist employed by the Mexican government to survey the Texas-U.S. border while Texas was still part of Mexico. He settled in Matamoros, where he established himself as a doctor and pharmacist; he eventually drowned while attempting to cross the San Fernando River.

Berlandier found this small tree of South Texas west of the Nueces River unusual among acacias in a couple of respects. The word *acacia* derives from a Greek term meaning "hard-pointed" or "thorny," but this small, ornamental tree feels soft to the touch with its drooping, fernlike foliage and does not develop spines—or at least not many. Second, guajillo blooms from November to March, the blossoms developing in little half-inch white puffballs. These fragrant, winter-blooming flowers produce a clear, excellent honey.

More recent studies of the plant's properties suggest that overconsumption by ruminants, such as domestic goats, can result in a condition called "guajillo wobbles," which begins with decreased reproductive efficiency and progresses to paralysis of the hind limbs.

GOLDEN BALL LEAD TREE   *Leucaena retusa*

LEAVES: Deciduous
HEIGHT: To 25 feet
GROWTH: Fast
VALUE: Landscape, wildlife
FAMILY: Legume (Fabaceae)
REGION(S): 7, 10

*T*HE GLOBULAR, DEEP Yellow pompoms responsible for the name golden ball burst into bloom after rain showers in late spring, summer, and fall. Long, flattened pods containing numerous shiny brown seeds replace the flowers, and delicate foliage invites cattle and deer to browse the compound leaves, often reducing the tree to a mere shrub. The hard, heavy wood inspired the name lead tree.

Golden ball lead tree is native to parts of the western Edwards Plateau, the Big Bend, and the Trans-Pecos. It also graces the states of New Mexico and Coahuila in Mexico. The tree performs best in full sun and well-drained locations.

Although some people refer to it as little leaf lead tree, the size of its leaflets exceeds that of its more southerly cousin, tepeguaje (p. 157). The flowers, too, develop into bigger, more deeply golden clusters—almost the color of a school bus. A fine landscape species in its dry range, golden ball lead tree can be cultivated from Houston to San Antonio and beyond.

TEPEGUAJE

LEAVES: Semi-evergreen
HEIGHT: To 50 feet
GROWTH: Fast
VALUE: Honey, landscape, wood uses
FAMILY: Legume (Fabaceae)
REGION(S): 2, 6, 7

FERNY FOLIAGE AND sweet-scented blossoms render tepeguaje ("teppe*wa*hay") a good ornamental or dappled-shade tree. The spherical white or pale yellow flower clusters emerge frequently throughout the warmer parts of the year and provide a rich source of honey. Long thin seedpods, with their seeds prominently bulging through papery skins, succeed the delicate blooms. Mexican girls sometimes string these seeds into pretty necklaces. The wood provides lumber and fence posts.

Tepeguaje, like ebony (p. 151), serves as a marker tree for the Lower Rio Grande Valley. Common in that region, it also grows down through northeastern Mexico and more rarely up the coast and into the Edwards Plateau. It attains about 50 feet in height and serves as a popular street tree in Brownsville and nearby communities. Easily freeze-killed, this tree does not adapt well outside its limited range. Other common names include Mexican lead tree and great lead tree, both of which pay tribute to this tree's hard, heavy wood.

HONEY AND SCREWBEAN MESQUITE

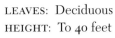

LEAVES: Deciduous
HEIGHT: To 40 feet
(Screwbean Mesquite: to 30 feet)
GROWTH: Slow
VALUE: Heritage, landscape,
wildlife, wood uses
FAMILY: Legume (Fabaceae)
REGION(S): 2–10
(Screwbean Mesquite: 10)

*L*EGEND HOLDS THAT a troop of Spanish conquistadors, camping under a tree long ago, were so plagued by mosquitoes that they named the tree mosquito, after their tormentors. Over time the word mutated into mesquite. A less romantic but more authoritative explanation appears in the *American Heritage Dictionary,* which holds that the name comes from the Spanish *mezquite,* in turn derived from the Náhuatl word *mizquitl.*

To the minds of people today, mesquite is the tree that typifies Texas. Once confined mostly to streambeds and river bottoms, honey mesquite now proliferates over almost all of the state except the Piney Woods. When ranchers introduced cattle into Texas, livestock became the tree's primary distributors, passing undigested seeds in ready fertilizer on overgrazed land.

Despite modern eradication techniques, mesquite survives and spreads. Its roots probe deeply to tap groundwater, and when landowners chop it down, it resprouts with multiple trunks.

Still, it cuts a striking figure, with lacy foliage and drooping branches, often leaning, wide spreading, with a crookedly rugged trunk. In spring and early summer it produces catkinlike racemes of tiny yellow blossoms.

Indians made use of mesquite beans by eating the sugary pulp of the pods and grinding the seeds into meal. Numerous birds and mammals also utilize this abundant food supply, and mesquite has developed quite a mystique as barbecue wood.

Screwbean mesquite, or *tornillo,* which is far less common in this state, grows in West Texas, thriving in flats, creek bottoms, and other relatively moist areas, sometimes forming thickets. It also grows in scattered locations across the Southwest to California and into northern Mexico. Screwbean's most obvious distinction, its spirally coiled pods, gives it its common name. Its foliage resembles that of honey mesquite except that it has fewer and smaller leaflets.

RETAMA

Parkinsonia aculeata

LEAVES: Deciduous
HEIGHT: To 35 feet
GROWTH: Fast
VALUE: Honey, landscape, wildlife
FAMILY: Legume (Fabaceae)
REGION(S): 2–7, 10

NATIVE TO south-central and West Texas, retama naturalizes as far east as Houston. It answers to a host of common names including paloverde but differs from true paloverde (p. 147) in its graceful, drooping demeanor and petite leaf structure. Nurseries often sell retama simply as "Parkinsonia."

This attractive small tree of the Southwest serves as a popular patio tree in sunny places. Its fernlike, pendulous leaves and bright yellow flowers make it a choice landscape species. It thrives in hot, dry climates and, like so many arid-country plants, protects itself with thorns, a fact reflected in its other popular name, Jerusalem thorn. The blossoms develop in spring, but scattered blooms also erupt after summer showers.

These flowers provide nectar for honey, and the beanlike pods that follow them offer nourishment to deer and other wildlife.

Melia azedarach

CHINABERRY

LEAVES: Deciduous
HEIGHT: To 30 feet
GROWTH: Fast
VALUE: Shade
FAMILY: Mahogany (Meliaceae)
REGION(S): Non-native

Warning: Invasive species, known poisonous properties

ONCE POPULAR FOR SHADE, chinaberry was a ubiquitous feature of bare-dirt chicken yards. Small, lilac-colored blossoms, which burst forth with the emerging leaves in spring, emit a delightful fragrance. But the copious yellow berries, about half an inch in diameter, prove highly problematic. Several species of birds, particularly mockingbirds, robins, and waxwings, avidly devour them, getting "drunk" and sometimes smashing into windows as a result. Those that survive disperse the seeds, causing chinaberry to proliferate and

become a troublesome invader. Today this Asian native naturalizes widely throughout the southern United States and the eastern half of Texas, sometimes becoming a weedy pest.

All parts of the tree are poisonous, especially the fruits. Eating as few as six of them can kill you, and even birds that eat too many berries may become paralyzed.

Although this tree belongs to the mahogany family, its weak wood has virtually no commercial value. The tree is reputed to have insect repellent characteristics, and growers originally introduced it to this country partly for that reason.

In the 1890s, botanists found a mutation of chinaberry, called umbrella tree, near the San Jacinto battlefield. That variety usually makes a dense, umbrella-like shade at about 15 or 20 feet.

GOLDEN RAIN TREE

GOLDEN RAIN TREE

LEAVES: Deciduous
HEIGHT: To 35 feet
GROWTH: Fast
VALUE: Landscape, shade
FAMILY: Soapberry (Sapindaceae)
REGION(S): Non-native

See color illustration, p. vii

THE FLOWERS OF GOLDEN rain tree revive memories of spring as their large yellow clusters cover the tree in autumn. These "rain" down when they mature, spreading a golden carpet beneath the tree. The puffy, rosy pink capsules that follow are at least as pretty and charming as the blossoms.

This lovely tree of oriental origin grows rapidly and flowers at a young age, making it an excellent lawn or street tree within its hardiness zone, and many people in the Gulf Coast region plant it on their property. Hardy to Houston and San Antonio, it may freeze back in severe winters, but it naturalizes here to some extent.

The genus name honors Joseph Gottlieb Köhlreuter (1733–1806), professor of natural history at Karlsruhe, Germany. The species name *paniculata* refers to the tree's showy flower panicles.

HONEY LOCUST

HONEY LOCUST

LEAVES: Deciduous
HEIGHT: To 70 feet
GROWTH: Fast
VALUE: Heritage, landscape, wildlife
FAMILY: Legume (Fabaceae)
REGION(S): 1–5, 7

*H*ONEY LOCUST EARNS distinction as one of nature's best-armed trees. The often three-pronged thorns on its trunk and branches grow up to a foot long. They mostly point downward, protecting the bark and preventing harmful animals from scaling the tree.

The interesting foot-long beans curl spirally and, after falling, roll in the wind, slowly releasing their seeds. These beans provide wonderful wildlife food and often don't survive for long on the ground. Native Americans ate the sugary substance in the pods between the seeds and made fish hooks from the thorns. Pioneers also used these thorns for pinning sacks and sometimes brewed a beverage called locust beer from the pods. The wood resists rot, making it ideal for fence posts.

This well-protected species grows over most of the eastern United States, including at least the eastern third of Texas. Homeowners prize honey locust for its rapid growth and attractive compound leaves, prompting nurseries to cultivate several thornless varieties. However, botanists warn that even these trees may develop thorns with age.

WATER LOCUST

LEAVES: Deciduous
HEIGHT: To 60 feet
GROWTH: Fast
VALUE: Wood uses
FAMILY: Legume (Fabaceae)
REGION(S): 1–3

*T*HIS COUSIN OF HONEY locust (pp. 164–65) inhabits swamps and waterways in East Texas, occasionally growing as tall as 60 feet, although it usually attains a more modest size. The flowers are inconspicuous, but the fruits consist of interesting small, two-toned brown pods, usually containing only one flat round seed.

Water locust thorns are not three-pronged like those of honey locust but form an impressive display in their own right as they jut, thick and glossy, from the zigzag branches.

Some people use the tree's heavy, close-grained wood for fuel and posts, and its ability to take a high polish makes it ideal for woodenware.

BLACK LOCUST

Robinia pseudoacacia

NE OF THE MOST
unique American trees, black locust
originates in the Appalachians, the
Ozarks, and the Ohio Valley. It is
probably not indigenous to Texas, but
people have planted it here for so long
that it has become well established in
various parts of the state. It naturalizes
and forms groves by way of root
suckers.

Europeans have cultivated black
locust since the early 1600s, and they
greatly admire it for both its beauty
and its resistance to pollution. The
white, wisteria-like clusters of spring
flowers compete with the lacy
compound leaves for attention.
Most noteworthy, however, are the
properties of locust wood.

Black locust yields the absolute
favorite wood of any tree for fence
posts. Extremely durable in the
ground, it will outlast the wire
attached to it. It also provides the very
finest firewood in America, having a
heat index superior even to that of
hickory. It was once the preferred
wood for ship nails, marine timbers,
wagon hubs, and railroad ties.

Some cooks use the flowers in
salads and fritters, but other parts of
the tree are considered toxic. Black
locust makes a beautiful yard tree for
anyone prepared to deal with the
sprouts. When the tree is cut down, the
stump will endure for many decades.

The tree borrows its genus name
from Jean (1550–1629) and Vespian
(1579–1600) Robin, who served as
herbalists to King Henry IV of
France. *Pseudoacacia,* of course,
means "false acacia."

LEAVES: Deciduous
HEIGHT: To 50 feet
GROWTH: Fast
VALUE: Landscape, wood uses
FAMILY: Legume (Fabaceae)
REGION(S): Non-native

Warning:
Known poisonous properties

LEAVES: Evergreen
HEIGHT: To 30 feet
GROWTH: Fast
VALUE: Culinary, landscape, medicinal, wildlife
FAMILY: Citrus (Rutaceae)
REGION(S): 2, 6

*C*OLIMA, OFTEN CALLED lime prickly ash, should not be confused with *Zanthoxylum hirsutum* (p. 174), also known by that common name. The crushed leaves of both exude a strong citrus smell, but while the trees share a moniker and membership in the same genus, they do not look at all alike. You can readily identify colima by its dark evergreen foliage—each leaflet a tiny disc—and by the winged edges on the midrib of the leaves.

The fruits of colima turn brown when ripe, with a single shiny black seed inside. They mature in late summer or autumn and prove popular with many species of birds. Locals occasionally dry the leaves of colima for use as a seasoning, and in Mexico people regard them as the source of a nerve tonic and sleep inducer.

This cousin of Hercules' club (p. 197) occurs rather commonly in the Lower Rio Grande Valley and more sparsely up the coast to Galveston County. It usually appears as a small inclined tree but can attain a height of about 30 feet.

GUAYACAN

Guaiacum angustifolium

LEAVES: Evergreen
HEIGHT: To 20 feet
GROWTH: Slow
VALUE: Honey, landscape, medicinal
FAMILY: Caltrop (Zygophyllaceae)
REGION(S): 6, 7, 10

*I*N EARLY SPRING, THIS interesting little species develops petite purple flowers, which lie almost hidden among dense evergreen foliage. The unusual, heart-shaped capsules that follow the blossoms sport winged margins, and each contains two red, yellow, or orange seeds.

Merchants in Mexico sell the root bark of guayacan ("*wah*yahkahn") as "soap" for washing wool, and *curanderos* prescribe extracts of the root for the treatment of rheumatism. The flowers provide a good early source of honey, and guayacan wood serves well for tool handles and fence posts.

Also called Texas porlieria, this shrubby tree of the South Texas brush country grows westward to the Big Bend, northward to the southern Edwards Plateau, and southward into northern Mexico.

EVE'S NECKLACE

LEAVES: Deciduous
HEIGHT: To 25 feet
GROWTH: Fast
VALUE: Dye, landscape, wildlife
FAMILY: Legume (Fabaceae)
REGION(S): 4, 5, 7

Warning:
Known poisonous properties

*T*HIS TREE, WITH ITS unusual legumes constricted between the seeds so as to give them the appearance of a string of beads, evokes to some the humorous image of Eve strolling the Garden of Eden sparsely clad but fully accessorized. Little bonnet-shaped pink flowers appear in spring or early summer and hang in dangling clusters, heralding the prim little baubles.

While the pods, blossoms, and compound leaves endow the tree with ornamental properties suitable to paradise, gardeners should be aware of the poisonous nature of the seeds. Ring-tailed cats, however, can eat them, and deer browse the foliage. The wood also yields a yellow dye.

This dainty little cousin of Texas mountain laurel (p. 176) grows in a fairly narrow band from the Dallas area to around San Antonio and west to Kerrville.

TEXAS PISTACHE

Pistacia texana

LEAVES: Semi-evergreen
HEIGHT: To 40 feet
GROWTH: Moderate/fast
VALUE: Landscape, wildlife
FAMILY: Sumac (Anacardiaceae)
REGION(S): 7

WHILE TEXAS PISTACHE belongs to the sumac family, it represents one of only about ten pistachios worldwide. It occupies a very limited range in Texas, occurring in nature only near the confluence of the Pecos and Rio Grande rivers. Its pleasant appearance, however, leads to its propagation and sale by nurseries across the state. The horticultural department of Texas A&M University lists it as a good ornamental plant for El Paso, the *Dallas Morning News* recommends it as a hardy tree for north-central Texas, and the Travis Audubon Society suggests planting it in and around Austin to attract birds. Whether you call it American pistachio, wild pistachio, or *lentisco*, this tree enjoys a widespread following.

The fine, nearly evergreen foliage, with bright red new leaves in spring and clusters of red to blue-black nutlike drupes in summer, make it a good landscape choice in almost any part of the state. A cousin of Chinese pistache (p. 179), it thrives in full sun and tolerates dry conditions.

Amyris madrensis

SIERRA MADRE TORCHWOOD

LEAVES: Evergreen
HEIGHT: To 20 feet
GROWTH: Moderate/fast
VALUE: Landscape
FAMILY: Citrus (Rutaceae)
REGION(S): 6

*T*HIS RARE MEMBER of the citrus family makes its home in northern Mexico and in the Lower Rio Grande Valley. The species name *madrensis* refers to its presence in the Sierra Madre of Mexico. The genus name *Amyris* means "balsam-scented," alluding to the aromatic citrus smell exuded by all parts of the tree when bruised.

Sierra Madre torchwood belongs to the same genus as the shrubbier Texas torchwood (*Amyris texana*), and both species derive their common name from their easily ignited and hot-burning wood.

Shiny compound leaves and conspicuous gray-white trunks characterize this attractive plant. In midsummer it produces rather obscure clusters of tiny cream-colored flowers.

LIME PRICKLY ASH
Zanthoxylum hirsutum

LEAVES: Evergreen
HEIGHT: To 20 feet
GROWTH: Fast
VALUE: Landscape, medicinal, wildlife
FAMILY: Citrus (Rutaceae)
REGION(S): 2, 5–7

LIKE HERCULES' CLUB (p. 197), this tree numbs your mouth when you chew the leaves, twigs, or bark, thus alleviating toothaches. Because of this characteristic, it shares that tree's designations of tickle tongue and toothache tree. However, lime prickly ash differs from Hercules' club in several important respects.

The evergreen leaves are much smaller but emit a stronger, tangier smell and more potent lime taste. The tree also usually takes a more densely shrubby form, and its many thorns leave a stinging sensation long after you make contact with them.

Lime prickly ash grows along the central and lower coast, across the Edwards Plateau and Lower Rio Grande Valley, and southward into Mexico. Its habitat coincides with that of Hercules' club only in region 2, and Hercules' club has an otherwise more easterly distribution than lime prickly ash.

Herbalists, particularly in Latin America, make medicinal extracts from the tree for use as a sleep agent and nerve tonic. Many birds consume the berries, and the foliage furnishes valuable wildlife cover. *Zanthoxylum* means "yellow wood," and *hirsutum* refers to the usually hairy leaves.

FRAGRANT ASH

LEAVES: Deciduous
HEIGHT: To 20 feet
GROWTH: Fast
VALUE: Landscape
FAMILY: Olive (Oleaceae)
REGION(S): 7, 10

*U*NLIKE ANY OTHER ASH, this unique West Texas tree delivers showy sprays of delicate, highly aromatic flowers that completely cover the tree in a creamy white haze in the spring. These blossoms closely resemble those of the fringe tree (p. 30) of East Texas, except that fringe tree's blooms have somewhat longer flower petals.

Fragrant ash, which also grows in New Mexico, Arizona, and northern Mexico, seldom achieves more than 20 feet in height and sometimes forms thickets. While its native habitat is mountainous, it seems adaptable to other situations. Its exceptional ornamental beauty makes fragrant ash a perfect landscape choice in arid regions, and horticulturists are researching the possibility of propagating it for that purpose.

TEXAS MOUNTAIN LAUREL   *Sophora secundiflora*

LEAVES: Evergreen
HEIGHT: To 30 feet
GROWTH: Slow
VALUE: Heritage, landscape
FAMILY: Legume (Fabaceae)
REGION(S): 6, 7, 10

*T*HE DEEP VIOLET FLOWERS of Texas mountain laurel appear in late March and produce a fragrance faintly reminiscent of grape Kool-Aid. Bright red seeds, each about half an inch long, form in hard, lumpy pods, covered in velvety fuzz and hanging in stiff bunches. These seeds, called mescal beans, are highly toxic and hallucinogenic. Native Americans in the Southwest and in Mexico sometimes used a powder made from the beans in a drink during religious ceremonies to induce a mind-altered state and communicate with the spirit world. However, these were highly experienced practitioners; casual experimentation with this poisonous substance could lead to death and should never be tried.

Texas mountain laurel flaunts its vivid purple flower clusters from coastal South Texas across the Hill Country and westward. This beautiful tree commonly thrives in the poor limestone soil around Austin, but its admirers frequently plant it elsewhere as well. The flowers, seedpods, and glossy evergreen leaves combine to make this an attractive landscape plant as long as homeowners take note of the toxic properties of the seeds. These trees grow slowly and resist transplanting, but many nurseries around the state now offer them for sale.

Despite its name, this tree is not a laurel but a member of the legume family.

**Warning:
Known poisonous properties**

See color illustration, p. xx

Ailanthus altissima

TREE OF HEAVEN

Warning: Invasive species

LEAVES: Deciduous
HEIGHT: To 100 feet
GROWTH: Fast
VALUE: Landscape, shade, wildlife
FAMILY: Quassia (Simaroubaceae)
REGION(S): Non-native

LIKE MANY OTHER SPECIES, this Asian native made its way to the United States by way of Europe. In 1751, a French Jesuit priest brought the first specimens from Nanking, China, to England. Three and a half decades later, the eminent Philadelphian and amateur botanist William Hamilton (1745–1813) introduced this tree on his estate, the Woodlands, now a national historic landmark. Gardeners and homeowners have cultivated tree of heaven in the United States ever since and have planted it widely from coast to coast. It naturalizes readily not only from wind-dispersed seeds but also by way of root suckers.

Named for its fast, upright growth, it reaches toward the sky and attains more than 100 feet in height. Developers often plant it as a street tree because it endures exhaust fumes and pollution.

Long compound leaves and quick maturation make it a popular landscape choice, but male trees often emit a foul odor, and the tree can become weedy in some areas. Several species of birds, such as pine grosbeaks and crossbills, eat the seeds.

WESTERN SOAPBERRY
Sapindus saponaria var. *drummondii*

LEAVES: Deciduous
HEIGHT: To 30 feet
GROWTH: Moderate/fast
VALUE: Heritage, landscape
FAMILY: Soapberry (Sapindaceae)
REGION(S): 1–8, 10

Warning:
Known poisonous properties

*B*OTH THE COMMON and generic names of this tree refer to a unique quality of its fruits: the amber drupes contain rich amounts of saponins and, when crushed in water, produce a lather that rivals soap. Native Americans and early settlers often used them for this purpose, and in Mexico they still form an ingredient in some shampoos and laundry detergents.

At optimum ripeness, the fruits look like plump, translucent globes, the shiny black seeds visible inside. These fruits, which eventually shrivel and turn brown, are toxic to humans if ingested. Most wildlife also seems to avoid them. However, country folk once crafted the seeds into necklaces, rosaries, and buttons.

The compound leaves of soapberry somewhat resemble those of flameleaf or prairie flameleaf sumac (pp. 181, 180) but lack the winged midribs that characterize those species.

Western soapberry flourishes in almost every part of Texas except the Piney Woods, where it occurs only rarely. It survives and even thrives on many types of soil and with varied rainfall patterns. Because of its adaptability, the Texas Department of Agriculture recommends it as a good landscape and shade tree. Its rounded form, rapid growth, and attractive compound leaves enhance its ornamental value.

Pistacia chinensis

CHINESE PISTACHE

LEAVES: Deciduous
HEIGHT: To 40 feet
GROWTH: Moderate/slow
VALUE: Landscape, rootstock, wildlife
FAMILY: Sumac (Anacardiaceae)
REGION(S): Non-native

*C*HINESE PISTACHE BOASTS attractive foliage that turns dazzling shades of red, yellow, and orange in autumn and releases a bitter smell when crushed. The showy drupes, borne only on female trees, ripen through turquoise and pink before culminating in bright red. While birds relish these fruits, they are inedible to humans. However, the tree serves as a hardy grafting rootstock for the commercial pistachio (*Pistacia vera*).

This native of China enjoys popularity as an ornamental tree in Texas and sometimes naturalizes where birds drop the seeds. A compact tree that can reach 40 feet in height, it readily adapts to drier areas.

While in the sumac family, this tree distinguishes itself by a more compact and spreading habit than that of flameleaf (p. 181) or prairie flameleaf sumac (p.180), and by smaller, slightly more oval leaflets, though not as rounded as those of Texas pistache (p. 172). It also lacks the winged midribs so typical of other sumacs.

PRAIRIE FLAMELEAF SUMAC *Rhus lanceolata*

LEAVES: Deciduous
HEIGHT: To 30 feet
GROWTH: Fast
VALUE: Dye, edible parts, landscape, wildlife
FAMILY: Sumac (Anacardiaceae)
REGION(S): 5, 7, 8, 10

See color illustration, p. xi

A MORE WESTERLY, MORE finely configured cousin of flameleaf sumac (p. 181), prairie flameleaf sumac proliferates from the Dallas–Fort Worth area down into Central Texas and from there over into West Texas. Though botanists classify several sumacs as shrubs, this one definitely attains tree status, growing to a stout 30 feet. Like other sumacs, it reveals its true beauty in fall when the compound leaves turn scarlet. As a result of its rich autumn color, the tree enjoys increasing popularity in landscapes.

The attractive red drupes can be used either to make a pleasant, mildly acidic drink or to produce a black dye. The drink, however, will not stain your mouth. Many birds devour the fruits, which provide an especially important source of nourishment for quail and prairie chickens.

As is typical of most sumacs, the tree's compound leaves have winged midribs, helping to distinguish them from those of the similar western soapberry (p. 178), Texas walnut (p. 182), and Chinese pistache (p. 179).

FLAMELEAF SUMAC

LEAVES: Deciduous
HEIGHT: To 25 feet
GROWTH: Fast
VALUE: Edible parts, heritage, landscape, wildlife
FAMILY: Sumac (Anacardiaceae)
REGION(S): 1–4

WELL NAMED, THIS SUMAC'S leaves blaze into a fiery display of scarlet and orange in autumn. The pyramidal red fruit clusters add to the tree's aesthetic appeal. You can steep these drupes in hot water to make a drink that looks and tastes somewhat like pink lemonade (appendix G). The fruits also have the property of refreshing and clarifying water. Native Americans used them for that purpose when they had only muddy pools from which to drink. Several other species of red-fruited sumacs can be used in the same way. Poison sumac (*Rhus vernix*), by contrast, develops dirty-white berries and occurs in this state in only a few isolated swamps in extreme East Texas, near the Louisiana border. From there, poison sumac grows east to Florida and north to Quebec.

Flameleaf sumac commonly appears along wood edges and fence-rows in the eastern quarter of Texas, growing to 25 feet or more and often forming thickets by way of root sprouts. The tree does not live long, but it proliferates by making its fruits attractive to birds. Nicknamed shining sumac, it has leaflets larger than those of its more westerly counterpart, prairie flameleaf sumac; the winged midribs of its leaves distinguish this species from Texas walnut (p. 182), Chinese pistache (p. 179), and western soapberry (p. 178).

TEXAS WALNUT

Juglans microcarpa

A JUNIOR MEMBER of the walnut family, Texas walnut grows to only about 30 feet, often sprouting multiple trunks. The narrow leaflets resemble those of prairie flameleaf sumac (p. 180) but lack the winged margins on the leaves' midribs. As the name *microcarpa* implies, the nuts appear tiny by comparison to other walnuts, but they taste sweet, and squirrels, other rodents, and javelinas relish them.

Also called little walnut, *nogalito*, and river walnut, this tree grows in southwest Texas with widely scattered populations in the central, southern, and northwest parts of the state. It also occurs in Oklahoma and New Mexico.

The foliage of Texas walnut smells strongly aromatic and turns a pleasant yellow in autumn, giving the tree certain ornamental value, with the added attraction that it requires little care.

LEAVES: Deciduous
HEIGHT: To 30 feet
GROWTH: Moderate/fast
VALUE: Landscape, wildlife
FAMILY: Walnut (Juglandaceae)
REGION(S): 5–8, 10

LEAVES: Deciduous
HEIGHT: To 100 feet
GROWTH: Fast
VALUE: Edible parts, lumber, shade, wildlife
FAMILY: Walnut (Juglandaceae)
REGION(S): 1–8

SHIPWRECKED ON GALVESTON Island in 1528, Cabeza de Vaca reported in his *Relación* that the coastal Karankawa Indians sat under pecan trees when the nuts were ripe and did little else for weeks but crack and eat them. While this was probably an exaggeration, pecans are highly nutritious, and throughout their range they constituted an important item of diet for Native Americans.

The state tree of Texas, pecan grows to the largest size of any member of the walnut family. When it is not in fruit, you will recognize pecan by its longer, narrower, and more scythe-shaped leaflets and by its flakier bark.

Pecan is native to a large part of the United States and common in East, Central, and parts of South Texas. Many property owners also plant horticultural forms in and well beyond the tree's native range.

Nurseries breed these for their thin, easy-to-crack shells and usually sell them under the name "Paper-shell Pecan." These nuts remain by far the most important of any nut grown commercially in America. Consider their use in pies (appendix G), candies, ice cream, cookies, and other confections.

Pecan grows fairly rapidly and makes a handsome landscape and shade tree. Squirrels, raccoons, opossums, and javelinas eat the nuts. Several bird species, including crows and blue jays, also manage to crack them.

BLACK WALNUT

Juglans nigra

LEAVES: Deciduous
HEIGHT: To 80 feet
GROWTH: Fast
VALUE: Dye, edible parts, heritage, landscape, lumber, wildlife
FAMILY: Walnut (Juglandaceae)
REGION(S): 1–5, 7, 8

BLACK WALNUT produces some of the finest nuts of any member of its family, which includes hickories and pecans. However, the tough shells and surrounding husks make the nutmeats hard to obtain. Native Americans and pioneers valued them enough to spend serious time and energy extracting them, and today a black walnut cake (appendix G) should be regarded on the same scale as fine caviar or truffles.

This is a multiuse tree. The wood proves extremely valuable for cabinets, furniture, veneer, musical instruments, and gunstocks, often rendering a large walnut tree worth more than the acre on which it grows.

Walnut husks yield an excellent brown dye—and will stain your hands indelibly for a week. They also produce a strong narcotic effect on fish, and Native Americans, such as the Cherokees, frequently used them for fishing. Settlers, too, crushed walnut hulls, put them in towsacks, and immersed them in creeks, whereupon the fish would rise drunkenly to the surface to be scooped up in nets. That practice is now illegal.

Black walnut prefers rich bottomlands where it can grow without competition from taller trees. Its long, compound leaves and regular form make it a good landscape tree.

Juglans major

LEAVES: Deciduous
HEIGHT: To 50 feet
GROWTH: Fast
VALUE: Edible parts, landscape, shade, wildlife
FAMILY: Walnut (Juglandaceae)
REGION(S): 7, 10

*T*HIS HANDSOME, MODEST tree of Central and West Texas also grows in its namesake state and in New Mexico as well as northern Mexico. Its nuts develop to a size intermediate between those of Texas walnut (p. 182) and the larger nuts of black walnut (p. 184). The leaves have fewer leaflets than either of the other species.

Arizona walnut can attain 50 feet in height but more often reaches to only about 30 feet, with a trunk diameter of around 18 inches. Its graceful, rounded form casts a pleasant shade and renders it a good landscape choice in drier parts of the state.

The wood, though similar to that of black walnut, has limited uses because of the tree's smaller size; it serves mainly for posts. The tasty and edible nuts also supply valuable wildlife food, particularly for squirrels and other rodents. The tree bears large crops every two to three years.

MEXICAN BUCKEYE

Ungnadia speciosa

*M*EXICAN BUCKEYE produces rich foliage and pretty spring blossoms that resemble the fuchsia clusters of redbud (p. 127) flowers except that they are larger and sparser. The interesting seed-pods consist of three compartments, each holding a round, marble-sized black seed. These seeds are toxic to humans, but rural children found a use for them long ago—as marbles.

This attractive small tree often develops a shrublike form with several trunks. Despite its common name, it is not a true buckeye (p. 211) but rather a cousin of the western soapberry (p. 178).

Mexican buckeye thrives in Central, South, and West Texas, New Mexico, and northern Mexico. It has recently received more recognition as an ornamental, and today its admirers often plant it in landscapes outside its native range.

LEAVES: Deciduous
HEIGHT: To 20 feet
GROWTH: Fast
VALUE: Heritage, landscape
FAMILY: Soapberry (Sapindaceae)
REGION(S): 2–5, 7, 8, 10

Warning:
Known poisonous properties

See color illustration, p. viii, ix

186

ONSIDERED RARE OVER its range, which extends from East Texas across the Gulf States to South Carolina, nutmeg hickory grows in small, scattered stands. It can reach 100 feet in height but usually attains a much more modest stature. This tree bears heavily, producing little nuts that resemble their namesake, the nutmeg.

These nuts are certainly edible but require painstaking work to extract the nutmeats, and usually only small children will spend their time in this endeavor. Experts consider the wood inferior to that of other hickories and assign it little commercial value. The nuts, however, produce valuable wildlife food, and the trees, which are loaded with them, do have a certain charm.

LEAVES: Deciduous
HEIGHT: To 100 feet
GROWTH: Slow
VALUE: Shade, wildlife
FAMILY: Walnut (Juglandaceae)
REGION(S): 1–3, 7

BLACK HICKORY

Carya texana

LEAVES: Deciduous
HEIGHT: To 80 feet
GROWTH: Slow
VALUE: Edible parts, wildlife
FAMILY: Walnut (Juglandaceae)
REGION(S): 1, 3–5, 7

*B*LACK HICKORY BEARS the name of our state, but it grows north to Kansas and Illinois and east into Indiana. It prefers dry upland areas, frequently growing in the company of blackjack or post oak (pp. 95, 96). In Texas, it appears over the eastern portion of the state to around San Antonio and Fredricksburg, and you can find it sprouting from the jagged crevices on Enchanted Rock.

This species can grow to more than 80 feet tall but is usually much smaller. It typically develops short, rather contorted branches, and its slow growth may take a leaning habit to reach the sunlight.

The edible nuts of black hickory form inside extremely hard, thick shells, and you will need a hammer and nut pick to extract the sweet kernels. But squirrels and wild hogs can manage them when hungry.

See color illustration, p. xiv

LEAVES: Deciduous
HEIGHT: To 100 feet
GROWTH: Fast
VALUE: Shade, wood uses
FAMILY: Walnut (Juglandaceae)
REGION(S): 1–4

*T*HE NAME HICKORY derives from *pawcohiccora,* the Algonquin term for a food made from nuts. But while the husks of this hickory are thin and allow easy access to the nutmeats inside, the kernels taste so bitter that even squirrels eat them reluctantly. The Iroquois, however, managed to derive several food substances from them and mixed oil from the nuts with bear grease to make hair lotion and insect repellent. They employed the bark for furniture and snowshoes.

The species name *cordiformis* means "heart-shaped" and refers to the look of the nuts.

Lumber dealers consider bitternut hickory wood inferior to the wood of mockernut and shagbark hickory (pp. 198–99, 200), and sell it primarily for tool handles and implements.

One of East Texas' big hickories, bitternut hickory is also the fastest growing of its clan and resprouts easily from stumps. Its huge range includes the northernmost states from Maine to Minnesota.

ELDERBERRY AND MEXICAN ELDER

Sambucus canadensis and *Sambucus mexicana*

LEAVES: Deciduous
HEIGHT: To 30 feet
GROWTH: Fast
VALUE: Dye, edible parts, heritage, medicinal, wildlife
FAMILY: Honeysuckle (Caprifoliaceae)
REGION(S): 1–7 (Mexican Elder: 10)

ANY PEOPLE think of elderberry and its cousin, Mexican elder, as woody shrubs, but because they are so widespread and occasionally reach heights of up to 30 feet, we include them in this book on Texas trees.

Both species enjoy a rich history. Their flowers make delightful "elderblow" fritters. The cooked berries taste wonderful in jellies and pies, and the dark, rich wine made from them is legendary (appendix G). These plants also boast countless medicinal uses—treating colds, fevers, and rheumatism, to name just a few. However, botanists consider all parts of the plant other than the flowers and ripe fruit somewhat toxic.

Maple farmers once used the hollow stems of elderberry as "spiles" for tapping sugar maples, and the plants yield dyes in a variety of colors. The big heads of berries also serve as living bird feeders, and any bird lover who grows elderberry will attract many avian species.

Elderberry occurs in most of the eastern United States from the Gulf states into Canada and west to Kansas. In Texas, it occupies the eastern half of the state, growing on rich stream banks and along fencerows. Mexican elder, which has smaller and fewer leaflets than elderberry, is native from West Texas to California and south through Mexico. Since it frequently appears along desert streams and arroyos, it exhibits some value for erosion control.

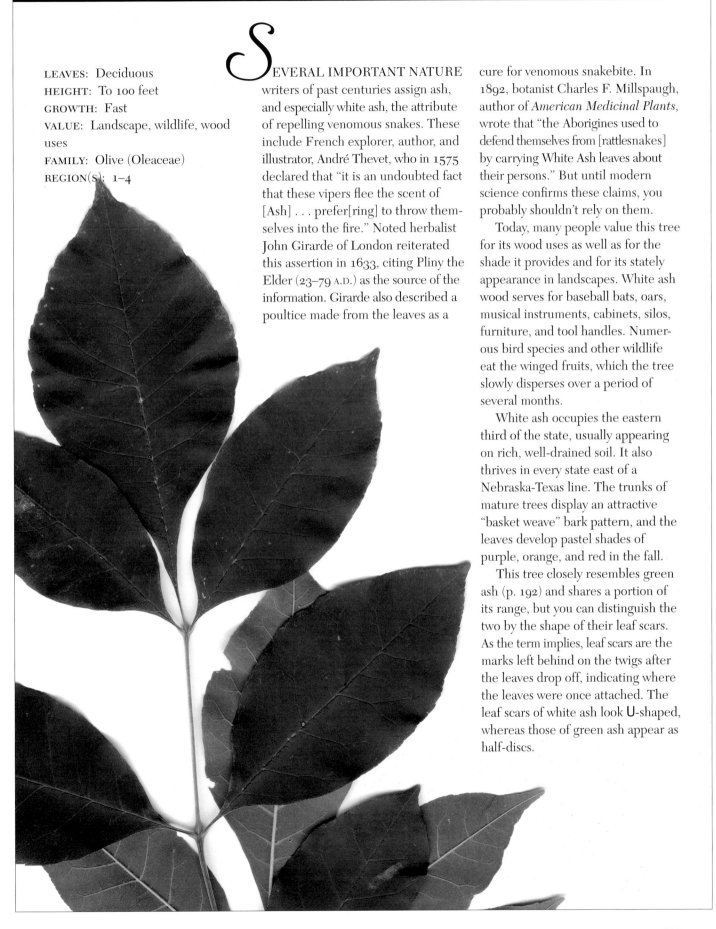

LEAVES: Deciduous
HEIGHT: To 100 feet
GROWTH: Fast
VALUE: Landscape, wildlife, wood uses
FAMILY: Olive (Oleaceae)
REGION(S): 1–4

$\mathcal{S}$EVERAL IMPORTANT NATURE writers of past centuries assign ash, and especially white ash, the attribute of repelling venomous snakes. These include French explorer, author, and illustrator, André Thevet, who in 1575 declared that "it is an undoubted fact that these vipers flee the scent of [Ash] . . . prefer[ring] to throw themselves into the fire." Noted herbalist John Girarde of London reiterated this assertion in 1633, citing Pliny the Elder (23–79 A.D.) as the source of the information. Girarde also described a poultice made from the leaves as a cure for venomous snakebite. In 1892, botanist Charles F. Millspaugh, author of *American Medicinal Plants,* wrote that "the Aborigines used to defend themselves from [rattlesnakes] by carrying White Ash leaves about their persons." But until modern science confirms these claims, you probably shouldn't rely on them.

Today, many people value this tree for its wood uses as well as for the shade it provides and for its stately appearance in landscapes. White ash wood serves for baseball bats, oars, musical instruments, cabinets, silos, furniture, and tool handles. Numerous bird species and other wildlife eat the winged fruits, which the tree slowly disperses over a period of several months.

White ash occupies the eastern third of the state, usually appearing on rich, well-drained soil. It also thrives in every state east of a Nebraska-Texas line. The trunks of mature trees display an attractive "basket weave" bark pattern, and the leaves develop pastel shades of purple, orange, and red in the fall.

This tree closely resembles green ash (p. 192) and shares a portion of its range, but you can distinguish the two by the shape of their leaf scars. As the term implies, leaf scars are the marks left behind on the twigs after the leaves drop off, indicating where the leaves were once attached. The leaf scars of white ash look U-shaped, whereas those of green ash appear as half-discs.

GREEN AND TEXAS ASH

Fraxinus pennsylvanica and *Fraxinus texensis*

LEAVES: Deciduous
HEIGHT: To 50 feet
(Texas Ash: to 30 feet)
GROWTH: Fast
VALUE: Landscape, lumber, shade, wildlife
FAMILY: Olive (Oleaceae)
REGION(S): 1–9 (Texas Ash: 7)

GREEN ASH'S HUGE habitat stretches from New England to Florida and west to the Rockies. In Texas, it grows over the eastern two thirds of the state. It prefers wet places and makes itself at home in creek and river bottoms.

In the past, farmers and ranchers often selected this tree for shelterbelt plantings across the prairie states. It casts deep shade and grows rapidly, and the bright green leaves turn a pleasing yellow in the fall. Green ash certainly presents a better landscape choice within its range than do the western ashes, since it resists storm damage and lives much longer. Carpenters employ the wood for cabinets, tool handles, and interior finishes.

A trick for distinguishing green ash from white ash (p. 191), is to look at the shape of the leaf scars or marks left behind on the twigs at the place where the leaves drop off. The leaf scars of green ash look like half-discs; those of white ash appear U-shaped.

Texas ash also resembles both white ash and green ash but differs from them by having only five (rarely seven) leaflets as opposed to the seven to nine leaflets of the other two species. Texas ash also remains smaller than its white and green cousins— substantially smaller than white ash— and prefers the limestone soil of the Edwards Plateau.

A number of birds eat the fruits, or "keys," of both species, and deer browse the foliage.

Fraxinus berlandieriana

BERLANDIER ASH

$\mathcal{T}$HIS NATIVE OF THE Edwards Plateau, South Texas, and Mexico bears the name of botanist Jean Louis Berlandier (ca. 1805–51). Chosen by eminent French botanist Auguste Pyrame DeCandolle to collect plant specimens in Mexico, Berlandier surveyed many parts of Texas and eventually settled in Matamoros. There he established himself as a physician before his life was cut short by a drowning accident in the San Fernando River.

Many people plant Berlandier ash outside its native range, often under the name Arizona ash, a name better applied to *Fraxinus velutina* (p. 195). The tree grows rapidly to form a broad crown, usually at about 30 feet, and so produces quick shade. For this reason, developers greatly overplant it. Experts generally do not consider this a valuable tree due to its short life span and its susceptibility to being blown over by storms.

Still, the tree is attractive, especially with its cascading sprays of cylindrical winged fruits known as "ash keys," and it can provide quick shade in bare places.

LEAVES: Deciduous
HEIGHT: To 40 feet
GROWTH: Fast
VALUE: Shade
FAMILY: Olive (Oleaceae)
REGION(S): 2, 6

CAROLINA ASH

Fraxinus caroliniana

LEAVES: Deciduous
HEIGHT: To 40 feet
GROWTH: Fast
VALUE: Landscape
FAMILY: Olive (Oleaceae)
REGION(S): 1

A TREE OF SWAMPS AND backwater areas, Carolina ash claims only a limited range in southeast Texas. It usually attains 30 feet or less in stature but can reach 40 feet under favorable conditions. Beyond this state it grows in scattered localities east to the Atlantic Coast and north to Virginia.

In addition to taking note of its specific habitat, you can distinguish this tree from other ashes by its unique fruit structure. The small elliptical seeds are completely enclosed in three-winged samaras that enable them to flutter or float.

A rather graceful little tree, Carolina ash has ornamental possibilities in moist places. The fruits, from 1 to 3 inches long, hang in pleasing clusters.

Fraxinus velutina

VELVET ASH

LEAVES: Deciduous
HEIGHT: To 40 feet
GROWTH: Fast
VALUE: Shade, wildlife
FAMILY: Olive (Oleaceae)
REGION(S): 10

*T*HE DOMINANT MEMBER of its genus west of the Pecos, velvet ash grows rapidly, usually with several main branches emanating from a short trunk to form a broad crown. It thrives across the American Southwest to California and southward into Mexico, where it goes by the name of *fresno.* Despite its unfortunate habit of shedding small limbs and copious winged fruits, many developers and homeowners plant velvet ash throughout Texas under the name Arizona ash. But the tree is so short-lived and susceptible to borers and high winds that most nurseries no longer promote it.

Nevertheless, many Texas home sites would be without shade were it not for velvet ash. Its rapid growth and attractive appearance can quickly fill an empty spot in the yard. You should note that some garden centers also offer Berlandier ash (p. 193) as "Arizona Ash," but you can distinguish the two by the velvety undersides of the leaflets on velvet ash.

Past uses of the wood of this tree include ax handles and wagons. Some herbivorous wildlife species browse the foliage.

YELLOW TRUMPET

Tecoma stans

LEAVES: Evergreen
HEIGHT: To 25 feet
GROWTH: Fast
VALUE: Heritage, honey, landscape, medicinal
FAMILY: Catalpa (Bignoniaceae)
REGION(S): 2, 6, 7, 10

*L*IKE HOPE, yellow trumpet springs eternal—or nearly so—blooming again and again during the warmer months of the year. Not surprisingly, its admirers in Mexico and along the Lower Rio Grande call it *esperanza*, the Spanish word for hope. Another common name is yellow bells.

This tree's abundant clusters of bright yellow, trumpet-shaped flowers convey a sense of pure joy and have transformed this plant into a common sight in gardens and landscapes north to Houston and San Antonio. Its native habitat covers southern and western parts of Texas and extends west to New Mexico and Arizona and south into tropical America. This species prefers full sun and can be pruned into a shrub or coaxed to attain tree status, with an ultimate height of nearly 25 feet. Even confined to a container, it will put forth wave after wave of delightful blossoms.

Herbalists use yellow trumpet medicinally as a treatment for diabetes and stomach cramps, and some people in Mexico brew the roots into a local beer. Indians once fashioned bows from the wood, and the flowers provide a plentiful source of honey.

See color illustration, p. xii

Zanthoxylum clava-herculis

HERCULES' CLUB

LEAVES: Deciduous
HEIGHT: To 20 feet
GROWTH: Moderate/slow
VALUE: Heritage, medicinal, wildlife
FAMILY: Citrus (Rutaceae)
REGION(S): 1–4

WITH OR WITHOUT its leaves, this tree is unmistakable: large conelike bumps topped by small prickles cover the bark. On older specimens the prickles disappear, leaving the corky knobs that transform the trunk into a caricature of the caveman's club.

Because the bark and leaves of Hercules' club contain a chemical compound that produces a distinct numbing sensation in the mouth, it earns the names toothache tree and tickle tongue. Native Americans and early settlers chewed these leaves to relieve toothaches, and mothers rubbed them on their babies' gums to ease teething pain.

The fruits of this little tree attract many avian species, and in late summer it converts into a living bird feeder. The birds, in turn, reward the tree's generosity by distributing its seeds—often while perching on barbed-wire fences. Hercules' club is common along fencerows in the eastern quarter of Texas, where it thrives in full sunshine. However, you will also find it in clearings and along forest edges.

MOCKERNUT HICKORY

Carya tomentosa (C. alba)   # MOCKERNUT HICKORY

LEAVES: Deciduous
HEIGHT: To 100 feet
GROWTH: Slow
VALUE: Shade, wildlife, wood uses
FAMILY: Walnut (Juglandaceae)
REGION(S): 1, 3

*T*HE SWEET BUT disappointingly small nuts of this hickory "mock" anyone who troubles to break through the incredibly thick, hard husks to get at them; hence the name mockernut. But deer, wild turkeys, squirrels, and other small mammals forage for the nuts anyway, since this hickory, together with the others, forms an integral part of their diet.

Mockernut has valuable wood, which is heavy, close-grained, and especially useful for tool handles, implements, and fuel. It makes excellent barbecue wood, and Native Americans used parts of the tree to concoct analgesics.

All hickory leaves have similar shapes: the leaflets tend to get bigger the farther out they are along the midrib. Mockernut leaves exaggerate this feature, their five to nine leaflets culminating in a truly sizable terminal one. The leaves also grow the largest, in general, of those of any hickory. The species name *tomentosa* means hairy, signifying that you can further distinguish mockernut from other hickories by the hairy upper and lower leaf surfaces. The foliage emits a spicy fragrance when crushed.

Mockernut is the most common hickory in the United States and in East Texas, and it also grows west-ward to near Austin. The tree attains a height of 100 feet or more and can live an astonishing 500 years.

SHAGBARK HICKORY

Carya ovata

LEAVES: Deciduous
HEIGHT: To 100 feet
GROWTH: Slow
VALUE: Edible parts, wildlife, wood uses
FAMILY: Walnut (Juglandaceae)
REGION(S): 1

*B*OTH HUMANS AND animals relish shagbark more than any other hickory for the sweet-tasting nuts, which were once a staple of the Native American diet. These nuts can develop to more than two inches in diameter and appear nearly round. Their high fat and protein content make them especially valuable to wildlife. As with all hickories, the kernels are tedious to extract, but the prize of a delicious hickory nut cake makes it well worth the effort. (See appendix G for a hickory nut brittle recipe.)

Widespread across eastern North America, shagbark hickory grows in rich forests and along streamsides in the East Texas Piney Woods, usually as isolated or scattered individuals. The gray bark looks smooth on young trees, but in older specimens it splits from the trunk in ragged strips. The upper and lower ends of these strips bow outward, giving this species its shaggy appearance and its common name.

Like most hickories, shagbark grows slowly but has a long life. Carpenters value the tough wood for tool handles, and outdoor chefs prize it for barbecue charcoal. Europeans grow shagbark, as well as bitternut (p. 189) and pignut hickory (p. 201), for timber.

Carya glabra

PIGNUT HICKORY

LEAVES: Deciduous
HEIGHT: To 100 feet
GROWTH: Slow
VALUE: Shade, wildlife, wood uses
FAMILY: Walnut (Juglandaceae)
REGION(S): 1, 3

THE COMMON NAME of this tree derives from the poor quality of the nuts. These usually taste bitter, except, apparently, to domestic and feral pigs, which relish them. People once used the tough, flexible wood of this tree for making brooms, giving it the common name broom hickory. The wood also serves for fuel, tool handles, and various implements.

You can distinguish pignut from shagbark hickory (p. 200) by its tight rather than shredded bark and by its leaves, which usually have five leaflets, compared to the seven leaflets of shagbark. Both of these species have smooth, or hairless, leaves. Pignut also has smooth nut husks, whereas those of shagbark tend to look lumpy.

Pignut grows slowly but can reach a very large size. Scattered across East Texas counties, it also extends over much of the eastern United States and north into Ontario, Canada.

WATER HICKORY

Carya aquatica

$\mathcal{W}$ATER HICKORY sometimes forms "hickory bogs," growing where few other trees can survive. In winter, rain transforms the bogs into shallow ponds, and Texas plays host to myriad migrating birds. Then wood ducks and mallards gorge on the little flattened hickory nuts that taste so bitter as to be inedible to humans.

This water-loving member of the walnut family thrives in the southern half of East Texas in areas that experience frequent flooding. Water hickory can grow to 100 feet but usually remains considerably smaller and often takes a leaning stance.

The wood exhibits less commercial value than that of other hickories. Its somewhat shredded looking bark sometimes supports a patch of resurrection fern—an epiphyte named for its ability to go dormant during dry spells and to revive after a rain.

LEAVES: Deciduous
HEIGHT: To 100 feet
GROWTH: Moderate/fast
VALUE: Wildlife
FAMILY: Walnut (Juglandaceae)
REGION(S): 1–3

LEAVES: Deciduous
HEIGHT: To 70 feet
GROWTH: Fast
VALUE: Heritage, shade, wildlife, wood uses
FAMILY: Maple (Aceraceae)
REGION(S): 1–5, 7

NOT AN ELDER AT ALL, this tree belongs to the maple family. It sports light green leaves and twigs, and even the younger branches remain green. The leaflets occur in sets of three, five, or seven, and their appearance causes many people to confuse young box elders with poison ivy (*Toxicodendron radicans*). You can easily distinguish them, however, if you know what to look for: box elder leaves grow opposite each other on the stems; poison ivy leaves grow alternately.

This tree prefers moist places but succeeds almost anywhere. It is fast growing but short-lived and forms colonies through aggressive reseeding, particularly around Central Texas homesteads. A box elder in the front yard with a swing hanging from one of its branches represents a fairly common sight in that region.

Box elder's weak wood provides boxes, cheap furniture, and interior finishes, and the tree was once popular for furnishing quick shade and shelterbelts. Years ago, people tapped box elder like sugar maple (p. 121) for its sap, but the tree produces inferior syrup. Squirrels and many bird species eat the fruits, or "keys."

CORAL BEAN TREE

LEAVES: Evergreen
HEIGHT: To 25 feet
GROWTH: Moderate/fast
VALUE: Landscape, wildlife
FAMILY: Legume (Fabaceae)
REGION(S): 6

Warning:
Known poisonous properties

ABOUT 112 SPECIES of coral trees, or *Erythrinas*, grow on numerous islands and on every major continent except Antarctica, but the mechanism of their worldwide distribution remains something of an enigma. Scientists speculate that the buoyant seeds traveled via ocean currents or were dispersed by migratory birds. The various species range from minor shrubs to the the large *Erythrina caffra* of South Africa, which reaches 70 feet in height. While botanists usually consider our eastern coral bean a shrub, this arboreal variety emerged in the Lower Rio Grande Valley, where temperatures remain warm throughout the year. Unlike its shrubby neighbor to the north, it does not freeze to the ground in winter. Instead it ascends to 25 feet with a trunk diameter of 10 inches.

Hummingbirds pollinate the gorgeous 2-inch-long tubular crimson flowers borne on leafless spikes. The flower spikes precede crinkled pods containing five to ten hard, bright red seeds.

Coral beans preserve their brilliant coral-red color, and in Africa and the Caribbean Islands people string the beans of local specimens into necklaces and good luck charms. But the beans of all *Erythrinas* contain a powerful alkaloid with an effect much like that of curare. This dangerous poison acts as a strong cardiac stimulant and respiratory paralytic. People in Mexico use the seeds as rat poison.

THE LOWER RIO GRANDE Valley's unique flora results from the fact that it represents an overlap point where Chihuahuan Desert species, such as mesquite (p. 158–59) and brazil (p. 16), and more northerly trees, such as Texas persimmon (p. 15) and sugar hackberry (p. 33), converge with plants from the semitropical Tamaulipan region of Mexico. This extreme southern part of Texas actually consists of eleven distinct biological communities.

Among them is the *barretal* of southeastern Starr County, where barreta produces thicketed colonies on dry caliche hilltops. Also found in northern Mexico, this small, evergreen tree coexists here with such diverse species as anacahuita (p. 72), chaparro prieto (p. 152), and Spanish dagger (p. 234).

Baretta has a slender form, and the glossy, trifoliate leaves, twigs, and other parts of the tree exude a pleasant aroma when crushed. The trunks of baretta also look interesting since the brown bark breaks off in large patches to expose the tan wood beneath. The tree produces little dry winged fruits.

Because of its delicate yet lush appearance, its diminutive size, and its ability to withstand drought conditions, botanists recommend this little tree for use in home landscapes.

LEAVES: Evergreen
HEIGHT: To 25 feet
GROWTH: Slow
VALUE: Landscape, wildlife
FAMILY: Citrus (Rutaceae)
REGION(S): 6

Poncirus trifoliata

TRIFOLIATE ORANGE

LEAVES: Semi-evergreen
HEIGHT: To 30 feet
GROWTH: Moderate/fast
VALUE: Landscape, rootstock, security hedge
FAMILY: Citrus (Rutaceae)
REGION(S): Non-native

NATIVE IN ASIA as far north as Korea, this small, naturalized tree may well rank as the hardiest of the citruses and is therefore also called hardy citrus. Because of this vigor, farmers often use it as rootstock for market citrus fruits. It escaped cultivation long ago and now grows, sometimes in large colonies, around East Texas and other parts of the South.

Armed with impressive thorns, this tree develops into a nuisance where it forms big patches of impenetrable thorn bush. Its potential to provide a degree of home security is obvious, and homeowners occasionally plant it as a hedge or for ornament. Its bare, thorny branches, twisted into a crown, make a moving prop for pre-Easter or Passion Week church services.

The pristine white spring flowers mature into little yellow "oranges" that also look attractive. However the fruits have little inside them except seeds, dry pith, and a bitter oil that makes them for all practical purposes inedible. The trifoliate leaves are remarkable for their winged petiole.

WAFER ASH

Ptelea trifoliata

LEAVES: Deciduous
HEIGHT: To 20 feet
GROWTH: Fast
VALUE: Heritage, landscape
FAMILY: Citrus (Rutaceae)
REGION(S): 1, 3–5, 7, 10

AFER ASH IS A CUTE little tree. It grows to a petite size and possesses charming and whimsical characteristics. Attractive trifoliate leaves form the backdrop to the real eye-catchers, the clusters of "wafers," which actually consist of seeds surrounded by papery wings. These remain light green until autumn when they turn off-white to tan in color. A bit of paint could make them look like tiny fried eggs.

On the negative side, all parts of this tree emit an offensive odor clearly reminiscent of skunk, hence the alternate common name skunk bush. Despite this smell, thirsty Texas settlers used the wafers as a substitute for hops in brewing beer—leading to the popular name hop tree.

Though called wafer ash by some, the tree is not an ash; rather it belongs to the citrus family. It grows in East, Central, and southwestern Texas but most commonly flourishes on the Edwards Plateau. Wafer ash provides a definite conversation piece in the landscape for any homeowner able to overlook the smell.

LEAVES: Deciduous
HEIGHT: To 25 feet
GROWTH: Fast
VALUE: Edible parts,
heritage, landscape
FAMILY: Verbena
(Verbenaceae)
REGION(S): Non-native

*T*HE SPECIES NAME *agnus-castus* means "pure lamb" or "chaste lamb." Although records of a wide variety of medicinal uses of this plant date back to Hippocrates (460–377 B.C.), both its species and common names derive from its historical use as an anti-aphrodisiac taken by women and by monks to help them maintain their chastity. Today, scientists study the properties of chaste tree for use in the treatment of various female reproductive disorders and ailments.

The leaves emit a pleasant fragrance, and South Americans occasionally employ these in their cooking to flavor foods. Another popular name, monk's pepper, resulted from use of the seeds as a spice by monks in southern Europe. Manufacturers also distill perfume from the flowers.

Chaste tree is native to southern Europe and Central Asia but has long been a favorite in American landscapes. In Texas, it escapes cultivation in many places, especially near streams and ditches. Its slender, palmately compound leaves resemble those of the cannabis plant, and growing it in your yard may shock your neighbors. As chaste tree develops, however, it forms a rounded crown to about 25 feet. The blue flower spikes, so prominent in the spring, may appear throughout the summer and attract multitudes of bees. The tree also comes in pink-, white-, and purple-flowering forms.

See color illustration, p. xvi

RED AND YELLOW BUCKEYE

LEAVES: Deciduous
HEIGHT: To 25 feet
GROWTH: Fast
VALUE: Heritage, landscape
FAMILY: Buckeye (Hippocastanaceae)
REGION(S): 1, 3, 4, 7
(Yellow Buckeye: 7)

Warning:
Known poisonous properties

USH, PALMATELY compound leaves and striking red or yellow tubular flowers characterize this attractive small tree or shrub. The first hummingbirds and butterflies of spring sip the nectar and pollinate the blooms.

The "buckeyes" that follow usually come in sets of three, pressed tightly into a thin-walled shell. They mature into large, lustrous, brown seeds that look something like chestnuts. Once people treated the big, waxy-feeling buckeyes as charms, carrying them in their pockets to rub for good luck. However, all parts of this tree are poisonous to humans, especially the seeds. Both Indians and settlers

crushed these seeds and immersed them in streams or ponds to intoxicate the fish, which then floated to the surface, where they were easily harvested. That practice is now illegal.

Red buckeye grows over much of the eastern United States, seldom in large numbers but scattered here and there by road edges or near streams. Yellow buckeye is restricted to the Edwards Plateau, and where the varieties' habitats overlap, they frequently hybridize to produce yellow flowers with red streaks. People sometimes plant buckeye in landscapes in recognition of its beauty.

Its species name *pavia* honors Dutch botanist and anatomy teacher Peter Paaw, latinized as Petrus Pavius (1564–1617).

SALT CEDAR

Tamarix gallica

LEAVES: Evergreen
HEIGHT: To 30 feet
GROWTH: Fast
VALUE: Erosion control, honey, wildlife
FAMILY: Tamarisk (Tamaricaceae)
REGION(S): Non-native

*T*HIS NATIVE OF THE Mediterranean coast was introduced to the United States long ago for erosion control and because of the beauty of its feathery foliage and dainty pink flowers. It quickly naturalized and spread across the southern part of the country from coast to coast. Salt cedar thrives in the salty soil, heat, and storms of the Gulf Coast and in the dry desert landscapes of western Texas. Several other tamarisk species have also naturalized in Texas, but they are nearly impossible to distinguish from salt cedar unless you study the tiny flowers under a microscope.

In many parts of the Southwest, this tree has become a problem because of its propensity for sucking up the groundwater needed by other plants. Its roots probe deeply in search of moisture, and it forms colonies that crowd out native species.

Salt cedar's positive traits include providing honeybees with nectar all summer long and offering excellent wildlife cover. It also appears as an ingredient in over-the-counter herbal products marketed for treatment of liver and kidney problems.

Warning: Invasive species

LEAVES: Evergreen
HEIGHT: To 30 feet
GROWTH: Slow
VALUE: Heritage, wildlife, wood uses
FAMILY: Cypress (Cupressaceae)
REGION(S): 5, 7, 8, 10

*C*ALLED CEDAR throughout its range, this small, rugged tree that so characterizes the Hill Country and Edwards Plateau is actually a juniper. Cedars do not occur naturally in the Americas. In fact, only three species of true cedars exist in the world: the cedars of Lebanon, the Atlas cedars of northwest Africa, and the deodars of the Himalayas. Try to explain that to a Hill Country native, however, and you will get some condescending looks. To Texans, Ashe juniper is just plain cedar.

Over the years, "cedar cutting" has employed a lot of people. Ashe juniper was once an important source of charcoal used not only for barbecuing but also for filtering water, heating flatirons, blacksmithing, and concocting medicine. Today the tree has spread so invasively throughout Central Texas that ranchers constantly struggle to eradicate it because it shades soil that could be producing grasses.

But the tree also has its virtues: the blue fruits, which are actually densely configured cones, serve as food for numerous birds and mammals. The endangered golden-cheeked warbler nests only in old-growth junipers, and several wildlife organizations have purchased properties on the Edwards Plateau in order to preserve this important habitat.

Several other junipers, namely eastern red cedar (p. 214), and the roseberry, redberry, and alligator junipers (pp. 216–18), share portions of this tree's range. However, you can distinguish Ashe juniper from these: eastern red cedar grows in a columnar shape that contrasts with the spreading habit of Ashe juniper. Roseberry, redberry, and alligator juniper all produce reddish rather than blue "berries."

Both the common and species names of this tree honor botanist and forester William Willard Ashe (1872–1932).

See color illustration, p. iii

Warning: Invasive species

EASTERN RED CEDAR

Juniperus virginiana

ANY BOTANICAL writings of the past refer to the use of junipers for curing venereal diseases. In 1633, London herbalist John Girarde recommended dried leaves of red cedar (which, despite its name, is actually a juniper) for treating conditions "gotten by dealings with uncleane women." Peter Kalm (1716–79), a Swedish botanist and student of Carl Linnaeus, described an equally practical use for the tree in his journal, *Travels in North America* (1771): "The best canoes, consisting of a single piece of wood, are made of Red Cedar."

You will easily spot this tree in the landscape, since it typically grows very erect in a column or cone-shaped form. Young specimens once made popular Christmas trees, and German settlers also planted these trees around their homes, churches, and cemeteries. A 100-year-old tree may have a trunk only 18 inches in diameter, and because of such slow growth, remnant rows of old cedars long bear witness to the past.

This species occurs in the eastern third of Texas and east of a line from there to the Dakotas. Historical uses of its wood include furniture, paneling, cabinets, pencils, and insect-repellent "cedar" chests. Woodworking hobbyists utilize it for crafts, and landowners have always valued it for long-lasting fence posts. Many bird species eat the blue "berries" —in reality small, tightly compacted cones.

LEAVES: Evergreen
HEIGHT: To 50 feet
GROWTH: Slow
VALUE: Heritage, landscape, wildlife, wood uses
FAMILY: Cypress (Cupressaceae)
REGION(S): 1, 3–5, 8, 9

Juniperus virginiana var. *silicicola*   # SOUTHERN RED CEDAR

LEAVES: Evergreen
HEIGHT: To 50 feet
GROWTH: Slow
VALUE: Landscape, wildlife, wood uses
FAMILY: Cypress (Cupressaceae)
REGION(S): 1, 2

DESPITE ITS NAME, this American tree belongs to the junipers and not to the cedars, which all originate in the Old World. Southern red cedar claims the sandy soil near the Gulf and South Atlantic coasts of the United States as its native habitat. In Texas, it grows in the southeastern portion of the state, westward to around Lake Texana.

Southern red cedar differs from eastern red cedar (p. 214) in developing a more irregular form, drooping branches, and smaller fruits. These tiny cones with tightly compacted scales masquerade as little blue berries and provide a food source for many species of birds. Juniper "berries" also lend flavor to gin, although those generally employed for that purpose come from a more northerly species, the common juniper (*Juniperus communis*).

The valuable wood of this tree, like that of eastern red cedar, serves for paneling, woodenware, posts, and insect-repellent "cedar" chests. Caddoan Indian tribes, such as the Wichita, employed forked cedar poles as the structural members for their domelike grass huts. Today, garden centers market a product made from juniper shavings as an effective natural insecticide.

Southern red cedar grows slowly but enjoys a long life and is always worthy of a place in the landscape.

ROSEBERRY JUNIPER

Juniperus coahuilensis

LEAVES: Evergreen
HEIGHT: To 15 feet
GROWTH: Slow
VALUE: Heritage, wildlife
FAMILY: Cypress (Cupressaceae)
REGION(S): 10

At the end of the last ice age, around 10,000 years ago, woodlands of oak and juniper covered most of the Trans-Pecos region. As the climate became drier, these forests retreated to high elevations and to mostly northern and eastern exposures in the mountain ranges.

Today, roseberry and redberry juniper (p. 217), together with gray oak (p. 87) and Emory oak (p. 104), dominate this remnant woodland at elevations above 4,000 feet in the Davis Mountains and other ranges of western Texas. Roseberry juniper also occurs in New Mexico and Arizona, and its species name hints at its presence in Coahuila, Mexico.

This tree, while closely related to redberry juniper, has a much more limited range in Texas, occurring in only a small portion of the Trans-Pecos.

You can most easily distinguish it from redberry juniper by the dusty rose color of its "berries" or tiny cones; those of redberry juniper are a true red. You will not confuse it with Ashe juniper (p. 213), which produces blue fruits. Finally, the shredded bark of roseberry juniper differentiates it from alligator juniper (p. 218), which has distinctive, close-fitting bark marked by regular horizontal and vertical furrows that make it resemble the tough scales of an alligator's hide.

A number of birds and mammals eat the rosy juniper berries. Indians once employed the soft bark for breechcloths and mats, and the wood provides posts and fuel.

Juniperus pinchotii

REDBERRY JUNIPER

LEAVES: Evergreen
HEIGHT: To 20 feet
GROWTH: Slow
VALUE: Wildlife
FAMILY: Cypress (Cupressaceae)
REGION(S): 7–10

*T*HE NAME OF THE FAMED Palo Duro Canyon of the Texas Panhandle recalls the hard, durable wood of redberry juniper. Common in that region, this juniper spreads southward from there over much of West Texas. While it occasionally grows into a spreading tree of 20 feet or more, it often appears as a shrubby colonizing growth that sprouts readily from cut or burned stumps.

As the name implies, this tree bears bright red, berrylike cones instead of the blue fruits borne by most other junipers. These red "berries" prove valuable to birds and other wildlife. Ashe juniper (p. 213) and redberry Juniper have overlapping ranges, but the latter is distinguished by more upright growth and, of course, its red berries. The cones of roseberry juniper (p. 216) appear dusty pink by comparison.

This tree is named for Gifford Pinchot (1865–1946), conservationist and chief forester of the U.S. Forest Service under Theodore Roosevelt. Pinchot's principle of "the greatest good of the greatest number in the long run" checked the fury of shortsighted overdevelopment and became a rallying cry for conservationists, as it still is today.

ALLIGATOR JUNIPER

Juniperus deppeana

LEAVES: Evergreen
HEIGHT: To 50 feet
GROWTH: Slow
VALUE: Landscape, wildlife
FAMILY: Cypress (Cupressaceae)
REGION(S): 10

*T*HIS TREE'S MOST conspicuous feature differentiates it from all other junipers: the trunk protects itself with a coat of scaly plates resembling the hide of an alligator. With its distinctive blue-green foliage, interesting bark, and reddish brown cones, alligator juniper makes a good landscape tree, especially in dry areas, and its slow growth enables it to live for five centuries or more. It can attain a height of 50 feet but typically develops into a broad tree to about 25 feet.

Alligator juniper resides in the arid mountains of the Trans-Pecos, growing at elevations of about 4,000 to 7,000 feet. This species also occurs in New Mexico, Arizona, and southward into Mexico. Squirrels, foxes, bears, and birds eat the berrylike cones. Wood uses include fuel and posts.

The species name of this tree honors German horticulturist Ferdinand Deppe (1794–1861), who traveled widely in Mexico, collecting plant specimens.

Cupressus arizonica

ARIZONA CYPRESS

LEAVES: Evergreen
HEIGHT: To 90 feet
GROWTH: Fast
VALUE: Erosion control, landscape, wildlife
FAMILY: Cypress (Cupressaceae)
REGION(S): 10

*T*HIS HANDSOME TREE occurs naturally in Texas only in the Chisos Mountains of the Big Bend. From there its habitat spreads across southern New Mexico and Arizona to California and into northern Mexico. Because of its beauty and drought-resistant qualities, homeowners plant it all over the West, and nurseries cultivate it for the Christmas tree market. The immature tree looks especially handsome with its conical form and scalelike, blue-green foliage. It develops a more open crown as it matures and can live for several centuries. Arizona cypress will succeed under many conditions but requires good drainage and a sunny location.

Ranchers and landowners sometimes plant it in shelterbelts or for erosion control and use the wood for posts. The tree also provided many of the timbers used by mining companies in the old West.

MONTEZUMA BALD CYPRESS   *Taxodium mucronatum*

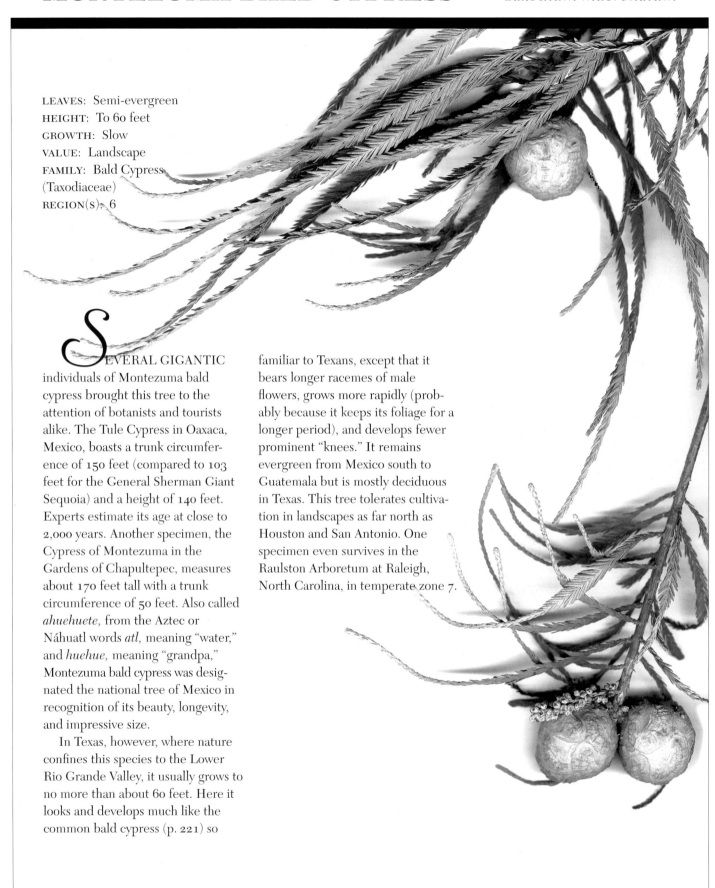

LEAVES: Semi-evergreen
HEIGHT: To 60 feet
GROWTH: Slow
VALUE: Landscape
FAMILY: Bald Cypress
(Taxodiaceae)
REGION(S): 6

SEVERAL GIGANTIC individuals of Montezuma bald cypress brought this tree to the attention of botanists and tourists alike. The Tule Cypress in Oaxaca, Mexico, boasts a trunk circumference of 150 feet (compared to 103 feet for the General Sherman Giant Sequoia) and a height of 140 feet. Experts estimate its age at close to 2,000 years. Another specimen, the Cypress of Montezuma in the Gardens of Chapultepec, measures about 170 feet tall with a trunk circumference of 50 feet. Also called *ahuehuete,* from the Aztec or Náhuatl words *atl,* meaning "water," and *huehue,* meaning "grandpa," Montezuma bald cypress was designated the national tree of Mexico in recognition of its beauty, longevity, and impressive size.

In Texas, however, where nature confines this species to the Lower Rio Grande Valley, it usually grows to no more than about 60 feet. Here it looks and develops much like the common bald cypress (p. 221) so familiar to Texans, except that it bears longer racemes of male flowers, grows more rapidly (probably because it keeps its foliage for a longer period), and develops fewer prominent "knees." It remains evergreen from Mexico south to Guatemala but is mostly deciduous in Texas. This tree tolerates cultivation in landscapes as far north as Houston and San Antonio. One specimen even survives in the Raulston Arboretum at Raleigh, North Carolina, in temperate zone 7.

BALD CYPRESS

LEAVES: Deciduous
HEIGHT: To 100 feet
GROWTH: Moderate/slow
VALUE: Heritage, landscape, wildlife
FAMILY: Bald Cypress (Taxodiaceae)
REGION(S): 1–3, 6, 7

A TREE OF SOUTHERN swamps and waterways, bald cypress is suited to a habitat where it has few competitors for sunshine. It thrives in standing water all year round, if necessary, something only a small and select group of trees on earth can do. Among its adaptations to water and soft mud you will note the flared and buttressed trunks and the unique "knees" that arise from the roots.

Construction companies once eagerly sought the wood of bald cypress for boat building, wharves, pilings, shingles, silos, and other uses that required resistance to rotting. Native Americans in the South favored it for dugout canoes.

This species grows to great size and age. While most of the really big cypresses in the United States were cut long ago, a few trees estimated at more than 1,000 years old still remain in Louisiana and Florida. Bald cypress also ranks among the small number of coniferous trees that shed their leaves. Its attractive ferny foliage turns russet brown before falling in autumn, causing some people to wonder if the tree has died. The genus name *Taxodium* derives from *Taxus*, meaning "yew," and refers to the yewlike foliage. The term *distichum* means "two-ranked," describing the two rows of leaves.

This tree grows fairly rapidly when young but slowly when old. An attractive landscape species, bald cypress can manage on only the water you apply to your lawn. Some birds, particularly ducks, eat the seeds borne in the small cones.

PINYON PINE

Pinus edulis

LEAVES: Evergreen
HEIGHT: To 35 feet
GROWTH: Slow
VALUE: Edible parts, heritage, medicinal, landscape, wildlife
FAMILY: Pine (Pinaceae)
REGION(S): 10

*E*DULIS MEANS EDIBLE, and the oval, reddish brown cones of pinyon pine or *piñón* contain large, edible seeds that were once an important part of the diet of southwestern Indians, including the Zuñi and Navajo people. Today, pine nuts appear alongside walnuts and pecans at many grocery stores. These seeds form an important crop in the tree's other native states of Colorado, New Mexico, and Arizona. Several species of birds also enjoy the nuts, as do squirrels, chipmunks, porcupines, and bears,

Additionally, both the needles and the pitch of the tree serve medicinal uses. You can boil the needles to make a flavorful tea, which functions as an expectorant or gentle diuretic. The Zuñi Indians used pinyon needles as a treatment for syphilis. After chewing and swallowing them, the patient would drink a quantity of cold water, run to induce profuse perspiration, and then be wrapped in warm blankets. Salves made with the pitch also promote healing, soothe skin irritations, work as sun block, and draw out embedded splinters.

At Christmas time, many tree lots in the Southwest offer pinyon pine among their selections, and the branches make delightfully aromatic wreaths and holiday arrangements.

Pinyon pine grows northward from West Texas through Colorado and Wyoming and westward to California. Less common in Texas than Mexican pinyon pine (p. 223), it occurs in this state only in the Guadalupe Mountains and the Sierra Diablo. It is also a smaller tree than Mexican pinyon pine, usually attaining only 35 feet or less in height.

MEXICAN PINYON PINE

LEAVES: Evergreen
HEIGHT: To 40 feet
GROWTH: Slow
VALUE: Edible parts, heritage, wildlife
FAMILY: Pine (Pinaceae)
REGION(S): 10

MEXICAN PINYON PINE has thick, blue-green foliage and small cones containing very large seeds. These have considerable market value, and people still gather them the way the Indians in Mexico and across the southwestern United States did in ancient times. You can eat pine nuts raw or roasted, plain or salted, according to your taste, but if you gather them yourself, you will have to be quick to beat the wildlife to the crop. Wild turkeys and quail eat these seeds, and squirrels, porcupines, chipmunks, and bears relish them as well.

The wood of Mexican pinyon pine provides posts and fuel. Native Americans once utilized the resin to waterproof baskets and to "cement" pots and other materials into place.

This tree occurs more commonly in Texas than pinyon pine (p. 222), and you can distinguish the two by their size and their needles: Mexican pinyon pine grows slightly larger, and its needles appear a bluer green. The yellow-green needles of pinyon pine usually come in bundles of two, whereas those of Mexican pinyon pine are generally bundled in groups of three and only rarely in pairs.

This small tree grows from the southern part of the Trans-Pecos and adjacent Edwards Plateau across the Southwest to California and into northern Mexico. It thrives at elevations of 4,000 to 7,000 feet.

DOUGLAS FIR

Pseudotsuga menziesii

THIS BEAUTIFUL TREE, commonly considered the most valuable timber tree in the United States, grows in Texas only at high elevations in the Chisos and Guadalupe mountains. There it reaches heights of nearly 80 feet; it attains an astonishing 200 feet or more in the Pacific Northwest. Neither a pine nor a fir, this tree belongs to its own genus, *Pseudotsuga,* which means "false hemlock." To identify Douglas fir, note the cones' distinctive bracts, sometimes called "mousetails," with their zigzag tips that extend past the scales and curl back.

The species name honors surgeon-naturalist Archibald Menzies (1754–1842), who accompanied Captain Vancouver on his round-the-world voyage on the *HMS Discovery.* Dr. Menzies collected the tree in 1791 or 1792 on what is now called Vancouver Island. Botanist David Douglas (1799–1834) found it again along the Oregon coast in 1825 and described

the tree with such vividness and admiration that it now bears his name in all common usage. This same Douglas discovered gold in California long before John A. Sutter did: he sent many botanical specimens home to England, and when his colleagues examined one shrub, they found gold flecks all over the roots. Unfortunately for Douglas, he could not remember where he had collected that specimen.

The wood of Douglas Fir contains no gold flecks, but it is highly valuable for home construction, shipbuilding, boxes, crates, furniture, and a multitude of other uses. Grouse and other birds eat the seeds, as do various western rodents. Many people plant this tree for ornament across the cooler parts of the United States and Europe, and growers cultivate it extensively for Christmas trees.

LEAVES: Evergreen
HEIGHT: To 80 feet
GROWTH: Fast
VALUE: Landscape, lumber, wildlife
FAMILY: Pine (Pinaceae)
REGION(S): 10

Pinus echinata

LEAVES: Evergreen
HEIGHT: To 100 feet
GROWTH: Fast
VALUE: Lumber, wildlife, wood uses
FAMILY: Pine (Pinaceae)
REGION(S): 1–3

*T*HE SPECIES NAME *ECHINATA* means "hedgehog-like," a good description of the short, stiff needles of this tree. They are usually only about 3 inches long and come in bundles of two or, infrequently, three. The cones appear tiny compared to those of loblolly (p. 226) and longleaf pine (p. 228), averaging only about 2 inches long.

Also called yellow pine, this tree grows very straight and makes a handsome specimen but produces little shade. Birds and rodents feed on the copious seeds. A valuable lumber tree, shortleaf pine yields softer and less resinous wood than other pines. It serves for veneer, plywood, pulp, woodenware, and a variety of other applications.

Shortleaf pine occurs throughout most of the East Texas Piney Woods and is more numerous northward into Oklahoma, Arkansas, and northern Louisiana. From there its habitat reaches to the southern edge of Pennsylvania. Shortleaf pine prefers dry, elevated sites but can be found scattered in various kinds of soil.

The tree hybridizes readily with loblolly pine and may eventually be absorbed into the loblolly species through continual hybridization and attrition.

LOBLOLLY PINE

Pinus taeda

LEAVES: Evergreen
HEIGHT: To 100 feet
GROWTH: Fast
VALUE: Heritage, lumber, wildlife
FAMILY: Pine (Pinaceae)
REGION(S): 1–3

*T*HE NAME LOBLOLLY derives from an old-fashioned term meaning a hodgepodge or mishmash of something. American sailors were nicknamed loblollies because they resorted to eating stews consisting of all kinds of leftover ingredients during their long voyages. The tall southern pine they frequently used for masts on their sailing ships became known as the loblollies' pine.

This tree grows very fast and under good conditions reaches 60 feet in only 20 years. A handsome species, it dominates in moist lowlands, usually rising well above the hardwoods around it. Its cones drop their winged fruits in fall, and numerous birds, squirrels, and rodents eat the seeds.

Homeowners sometimes cut down their tall pines, fearing that they will blow over in a storm. But the astonishingly deep taproot and flexible trunk render this pine among the most wind-resistant of trees. A loblolly will remain standing long after the surrounding water oaks (p. 17) have toppled. Much more dangerous than the occasional nervous property owner, the southern pine beetle does devastating damage to this species throughout East Texas.

Loblolly is the most common pine in the Texas Piney Woods and, collectively, the most valuable lumber tree there. Ranging all the way to the Atlantic Coast, it provides more cut timber than all other southern pines combined, ensuring that lumber companies will keep it widely planted. A forest of loblolly pines and associated species once spread in a contiguous swath all the way into Central Texas. Today, only a remnant colony of old loblollies survives near Bastrop in the Lost Pines area. To see some really large, old growth pines, visit the Alabama-Coushatta Indian Reservation between Livingston and Woodville.

LEAVES: Evergreen
HEIGHT: To 100 feet
GROWTH: Slow
VALUE: Landscape, wildlife
FAMILY: Pine (Pinaceae)
REGION(S): 10

*A*RIZONA PINE PROVIDES a fine example of how botanists can differ on the subject of classification. Some authorities spell the varietal name *stormiae* while others spell it *stromiae.* Some experts consider this variety a distinct species, while others regard *Pinus arizonica* var. *stormiae* as a synonym for the *scopulorum* variety of ponderosa pine (p. 229).

Suffice it to say that whatever its spelling and classification, this variety remains very localized, occurring naturally in the United States only in the Chisos Mountains of Texas, particularly in Pine Canyon. It grows far more commonly to the south, in Mexico. Additionally, its airy appearance and open form give it potential as a landscape plant, and people cultivate it in many other locations.

Large for a southwestern pine, this tree attains 100 feet in height. Its needles also grow longer than those of most regional species. Although it matures quite slowly, it provides good nesting and wildlife habitat in its region.

LONGLEAF PINE

Pinus palustris

LEAVES: Evergreen
HEIGHT: To 100 feet
GROWTH: Moderate/fast
VALUE: Landscape, lumber, wildlife
FAMILY: Pine (Pinaceae)
REGION(S): 1, 2

*I*F YOU SPOT A SEEDLING longleaf pine, you may confuse it with a tuft of grass. Only the long needles emerge from the soil at first; the little trunk appears over the course of several years. Nevertheless, this slow-growing pine provides the most valuable lumber, inch for inch, of any southern species.

Longleaf pine thrives in the deep, sandy, inland soil across the South, from the Trinity River Valley of Texas to the Atlantic Coast. Loblolly pine (p. 226) prefers the wet flatlands, and shortleaf pine (p. 225) dominates the hilly uplands. Longleaf forms a component of savannahs—grassy areas punctuated with a few trees and only sparse understory. Fire is a friend of this species, because it eliminates competition while doing little damage to this sturdy tree.

The beauty of longleaf pine inspires people to plant it widely outside its natural range. The 8- to 15-inch-long needles, which appear primarily at the ends of the branches, and the large cones, which measure up to 10 inches long, make this tree a striking landscape feature.

The wood offers great strength and durability and has many uses in heavy construction and for pilings, masts, pulp, and lumber. A number of species of birds eat the seeds, as do squirrels and other rodents.

Pinus ponderosa var. scopulorum

PONDEROSA PINE

LEAVES: Evergreen
HEIGHT: To 80 feet
GROWTH: Moderate/slow
VALUE: Landscape, lumber, wildlife
FAMILY: Pine (Pinaceae)
REGION(S): 10

ALSO CALLED INTERIOR ponderosa or Rocky Mountain ponderosa pine, this tree is one of three widely recognized varieties of this species. The other two are Pacific ponderosa (*Pinus ponderosa* var. *ponderosa*) and Arizona pine (*P. ponderosa* var. *arizonica,* p. 227). Together they represent the most widespread of western pines. This one occurs in Texas in the Davis, Guadalupe, and Chisos mountains, where it attains a height of about 80 feet. Its cousins in other parts of the West can exceed 200 feet in height.

Its distinctive cinnamon-red bark, long needles, and stately carriage make this an attractive landscape tree. Europeans also appreciate and plant it, and today many big ponderosa pines thrive in England. The valuable lumber has many construction uses and also serves for railroad crossties, mine timbers, and fencing.

Ponderosa pine communities provide critical habitat for a variety of birds such as owls and other cavity nesters as well as for wild turkeys. Aside from nest sites, the snags offer good forage in the form of insects that burrow into the dead wood. Almost all western squirrel species eat the pine nuts, which also supply important nourishment for grouse and quail.

SOAPTREE YUCCA

Yucca elata

LEAVES: Evergreen
HEIGHT: To 30 feet
GROWTH: Slow
VALUE: Edible parts, heritage, landscape, wildlife
FAMILY: Agave (Agavaceae)
REGION(S): 10

THIS THIN-LEAVED YUCCA with multiple heads derives its species name, *elata*, from its elevated growth, up to 30 feet tall, often topped with a 6-foot flower stalk. All of the approximately 40 species of yucca depend entirely and specifically on yucca moths to pollinate the creamy white flowers. Thanks to the moths, soaptree yucca grows widely throughout the Trans-Pecos and northern Mexico and claims the title of state flower of New Mexico.

Its common name comes from the use of the inner bark of the roots and stems as a soap substitute. Navajo Indians utilize this lather for washing their blanket wool. Native Americans have also employed both the flowers and the young flower stalks of this species for food. The leaves yield strong fibers, which southwestern Indians sun-bleach or dye to weave into colorful baskets.

Soaptree yucca leaves have filamentous margins and a fine-toothed keel on the underside. Fruit characteristics present another aid to identification: all yuccas produce either dry or fleshy fruit capsules. Those of soaptree yucca are fleshy and dehiscent; that is, they split open along well-defined seams, releasing their oval seeds.

Like other yuccas, soaptree has some landscape value, particularly in arid settings. However, its rhizome root system develops downward rather than horizontally, making this species difficult to transplant.

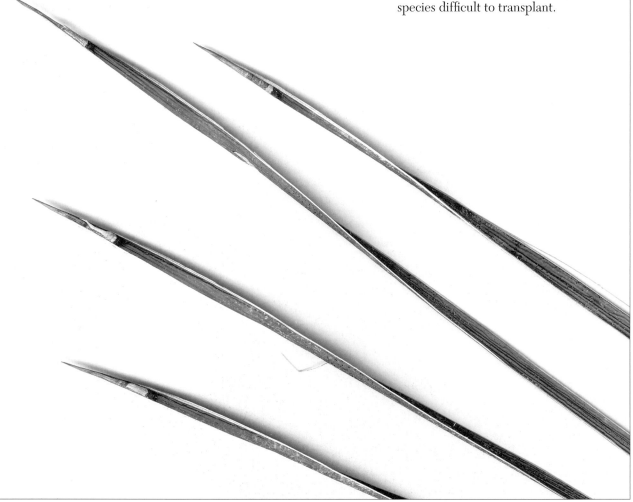

Yucca rostrata

BEAKED YUCCA

LEAVES: Evergreen
HEIGHT: To 15 feet
GROWTH: Slow
VALUE: Edible parts, heritage, landscape, wildlife
FAMILY: Agave (Agavaceae)
REGION(S): 10

BOTANISTS USUALLY describe yuccas as either broad-leaved or thin-leaved. Beaked yucca ranks among the thin-leaved species and occurs naturally in Texas only in Brewster County. However, it also grows in the Mexican states of Coahuila and Chihuahua, and its beauty has prompted its admirers to cultivate it in many other areas.

This yucca usually achieves about 15 feet in height but has been recorded as tall as 30 feet. The leaves have yellow margins like those of Thompson yucca (p. 232), but unlike Thompson yucca leaves, they exhibit no marginal teeth. Beaked yucca often sprouts several branching heads and produces spires of off-white flowers that rely entirely on a species of yucca moth for pollination. However, the most distinctive feature of this plant is the fruit capsule, which has three erect "beaks" and contains many small black seeds. The species name *rostrata* refers to these beaks.

Like other yuccas, this tree provided food and fiber for Native Americans, who still utilize it for those purposes in some regions.

THOMPSON YUCCA

Yucca thompsoniana

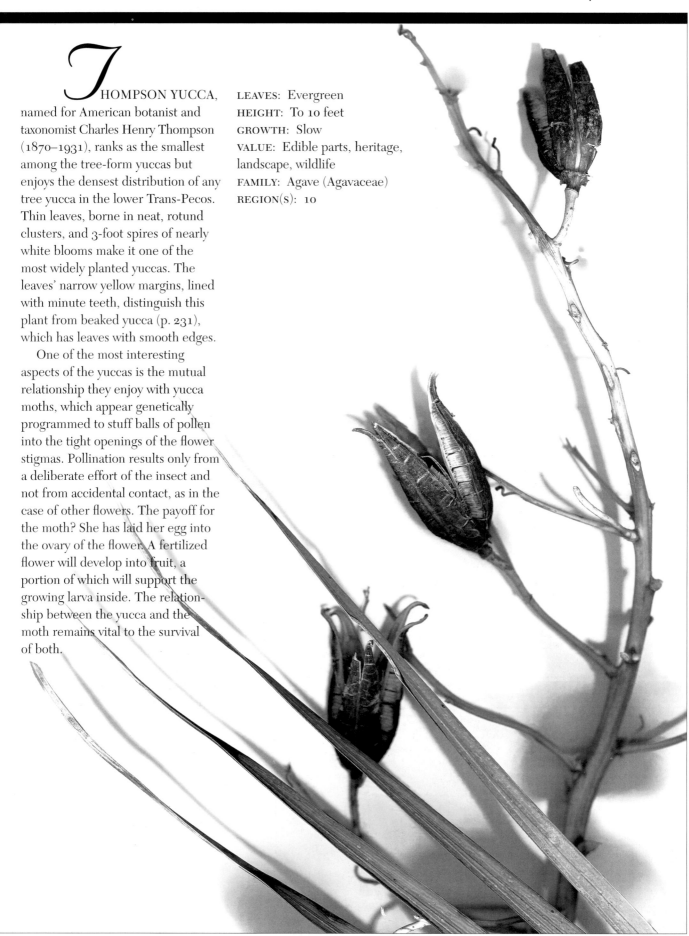

THOMPSON YUCCA, named for American botanist and taxonomist Charles Henry Thompson (1870–1931), ranks as the smallest among the tree-form yuccas but enjoys the densest distribution of any tree yucca in the lower Trans-Pecos. Thin leaves, borne in neat, rotund clusters, and 3-foot spires of nearly white blooms make it one of the most widely planted yuccas. The leaves' narrow yellow margins, lined with minute teeth, distinguish this plant from beaked yucca (p. 231), which has leaves with smooth edges.

One of the most interesting aspects of the yuccas is the mutual relationship they enjoy with yucca moths, which appear genetically programmed to stuff balls of pollen into the tight openings of the flower stigmas. Pollination results only from a deliberate effort of the insect and not from accidental contact, as in the case of other flowers. The payoff for the moth? She has laid her egg into the ovary of the flower. A fertilized flower will develop into fruit, a portion of which will support the growing larva inside. The relationship between the yucca and the moth remains vital to the survival of both.

LEAVES: Evergreen
HEIGHT: To 10 feet
GROWTH: Slow
VALUE: Edible parts, heritage, landscape, wildlife
FAMILY: Agave (Agavaceae)
REGION(S): 10

TORREY YUCCA

LEAVES: Evergreen
HEIGHT: To 20 feet
GROWTH: Slow
VALUE: Edible parts, heritage, landscape, wildlife
FAMILY: Agave (Agavaceae)
REGION(S): 6, 7, 10

ONLY NORTH AMERICA and the Caribbean Islands can claim the yuccas as native plants. These desert-adapted members of the Agave family received their name from the Haitian term *yuca*, which originally applied to the cassava or tapioca plant (*Manihot esculenta*), an unrelated species. The name was later somehow transferred to this genus. Both the common and species names of this particular yucca honor John Torrey (1796–1873) who served as professor of chemistry at the College of Physicians and Surgeons in New York and, at the same time, as professor of chemistry and natural history at Princeton, while still finding time to establish himself as a preeminent American botanist.

Torrey yucca appears widespread throughout the Trans-Pecos and also grows in scattered locations on the Edwards Plateau and Rio Grande Plains. Its range extends into Mexico and New Mexico. This yucca, like the others, depends upon one of several species of yucca moths for pollination and propagation. Yuccas cultivated in Europe, where no yucca moths exist, will not produce seed without human intervention.

The upper leaves of Torrey yucca remain more erect than those of other species, while the spent lower leaves hang downward in a disheveled manner from the stalk. This forms a good protective device for the plant and gives rise to the common name old shag. Native Americans used the flowers and fruits of Torrey yucca for food and the leaves for fiber. The plant also provided a source of cough medicine and a soap substitute.

SPANISH DAGGER

Yucca treculeana

LEAVES: Evergreen
HEIGHT: To 20 feet
GROWTH: Slow
VALUE: Edible parts, heritage, landscape, wildlife
FAMILY: Agave (Agavaceae)
REGION(S): 2, 6, 7

*A*LL OF THE FORTY or so species of yucca originate in North America, about half of them in Texas. Several of these reach tree status, including Trecul yucca, named for French botanist Auguste Adolphe Lucien Trecul (1818–96). This handsome plant, which can achieve 20 feet or more, thrives from around San Antonio southward across the Rio Grande Plains.

Also known as *palmito,* the tree lends its name to Palmito Hill in Cameron County, where the last battle of the Civil War erupted on May 13, 1865. (The news of Lee's surrender had not yet reached the area.) But the name most often applied to the plant is Spanish dagger.

The huge flower stalk of Spanish dagger, up to 3 feet tall and containing many fragrant, white, lily-like flowers, looks very impressive. The sharp spiny leaves of this yucca, which prevent browsing by larger mammals, form a haven for small animals and insects, many of which nibble the blooms. People, too, can eat the flowers, either raw or boiled. Indians used a lather made from the roots to wash clothes and hair. The tough fiber from the leaves yields cordage for weaving mats, sandals, and thatch, and homeowners frequently plant Spanish dagger for ornament.

GIANT DAGGER

LEAVES: Evergreen
HEIGHT: To 30 feet
GROWTH: Moderate/slow
VALUE: Edible parts, heritage, landscape, wildlife
FAMILY: Agave (Agavaceae)
REGION(S): 10

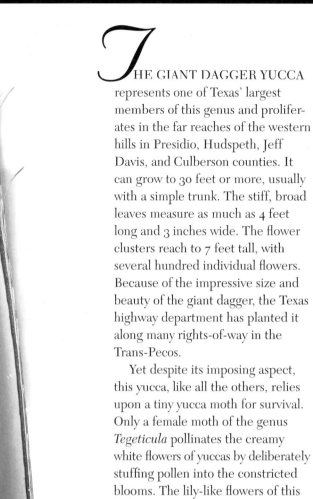

THE GIANT DAGGER YUCCA represents one of Texas' largest members of this genus and proliferates in the far reaches of the western hills in Presidio, Hudspeth, Jeff Davis, and Culberson counties. It can grow to 30 feet or more, usually with a simple trunk. The stiff, broad leaves measure as much as 4 feet long and 3 inches wide. The flower clusters reach to 7 feet tall, with several hundred individual flowers. Because of the impressive size and beauty of the giant dagger, the Texas highway department has planted it along many rights-of-way in the Trans-Pecos.

Yet despite its imposing aspect, this yucca, like all the others, relies upon a tiny yucca moth for survival. Only a female moth of the genus *Tegeticula* pollinates the creamy white flowers of yuccas by deliberately stuffing pollen into the constricted blooms. The lily-like flowers of this and other yuccas cause some experts to classify them as members of the lily family rather than the agave family.

Giant dagger had many historical uses among Native Americans: the flowers provided a tasty food, as did the young fruits. The leaves yield long, stiff fibers, which the southwestern Indians wove into nets, sandals, blankets, and ropes. They also used the root to make a soapy lather, which they claimed prevented baldness.

In its habitat, giant dagger offers valuable shelter for wildlife.

LOUISIANA PALM

LEAVES: Evergreen
HEIGHT: To 10 feet
GROWTH: Slow
VALUE: Heritage, wildlife
FAMILY: Palm (Arecaceae)
REGION(S): 1, 2

THIS SHORT-TRUNKED PALM resides in several East Texas areas and in scattered locations along the coast southward to Rockport. Botanists debate its relationship with *Sabal minor,* the little trunkless dwarf palm, or "palmetto," so common in wet, flood-prone places throughout the eastern part of the state. However, this palm grows much larger—large enough to earn inclusion in a book on Texas trees. The otherworldly beauty of a palmetto flat composed of Louisiana palms draws in and dwarfs the intruder.

Researchers have recorded the trunks of Louisiana palm to 18 feet high, although they usually remain much shorter. The huge fronds often measure more than 6 feet wide, and the length of their stems exceeds that of the blades. *Sabal minor,* by comparison, develops no above-ground trunk at all, and the length of the frond stems does not exceed that of the blades.

Many coastal Indians in the South, such as the Akokisa and Attakapa, used the leaves of Louisiana palm to thatch their dwellings. The fronds perform excellently for that purpose, shedding rain efficiently and holding in the warmth. To see several examples of the kinds of structures built by the Akokisa using these fronds, visit Jesse H. Jones Park and Nature Center in Humble, north of Houston.

Texas settlers, too, utilized the fronds to make brush arbors for church meetings. Formerly, people also cut, shipped, and sold them for use in Palm Sunday observances.

SABAL PALM

LEAVES: Evergreen
HEIGHT: To 50 feet
GROWTH: Moderate/slow
VALUE: Edible parts, landscape, wildlife
FAMILY: Palm (Arecaceae)
REGION(S): 6

TEXAS' ONLY TALL-GROWING native palm, this tree's habitat covered 40,000 acres as recently as 1925. Today, agricultural development has reduced it to a narrow band along the lower Rio Grande on both sides of the river. The Audubon Society's Sabal Palm Grove Sanctuary of 527 acres contains the last remaining large stand of these mature trees in Texas, covering a mere 32 acres of the park. Located near the extreme southern tip of the state, in Cameron County, the sanctuary hosts other flora and fauna unique to the Lower Valley, including some interesting birds, such as chachalacas, green jays, and buff-bellied hummingbirds, and mammals such as the endangered jaguarundi and ocelot. Several subtropical bat species use the drooping leaves of sabal palm as roosting places.

Fortunately, many people plant this tree for ornament, and it normally appears hardy slightly north of its native habitat. You can distinguish sabal palm from other palms with hand-shaped fronds by its smooth petioles or leaf stems.

Merchants sell the edible fruits of this palm in Mexican markets as *micharos,* and the fronds provide thatch and weaving material.

WASHINGTON PALM

Washingtonia filifera

WASHINGTON PALM

LEAVES: Evergreen
HEIGHT: To 50 feet
GROWTH: Fast
VALUE: Edible parts, heritage, landscape, wildlife
FAMILY: Palm (Arecaceae)
REGION(S): Non-native

*T*EXANS PLANT this indigenous tree of California, Arizona, and northern Mexico more than any other palm. They cultivate it so often in the Lower Rio Grande Valley that this non-native has come to symbolize the region. The Texas highway department plays a major role in promoting the tree by planting it along roads in the Valley, where it towers over the mostly low-growing trees and shrubs of the area. As you head south for a family vacation, the inevitable question "Are we there yet?" will be answered by Washington palm. The tree also naturalizes here under some circumstances and remains hardy as far north as Houston, College Station, and San Antonio, except in extreme winters.

This tree's other common name, petticoat palm, derives from the skirt of dead fronds that, if left untrimmed, will cover the trunk virtually to the ground. This petticoat serves to protect the tree from freezes and may offer resistance to relatively cool, fast-moving fires, which consume the dead fronds but spare the trunk. Birds eat the fruit and use the thick skirt of dead leaves for nesting sites.

The species name *filifera* means "bearing filaments or threads" and refers to the filamentous leaf margins.

Southwestern Indians, such as the Cahuilla of southeastern California and the Cocopa of Arizona, employed the fronds of Washington palm for thatch and utilized the strong fibers from the leaves for ropes and baskets. They ate the fruits either fresh or dried and made a beverage from them. The Cahuilla also ground the seeds into a mush. This palm presented such an important resource to the natives of the Desert Southwest that some botanists believe the tree's distribution relates, at least in part, to human dispersal.

Agave (Agavaceae)
  Giant Dagger
  Spanish Dagger
  Yucca, Beaked
  Yucca, Soaptree
  Yucca, Thompson
  Yucca, Torrey
Bald Cypress (Taxodiaceae)
  Cypress, Bald
  Cypress, Montezuma Bald
Beech (Fagaceae)
  Beech, American
  Chinquapin, Allegheny
  Oak, Black
  Oak, Blackjack
  Oak, Bluejack
  Oak, Bottomland Post
  Oak, Bur
  Oak, Chinkapin
  Oak, Chisos Red
  Oak, Diamond Leaf
  Oak, Emory
  Oak, Gambel
  Oak, Gray
  Oak, Havard Shin
  Oak, Lacey
  Oak, Laurel
  Oak, Live
  Oak, Mexican
  Oak, Mohr
  Oak, Nuttall
  Oak, Overcup
  Oak, Plateau Live
  Oak, Post
  Oak, Sandpaper
  Oak, Scrub
  Oak, Shumard
  Oak, Silver Leaf
  Oak, Southern Red
  Oak, Swamp Chestnut
  Oak, Texas
  Oak, Vasey
  Oak, Water
  Oak, Wavy Leaf
  Oak, White

Oak, White Shin
Oak, Willow
Birch (Betulaceae)
  Alder, Smooth
  Birch, River
  Hornbeam, American
  Hornbeam, Wooly Hop
Borage (Boraginaceae)
  Anacahuita
  Anaqua
Buckeye (Hippocastanaceae)
  Buckeye, Red
  Buckeye, Yellow
Buckthorn (Rhamnaceae)
  Brazil
  Buckthorn, Carolina
  Coyotillo
Caltrop (Zygophyllaceae)
  Guayacan
Catalpa (Bignoniaceae)
  Catalpa, Northern
  Catalpa, Southern
  Desert Willow
  Yellow Trumpet
Chocolate (Sterculiaceae)
  Chinese Parasol Tree
Citrus (Rutaceae)
  Baretta
  Colima
  Hercules' Club
  Lime Prickly Ash
  Orange, Trifoliate
  Torchwood, Sierra Madre
  Wafer Ash
Custard Apple (Annonaceae)
  Pawpaw
Cypress (Cupressaceae)
  Cedar, Eastern Red
  Cedar, Southern Red
  Cypress, Arizona
  Juniper, Alligator
  Juniper, Ashe
  Juniper, Redberry
  Juniper, Roseberry
Cyrilla (Cyrillaceae)
  Titi

Dogwood (Cornaceae)
  Dogwood, Flowering
  Dogwood, Rough Leaf
Ebony (Ebenaceae)
  Persimmon
  Persimmon, Texas
Elm (Ulmaceae)
  Elm, American
  Elm, Cedar
  Elm, Chinese
  Elm, Slippery
  Elm, Winged
  Granjeno
  Hackberry, Lindheimer
  Hackberry, Net Leaf
  Hackberry, Sugar
Flacourtia (Flacourtiaceae)
  Xylosma
Ginkgo (Ginkgoaceae)
  Ginkgo
Ginseng (Araliaceae)
  Devil's Walking Stick
Heath (Ericaceae)
  Farkleberry
  Madrone, Texas
Holly (Aquifoliaceae)
  Holly, American
  Holly, Deciduous
  Holly, Winterberry
  Holly, Yaupon
Honeysuckle (Caprifoliaceae)
  Elder, Mexican
  Elderberry
  Viburnum, Rusty Blackhaw
Laurel (Lauraceae)
  Camphor Tree
  Red Bay
  Sassafras
Legume (Fabaceae)
  Acacia, Gregg
  Acacia, Roemer
  Acacia, Wright
  Anacacho Bauhinia
  Chaparro Prieto
  Coral Bean Tree

Ebony, Texas
Eve's Necklace
Guajillo
Huisache
Huisachillo
Lead Tree, Golden Ball
Locust, Black
Locust, Honey
Locust, Water
Mesquite, Honey
Mesquite, Screwbean
Mimosa
Paloverde
Poinciana, Mexican
Redbud, Eastern
Redbud, Texas
Retama
Tenaza
Tepeguaje
Texas Mountain Laurel
Linden (Tiliaceae)
Linden, Carolina
Loosestrife (Lythraceae)
Crapemyrtle
Madder (Rubiaceae)
Button Bush
Magnolia (Magnoliaceae)
Magnolia, Southern
Magnolia, Sweet Bay
Mahogany (Meliaceae)
Chinaberry
Maple (Aceraceae)
Elder, Box
Maple, Bigtooth
Maple, Chalk
Maple, Red
Maple, Silver
Maple, Southern Sugar
Maple, Trident
Mulberry (Moraceae)
Mulberry, Red
Mulberry, White
Osage Orange
Nightshade (Solanaceae)
Potato Tree
Tobacco Tree
Oak: see Beech (Fagaceae)
Olive (Oleaceae)
Ash, Berlandier
Ash, Carolina

Ash, Fragrant
Ash, Green
Ash, Velvet
Ash, White
Fringe Tree
Ligustrum, Japanese
Ligustrum, Wax leaf
Privet
Privet, Swamp
Palm (Arecaceae)
Palm, Louisiana
Palm, Sabal
Palm, Washington
Pine (Pinaceae)
Fir, Douglas
Pine, Arizona
Pine, Loblolly
Pine, Longleaf
Pine, Mexican Pinyon
Pine, Pinyon
Pine, Ponderosa
Pine, Shortleaf
Quassia (Simaroubaceae)
Tree of Heaven
Rose (Rosaceae)
Cherry Laurel
Cherry, Black
Cherry, Escarpment Black
Cherry, Southwestern Choke
Crabapple, Southern
Crabapple, Texas
Hawthorn, Big Tree
Hawthorn, Cockspur
Hawthorn, Downy
Hawthorn, Green
Hawthorn, Little Hip
Hawthorn, Mountain
Hawthorn, Parsley
Hawthorn, Texas
Loquat
Mahogany, Mountain
Mayhaw
Plum, Mexican
Sapodilla (Sapotaceae)
Coma
Gum Bumelia
Soapberry (Sapindaceae)
Golden Rain Tree
Mexican Buckeye

Soapberry, Western
Spurge (Euphorbiaceae)
Tallow Tree, Chinese
Tung Oil Tree
Storax (Styracaceae)
Silver Bell, Carolina
Silver Bell, Two Wing
Sumac (Anacardiaceae)
Pistache, Chinese
Pistache, Texas
Smoke Tree, American
Sumac, Flameleaf
Sumac, Prairie Flameleaf
Sweet Leaf (Symplocaceae)
Sweet Leaf
Sycamore (Platanaceae)
Sycamore, American
Tamarisk (Tamaricaceae)
Salt Cedar
Tupelo (Nyssaceae)
Gum, Black
Tupelo, Water
Verbena (Verbenaceae)
Fiddlewood, Tamaulipan
Chaste Tree
Walnut (Juglandaceae)
Hickory, Bitternut
Hickory, Black
Hickory, Mockernut
Hickory, Nutmeg
Hickory, Pignut
Hickory, Shagbark
Hickory, Water
Pecan
Walnut, Arizona
Walnut, Black
Walnut, Texas
Waxmyrtle (Myrtaceae)
Waxmyrtle, Southern
Willow (Salicaceae)
Aspen, Quaking
Cottonwood, Arizona
Cottonwood, Eastern
Cottonwood, Plains
Cottonwood, Rio Grande
Willow, Black
Willow, Yew Leaf
Witch Hazel (Hamamelidaceae)
Sweetgum

The common names used in the tree profiles in this book are given in **bold**. Please note that the following list of common names is not exhaustive. Note also that the same common name is sometimes applied to more than one tree species and that some Spanish tree names are not given in italics because they are locally in use in English.

Acacia berlandieri
  Berlandier Acacia
  Guajillo
Acacia farnesiana
  Cassie
  Huisache
  Sweet Acacia
  Texas Huisache
Acacia greggii
  Catclaw
  Devil's Claw
  Gregg Acacia
  Gregg Catclaw
  Texas Catclaw
  Uña de gato
Acacia rigidula
  Blackbrush Acacia
  Catclaw
  Chapparro Prieto
Acacia roemeriana
  Catclaw
  Roemer Acacia
Acacia schaffneri
  Dwarf Huisache
  Huisachillo
  Little Huisache
  Medusa Acacia
  Schaffner's Acacia
  Schaffner's Wattle
  Twisted Acacia
Acacia smallii (see *Acacia farnesiana*)
Acacia wrightii
  Catclaw
  Texas Catclaw
  Uña de gato
  Wright Acacia
Acer barbatum
  Florida Maple
  Hard Maple
  Southern Sugar Maple
Acer grandidentatum
  Bigtooth Maple
  Canyon Maple
  Sabinal Maple

  Southwestern Bigtooth Maple
  Uvalde Bigtooth Maple
  Western Sugar Maple
Acer leucoderme
  Chalk Maple
  Whitebark Maple
Acer negundo
  Ashleaf Maple
  Box Elder
  Red River Maple
Acer rubrum
  Drummond Red Maple
  Red Maple
  Scarlet Maple
  Soft Maple
  Swamp Maple
  Water Maple
Acer rubrum var. *tridens*
  Red Maple
  Scarlet Maple
  Soft Maple
  Swamp Maple
  Trident Maple
  Water Maple
Acer saccharinum
  Silver Maple
  Soft Maple
  Swamp Maple
  White Maple
Aesculus pavia var. *flavescens*
  Hill Country Buckeye
  Yellow Buckeye
Aesculus pavia var. *pavia*
  Firecracker Plant
  Red Buckeye
Ailanthus altissima
  Tree of Heaven
Albizia julibrissin
  Mimosa
  Powderpuff Tree
  Silk Tree
Aleurites fordii
  Tung Oil Tree
  Varnish Tree

Alnus serrulata
    Black Alder
    Common Alder
    Hazel Alder
    Smooth Alder
    Tag Alder
Amyris madrensis
    Mexican Torchwood
    Mountain Torchwood
    Sierra Madre Torchwood
Aralia spinosa
    Angelica Tree
    Devil's Walking Stick
    Hercules' Club
    Pigeon Tree
    Prickly Ash
    Prickly Elder
    Shotbush
    Toothache Tree
Arbutus xalapensis
    Lady's Legs
    Madroña or *Madroño*
    Naked Indian
    Texas Arbutus
    Texas Madrone
Asimina triloba
    Custard Apple
    Pawpaw
    Wild Banana
Bauhinia lunarioides
    Anacacho Bauhinia
    Orchid Tree
Betula nigra
    Black Birch
    Red Birch
    River Birch
    Water Birch
Bumelia celestrina (see *Sideroxylon celestrina*)
Bumelia lanuginosa (see *Sideroxylon lanuginosum*)
Caesalpinia mexicana
    Mexican Bird of Paradise
    Mexican Caesalpinia
    Mexican Poinciana
Carpinus caroliniana
    American Hornbeam
    Blue Beech
    Ironwood
    Musclewood
    Water Beech

Carya alba (see *Carya tomentosa*)
Carya aquatica
    Bitter Hickory
    Bitter Pecan
    Swamp Hickory
    Water Hickory
    Water Pignut
    Wild Pecan
Carya cordiformis
    Bitternut Hickory
    Bitter Pecan
    Bitter Walnut
    Pignut Hickory
    Red Hickory
    Swamp Hickory
    White Hickory
Carya glabra
    Broom Hickory
    Coast Pignut Hickory
    Pignut Hickory
    Red Hickory
    Smoothbark Hickory
    Swamp Hickory
    Sweet Pignut
    Switch Hickory
Carya illinoinensis
    Pecan
Carya myristiciformis
    Bitter Water Hickory
    Bitter Waternut
    Nutmeg Hickory
    Swamp Hickory
Carya ovata
    Carolina Hickory
    Scalybark Hickory
    Shagbark Hickory
    Shellbark Hickory
    Upland Hickory
Carya texana
    Black Hickory
    Buckley Hickory
    Pignut Hickory
    Texas Hickory
Carya tomentosa
    Bigbud Hickory
    Bullnut
    Fragrant Hickory
    Hardbark Hickory
    Hognut
    Mockernut Hickory

    White Hickory
    Whiteheart Hickory
Castanea pumila
    Allegheny Chinquapin
Catalpa bignonioides
    Catawba
    Cigar Tree
    Indian Bean
    Southern Catalpa
Catalpa speciosa
    Catawba
    Cigar Tree
    Indian Bean
    Northern Catalpa
Celtis laevigata
    Lowland Hackberry
    Palo Blanco
    Southern Hackberry
    Sugar Hackberry
    Sugarberry
    Texas Sugarberry
Celtis lindheimeri
    Lindheimer Hackberry
Celtis pallida
    Desert Hackberry
    Granjeno
    Granjeno Huasteco
    Spiny Hackberry
Celtis reticulata
    Net Leaf Hackberry
    Net Leaf Sugar Hackberry
    Palo Blanco
    Sugarberry
    Western Hackberry
Cephalanthus occidentalis
    Button Bush
    Button Willow
    Common Button Bush
    Honey Bells
    Honeyball
    Spanish Pincushion
Cercis canadensis
    Eastern Redbud
    Judas Tree
Cercis canadensis var. *texana*
    Texas Redbud
Cercocarpus montanus
    Mountain Mahogany
    Silver Mountain Mahogany
    True Mountain Mahogany

Chilopsis linearis
   Bow Willow
   Catalpa Willow
   Desert Catalpa
   Desert Willow
   False Willow
   Flor de mimbre
   Flowering Willow
   Jano
   Mimbre
   Willow Leaf Catalpa
Chionanthus virginica
   Flowering Ash
   Fringe Tree
   Grandfather Graybeard
   Graybeard Tree
   Old Man's Beard
   Poison Ash
   Shavings
   Snowflower Tree
   Sunflower Tree
   White Fringe Tree
Cinnamomum camphora
   Camphor Laurel
   Camphor Tree
Citharexylum berlandieri
   Berlandier Fiddlewood
   Negrito
   Tamaulipan Fiddlewood
   Zitherwood
Condalia hookeri
   Bluewood Condalia
   Brazil
   Capul Negro
   Capulin
   Chaparral
   Logwood
   Purple Haw
Cordia boissieri
   Anacahuita
   Mexican Olive
   Texas Olive
   Wild Olive
Cornus drummondii
   Rough Leaf Dogwood
   White Cornel
Cornus florida
   Arrowwood
   Boxwood
   False Box

   Florida Dogwood
   Flowering Dogwood
   Virginia Dogwood
   White Cornell
Cotinus aboratus
   American Smoke Tree
   Chittamwood
   Smokebush
   Smoke Tree
   Wild Smoke Tree
Crataegus berberifolia
   Barberry Hawthorn
   Big Tree Hawthorn
Crataegus crus-galli
   Cockspur Hawthorn
   Cockspur Thorn
   Hog Apple
   Newcastle Thorn
Crataegus marshallii
   Parsley Hawthorn
   Parsley Leaf Hawthorn
Crataegus mollis
   Downy Hawthorn
   Red Haw
Crataegus opaca
   Apple Haw
   May Hawthorn
   Mayhaw
   Riverflat Hawthorn
   Western Mayhaw
Crataegus spathulata
   Little Hip Hawthorn
   Pasture Haw
   Small Fruit Hawthorn
Crataegus texana
   Texas Hawthorn
Crataegus tracyi
   Mountain Hawthorn
   Tracy Hawthorn
Crataegus viridis
   Green Hawthorn
   Southern Hawthorn
Cupressus arizonica
   Arizona Cypress
   Arizona Rough Cypress
   Cedro blanco
   Rough Bark Arizona Cypress
Cyrilla racemiflora
   American Cyrilla
   Black Titi
   Burnwood Bark

   Leatherwood
   Red Titi
   Titi
   White Titi
Diospyros texana
   Black Persimmon
   Chapote negro
   Mexican Persimmon
   Texas Persimmon
Diospyros virginiana
   Common Persimmon
   Date Plum
   Eastern Persimmon
   Jove's Fruit
   Persimmon
   Possumwood
   Winter Plum
Ehretia anacua
   Anacahuita
   Anacua
   Anaqua
   Knockaway
   Manzanillo
   Manzanita
   Sandpaper Tree
   Sugarberry
   Vogelbeerbaum
Eriobotrya japonica
   China Plum
   Loquat
   Japanese Plum
Erythrina herbacea var. *arborea*
   Cardinal Spear
   Cherokee Bean
   Coral Bean Tree
   Eastern Coral Bean
   Mamou
   Red Cardinal
Fagus grandifolia
   American Beech
   Beech Nut
   Red Beech
   Ridge Beech
   White Beech
Firmiana simplex
   Bottle Tree
   Chinese Parasol Tree
   Japanese Varnish Tree
   Phoenix Tree
   Varnish Tree

Forestiera acuminata
Swamp Privet
Texas Privet
Frangula caroliniana
Alder Buckthorn
Carolina Buckthorn
Indian Cherry
Southern Buckthorn
Yellow Buckthorn
Yellow Wood
Fraxinus americana
Biltmore Ash
Cane Ash
Smallseed White Ash
White Ash
Fraxinus berlandieriana
Arizona Ash
Berlandier Ash
Fresno
Mexican Ash
Plumero
Fraxinus caroliniana
Carolina Ash
Florida Ash
Poppy Ash
Swamp Ash
Water Ash
Fraxinus cuspidata
Flowering Ash
Fragrant Ash
Fresno
Fraxinus pennsylvanica
Darlington Ash
Green Ash
Red Ash
River Ash
Swamp Ash
Water Ash
Fraxinus texensis
Mountain Ash
Texas Ash
Fraxinus velutina
Arizona Ash
Desert Ash
Fresno
Leather Leaf Ash
Modesto Ash
Smooth Ash
Standley Ash

Toumey Ash
Velvet Ash
Ginkgo biloba
Ginkgo
Maidenhair Tree
Gleditsia aquatica
Swamp Locust
Water Locust
Gleditsia triacanthos
Honey Locust
Honey Shucks Locust
Sweet Bean Tree
Sweet Locust
Thorny Locust
Guaiacum angustifolium
Guayacan
Soapbush
Texas Porlieria
Halesia caroliniana
Carolina Silver Bell
Little Silver Bell
Halesia diptera
American Silver Bell
Cowlicks
Snow Bell
Snow Drop Tree
Two Wing Silver Bell
Helietta parvifolia
Baretta
Ilex decidua
Bearberry
Deciduous Holly
Meadow Holly
Possum Haw
Prairie Holly
Swamp Holly
Welk Holly
Winterberry
Ilex opaca
American Holly
Christmas Holly
Evergreen Holly
Prickly Holly
White Holly
Yule Holly
Ilex verticillata
Black Alder
Common Winterberry
Coralberry
Michigan Holly
Winterberry Holly

Ilex vomitoria
Cassine Holly
Cassio Berry Bush Tea
Emetic Holly
Evergreen Cassena
Evergreen Holly
Indian Blackdrink
Yaupon Holly
Juglans major
Arizona Black Walnut
Arizona Walnut
Mountain Walnut
Nogal silvestre
River Walnut
Juglans microcarpa
Little Walnut
Namboca
Nogalito
River Walnut
Texas Black Walnut
Texas Walnut
Juglans nigra
American Black Walnut
Black Walnut
Eastern Black Walnut
Juniperus ashei
Ashe Juniper
Break Cedar
Cedar
Mexican Juniper
Mountain Cedar
Post Cedar
Rock Cedar
Sabino
Texas Cedar
Juniperus coahuilensis
Cedar
Roseberry Juniper
Juniperus deppeana
Alligator Juniper
Checkerbark
Mountain Cedar
Oakbark Cedar
Tascate
Thickbark Cedar
Western Juniper
Juniperus pinchotti
Cedar
Christmas Berry Juniper
Pinchot Juniper

Redberry Juniper
Texas Juniper
Juniperus virginiana var. *silicicola*
Coast Juniper
Sand Cedar
Southern Red Cedar
Juniperus virginiana
Baton Rouge
Carolina Cedar
Eastern Red Cedar
Pencil Cedar
Red Juniper
Red Savin
Virginia Juniper
Karwinskia humboldtiana
Coyotillo
Humboldt Coyotillo
Koelreuteria paniculata
Golden Rain Tree
Panicled Golden Rain Tree
Rose Lantern
Varnish Tree
Lagerstroemia indica
Crapemyrtle
Lilacs of the South
Leucaena pulverulenta
Great Lead Tree
Great Leucaena
Mexican Lead Tree
Tepeguaje
Leucaena retusa
Golden Ball Lead Tree
Lemonball
Little Leaf Lead Tree
Little Leucaena
Wahoo Tree
Ligustrum japonicum
Japanese Ligustrum
Japanese Privet
Privet Berry
Ligustrum lucidum
Tree Privet
Wax Leaf Ligustrum
Ligustrum sinense
Chinese Privet
Liquidamber styraciflua
Alligator Tree
American Sweetgum
Blisted
Red Gum
Satin Walnut

Star-Leaved Gum
Sweetgum
White Gum
Maclura pomifera
Bodark
Bois d' Arc
Bow Wood
Hedge Apple
Horse Apple
Naranjo chino
Osage Orange
Yellow Wood
Magnolia grandiflora
Big Laurel
Bull Bay Magnolia
Evergreen Magnolia
Great Laurel Magnolia
Loblolly Magnolia
Southern Magnolia
Magnolia virginiana
Bay
Beaver Tree
Big Laurel
Black Lin
Bullbay
Cucumberwood
Evergreen Magnolia
Indian Bark
Laurel Magnolia
Mountain Magnolia
Small Magnolia
Southern Sassafras
Southern Sweetbay
Swamp Bay Magnolia
Swamp Laurel
Swamp Magnolia
Swamp Sassafras
Sweet Bay Magnolia
Sweet Magnolia
Virginia Magnolia
White Laurel
White Bay Magnolia
Malus angustifolia
Narrow Leaf Crabapple
Southern Crabapple
Malus ioensis var. *texana*
Blanco Crabapple
Iowa Crab
Prairie Crabapple
Texas Crabapple
Western Crabapple

Melia azedarach
Chinaberry
Umbrella Tree
Morus alba
Moral blanco
Russian Mulberry
Silkworm Mulberry
White Mulberry
Morus rubra
Lampassas Mulberry
Moral
Red Mulberry
Myrica cerifera
Bayberry
Candleberry
Southern Bayberry
Southern Waxmyrtle
Tallow Shrub
Wax Myrtle
Nicotiana glauca
Tobacco Tree
Tree Tobacco
Yellow Tree Tobacco
Nyssa aquatica
Cotton Gum
Swamp Tupelo
Sour Gum
Water Gum
Water Tupelo
Nyssa sylvatica
Black Gum
Black Tupelo
Pepperidge
Sour Gum
Ostrya virginiana
American Hop Hornbeam
Deerwood
Eastern Hop Hornbeam
Eastern Ironwood
Ironwood
Leverwood
Roughbark Ironwood
Wooly Hop Hornbeam
Parkinsonia aculeata
Horse Bean
Jerusalem Thorn
Mexican Paloverde
Paloverde
Parkinsonia
Retama

Parkinsonia texana var. *macra*
    Border Paloverde
    Paloverde
    Retama China
    Texas Paloverde
Persea borbonia
    Laurel Tree
    Red Bay
    Red Bay Persea
    Silk Bay
    Sweet Bay
Pinus arizonica var. *stormiae* (*stromiae*)
    Arizona Pine
Pinus cembroides
    Mexican Pinyon Pine
    Nut Pine
    Piñón
Pinus echinata
    Arkansas Pine
    Longtag Pine
    Shortleaf Pine
    Short Straw Pine
    Southern Yellow Pine
    Yellow Pine
Pinus edulis
    Colorado Pinyon Pine
    New Mexico Pinyon Pine
    Nut Pine
    Piñón
    Pinyon Pine
    Two Leaf Pinyon
Pinus palustris
    Hard Pine
    Heart Pine
    Hill Pine
    Longleaf Pine
    Long Straw Pine
    Pitch Pine
    Southern Yellow Pine
    Yellow Pine
Pinus ponderosa var. *scopulorum*
    Black Hill Ponderosa Pine
    Interior Ponderosa Pine
    Ponderosa Pine
    Rocky Mountain Ponderosa Pine
Pinus taeda
    Loblolly Pine
    Oldfield Pine
Pistacia chinensis
    Chinese Pistache

Pistacia texana
    American Pistachio
    Lentisco
    Texas Pistache
    Wild Pistachio
Pithecellobium flexicaule
    Ape's Earring
    Ebano
    Ebony Blackbeard
    Texas Ebony
Pithecellobium pallens
    Ape's Earring
    Tenaza
Platanus occidentalis
    American Plane Tree
    American Sycamore
    Buttonball Tree
    Buttonwood
    Eastern Sycamore
    Plane Tree
Poncirus trifoliata
    Bitter Orange
    Chinese Citron
    Hardy Orange
    Mock Orange
    Trifoliate Orange
Populus deltoides
    Alamo
    Carolina Poplar
    Eastern Cottonwood
    Eastern Poplar
    Necklace Poplar
    Southern Cottonwood
Populus fremontii var. *mesetae*
    Arizona Cottonwood
    Meseta Cottonwood
Populus sargentii
    Northern Cottonwood
    Plains Cottonwood
    Texas Cottonwood
Populus tremuloides
    Alamo blanco
    Golden Aspen
    Quaking Aspen
    Trembling Poplar
Populus wislizenii
    Alamo
    Rio Grande Cottonwood
    Valley Cottonwood
    Wislizenus Cottonwood

Prosopis glandulosa
    Algaroba
    Glandular Mesquite
    Honey Mesquite
Prosopis pubescens
    Fremont Screwbean
    Screwbean Mesquite
    Screwpod Mesquite
    Tornillo
    Twisted Bean
Prunus caroliniana
    Carolina Cherry
    Carolina Cherry Laurel
    Cherry Laurel
    Laurel Cherry
    Mock Orange
    Wild Peach
Prunus mexicana
    Big Tree Plum
    Inch Plum
    Mexican Plum
Prunus serotina
    Rum Cherry
    Black Cherry
    Wild Black Cherry
    Wild Cherry
Prunus serotina var. *eximia*
    Edward's Plateau Black Cherry
    Escarpment Black Cherry
Prunus serotina var. *rufula*
    Capulin
    Chisos Wild Cherry
    Southwestern Choke Cherry
Pseudotsuga menziesii
    Blue Douglas Fir
    Colorado Douglas Fir
    Douglas Fir
    Inland Douglas Fir
    Interior Douglas Fir
    Pino real colorado
    Rocky Mountain Douglas Fir
Ptelea trifoliata
    Hop Tree
    Skunk Bush
    Wafer Ash
Quercus alba
    Fork Leaf White Oak
    Ridge White Oak
    Stave Oak
    White Oak

Quercus buckleyi
  Buckley Oak
  Spanish Oak
  Spotted Oak
  Texas Oak
  Texas Red Oak
Quercus emoryi
  Apache Oak
  Bellota
  Black Oak
  Desert Live Oak
  Emory Oak
  Holly Oak
  Roble negro
  Western Black Oak
Quercus falcata
  Bottomland Red Oak
  Cherrybark Oak
  Pagoda Oak
  Southern Red Oak
  Spanish Oak
  Swamp Red Oak
  Swamp Spanish Oak
  Three Lobe Red Oak
Quercus fusiformis
  Escarpment Live Oak
  Live Oak
  Plateau Live Oak
  Scrub Live Oak
  Spanish Live Oak
  West Texas Live Oak
Quercus gambelii
  Gambel Oak
Quercus gravesii
  Chisos Red Oak
  Graves Oak
  Mountain Oak
  Rock Oak
  Texas Red Oak
Quercus grisea
  Encino prieta
  Gray Oak
Quercus havardii
  Havard Shin Oak
  Sand Shin Oak
  Shinnery
Quercus hypoleucoides
  Silver Leaf Oak
  White Leaf Oak

Quercus incana
  Bluejack Oak
  Cinnamon Oak
  Sandjack Oak
  Shin Oak
  Turkey Oak
  Upland Willow Oak
Quercus laceyi
  Blue Oak
  Canyon Oak
  Lacey Oak
  Rock Oak
  Smokey Oak
Quercus laurifolia
  Darlington Oak
  Diamond Leaf Oak
  Laurel Leaf Oak
  Laurel Oak
  Obtusa Oak
  Swamp Laurel Oak
Quercus lyrata
  Overcup Oak
  Swamp Post Oak
  Swamp White Oak
  Water White Oak
Quercus macrocarpa
  Bur Oak
  Mossycup Oak
  Prairie Oak
Quercus marilandica
  Barron Oak
  Black Oak
  Blackjack Oak
  Iron Oak
  Jack Oak
Quercus michauxii
  Basket Oak
  Cow Oak
  Swamp Chestnut Oak
  Swamp White Oak
Quercus mohriana
  Mohr Oak
  Scrub Oak
  Shin Oak
Quercus muhlenbergii
  Chestnut Oak
  Chinkapin Oak
  Rock Chestnut Oak
  Rock Oak
  Yellow Chestnut Oak
  Yellow Oak

Quercus nigra
  Duck Oak
  Pin Oak
  Possum Oak
  Punk Oak
  Spotted Oak
  Water Oak
Quercus nuttallii
  Nuttall Oak
  Pin Oak
  Red Oak
  Red River Oak
  Striped Oak
Quercus obtusa (see *Quercus laurifolia*)
Quercus phellos
  Peach Oak
  Pin Oak
  Swamp Willow Oak
  Willow Oak
Quercus polymorpha
  Coahuila Oak
  Encino
  Mexican Oak
  Mexican White Oak
  Monterrey Oak
Quercus pungens
  Encino
  Sandpaper Oak
  Scrub Oak
  Shin Oak
  Shrub Live Oak
Quercus shumardii
  Shumard Oak
  Shumard Red Oak
  Spotted Oak
  Swamp Red Oak
Quercus similes
  Bottomland Post Oak
  Delta Post Oak
  Mississippi Valley Oak
  Swamp Post Oak
  Yellow Oak
Quercus sinuate var. *breviloba*
  Bigelow Oak
  Scalybark Oak
  Scrub Oak
  Shin Oak
  Shinnery
  White Shin Oak

Quercus stellata
  Cross Oak
  Iron Oak
  Post Oak
Quercus turbinella
  Encino
  Scrub Oak
  Shrub Live Oak
  Turbinella Oak
Quercus undulata
  Encino
  Scrub Live Oak
  Scrub Oak
  Shin Oak
  Wavy Leaf Oak
Quercus vaseyana
  Scrub Oak
  Shin Oak
  Shinnery
  Vasey Oak
Quercus velutina
  Black Oak
  Quercitron
  Smoothbark Oak
  Yellow Oak
  Yellowbark Oak
Quercus virginiana
  Coast Live Oak
  Encino
  Live Oak
  Southern Live Oak
  Virginia Live Oak
Rhus copalina
  Black Sumac
  Flameleaf Sumac
  Mountain Sumac
  Shining Sumac
  Upland Sumac
  Wing Rib Sumac
Rhus lanceolata
  Lance-leaved Sumac
  Limestone Sumac
  Prairie Flameleaf Sumac
  Prairie Shining Sumac
  Texas Sumac
  Tree Sumac
Robinia pseudoacacia
  Black Locust
  False Acacia
  Green Locust

  Locust Tree
  Post Locust
  Ship Mast Locust
  White Locust
  Yellow Locust
Sabal louisiana
  Louisiana Palm
  Palmetto
Sabal mexicana
  Mexican Palmetto
  Palma de micharos
  Rio Grande Palmetto
  Sabal Palm
  Texas Palmetto
  Victoria Palmetto
Salix nigra
  Black Willow
  Gooding Willow
  Gulf Black Willow
  Lindheimer Black Willow
  Sauz
  Southwestern Black Willow
  Swamp Willow
  Western Black Willow
Salix taxifolia
  Yew Willow
  Yew Leaf Willow
Sambucus canadensis
  American Elder
  Common Elder
  Elderberry
  Sweet Elder
Sambucus mexicana
  Blue Elderberry
  Mexican Elder
Sapindus saponaria var. *drummondii*
  Indian Soap Plant
  Jaboncillo
  Western Soapberry
  Wild Chinaberry
  Wild Chinatree
Sapium sebiferum
  Chinese Tallow Tree
Sassafras albidum
  Ague Tree
  Gumbo Filé
  Rootbeer Tree
  Saloop
  Sassafras
  White Sassafras

Sideroxylon celestrina
  Anstwood
  Coma
  Downward Plum
  La coma
  Milk Buckthorn
  Saffron Plum
  Tropical Buckthorn
Sideroxylon lanuginosum
  Chittamwood
  Coma
  False Buckthorn
  Gum Bumelia
  Gum Elastic
  Gum Woolybucket
  Ironwood
  Shittamwood
  Wooly Buckthorn
  Wooly Bumelia
  Woolybucket Bumelia
Solanum erianthum
  Mullein
  Potato Tree
  Shrub Nightshade
Sophora affinis
  Eve's Necklace
  Necklace Tree
  Pink Sophora
  Texas Sophora
Sophora secundiflora
  Frijolito
  Mescalbean
  Texas Mountain Laurel
Symplocos tinctoria
  Horse Sugar
  Sweet Leaf
  Yellow Wood
  Wild Laurel
Tamarix gallica
  French Tamarisk
  Manna Plant
  Salt Cedar
  Tamarindo
  Tamarisco
  Tamarisk
Taxodium distichum
  Bald Cypress
  Gulf Cypress
  Red Cypress
  Southern Cypress
  Swamp Cypress

Tidewater Red Cypress
White Cypress
Yellow Cypress
Taxodium mucronatum
  Ahuehuete
  Cipres
  Mexican Cypress
  Montezuma Bald Cypress
  Sabino
Tecoma stans
  Esperanza
  Trumpet Bush
  Yellow Bells
  Yellow Trumpet
Tilia caroliniana
  Basswood
  Carolina Basswood
  Carolina Linden
  Florida Basswood
  Florida Linden
  Lime Tree
Ulmus alata
  Cork Elm
  Wahoo Elm
  Winged Elm
  Witch Elm
Ulmus americana
  American Elm
  Common Elm
  Soft Elm
  Water Elm
  White Elm
Ulmus crassifolia
  Basket Elm
  Cedar Elm
  Lime Elm
  Olmo
  Scrub Elm
  Southern Rock Elm
  Texas Elm
Ulmus parvifolia
  Chinese Elm
  Lace Bark Elm
Ulmus rubra
  Indian Elm
  Moose Elm
  Red Elm
  Rock Elm
  Slippery Elm
  Sweet Elm

Ungnadia speciosa
  Mexican Buckeye
  Monillo
  Texas Buckeye
Vaccinium arboreum
  Farkleberry
  Huckleberry
  Sparkleberry
  Tree Huckleberry
  Winter Huckleberry
Viburnum rufidulum
  Blackhaw
  Bluehaw
  Nannyberry
  Rusty Blackhaw Viburnum
  Rusty Nannyberry
  Southern Blackhaw
  Southern Nannyberry
Vitex agnus-castus
  Chaste Berry
  Chaste Tree
  Hemp Tree
  Monk's Pepper
Washingtonia filifera
  American Cotton Palm
  California Fan Palm
  Cotton Palm
  Desert Fan Palm
  Palmera de Abanicos
  Petticoat Palm
  Washington Palm
Xylosma flexuosa
  Coronilla
  Manzanillo
  Xylosma
Yucca elata
  Amole
  Palmilla
  Soaptree Yucca
  Soapweed Yucca
Yucca faxonia
  Faxon Yucca
  Giant Dagger
  Palma
  Spanish Bayonet
  Spanish Dagger
Yucca rostrata
  Beaked Yucca
  Big Bend Yucca
  Palmita
  Soyate

Yucca thompsoniana
  Palmilla
  Thompson Yucca
Yucca torreyi
  Old Shag
  Palma
  Spanish Bayonet
  Spanish Dagger
  Torrey Yucca
Yucca treculeana
  Palma de datil
  Palma pita
  Palmito
  Spanish Bayonet
  Spanish Dagger
  Trecul Yucca
Zanthoxylum clava-herculis
  Hercules' Club
  Pepperbark
  Prickly Ash
  Tickle Tongue
  Toothache Tree
Zanthoxylum fagara
  Colima
  Lime Prickly Ash
  Wild Lime
Zanthoxylum hirsutum
  Lime Prickly Ash
  Limoncillo
  Texas Hercules' Club
  Tickle Tongue
  Toothache Tree

INTRODUCED SPECIES

Appendix C

BY SCIENTIFIC NAME

Acer saccharinum (Silver Maple)
Ailanthus altissima (Tree of Heaven)
Albizia julibrissin (Mimosa)
Aleurites fordii (Tung Oil Tree)
Catalpa bignonioides (Southern Catalpa)
Cinnamomum camphora (Camphor Tree)
Eriobotrya japonica (Loquat)
Firmiana simplex (Chinese Parasol Tree)
Ginkgo biloba (Ginkgo)
Koelreuteria paniculata (Golden Rain Tree)
Lagerstroemia indica (Crapemyrtle)
Ligustrum japonicum (Japanese Ligustrum)
Ligustrum lucidum (Wax Leaf Ligustrum)
Ligustrum sinense (Chinese Privet)
Melia azedarach (Chinaberry)
Morus alba (White Mulberry)
Nicotiana glauca (Tobacco Tree)
Pistacia chinensis (Chinese Pistache)
Poncirus trifoliata (Trifoliate Orange)
Robinia pseudoacacia (Black Locust)
Sapium sebiferum (Chinese Tallow Tree)
Tamarix gallica (Salt Cedar)
Ulmus parvifolia (Chinese Elm)
Vitex agnus-castus (Chaste Tree)
Washingtonia filifera (Washington Palm)

BY COMMON NAME

Camphor Tree (*Cinnamomum camphora*)
Catalpa, Southern (*Catalpa bignonioides*)
Cedar, Salt (*Tamarix gallica*)
Chaste Tree (*Vitex agnus-castus*)
Chinaberry (*Melia azedarach*)
Chinese Parasol Tree (*Firmiana simplex*)
Crapemyrtle (*Lagerstroemia indica*)
Elm, Chinese (*Ulmus parvifolia*)
Ginkgo (*Ginkgo biloba*)
Golden Rain Tree (*Koelreuteria paniculata*)
Ligustrum, Japanese (*Ligustrum japonicum*)
Ligustrum, Wax Leaf (*Ligustrum lucidum*)
Locust, Black (*Robinia pseudoacacia*)
Loquat (*Eriobotrya japonica*)
Maple, Silver (*Acer saccharinum*)
Mimosa (*Albizia julibrissin*)
Mulberry, White (*Morus alba*)
Orange, Trifoliate (*Poncirus trifoliata*)
Palm, Washington (*Washingtonia filifera*)
Pistache, Chinese (*Pistacia chinensis*)
Privet, Chinese (*Ligustrum sinense*)
Tallow Tree, Chinese (*Sapium sebiferum*)
Tobacco Tree (*Nicotiana glauca*)
Tree of Heaven (*Ailanthus altissima*)
Tung Oil Tree (*Aleurites fordii*)

See Map of Vegetation Regions, p. xxi

Region 1:
Piney Woods

Alder, Smooth
Ash, Carolina
Ash, Green
Ash, White
Beech, American
Birch, River
Black Gum
Box Elder
Buckeye, Red
Buckthorn, Carolina
Button Bush
Catalpa, Northern
Cedar, Eastern Red
Cedar, Southern Red
Cherry Laurel
Cherry, Black
Chinquapin, Allegheny
Cottonwood, Eastern
Crabapple, Southern
Cypress, Bald
Devil's Walking Stick
Dogwood, Flowering
Dogwood, Rough Leaf
Elderberry
Elm, American
Elm, Cedar
Elm, Slippery
Elm, Winged
Farkleberry
Fringe Tree
Gum Bumelia
Hackberry, Sugar
Hawthorn, Big Tree
Hawthorn, Cockspur
Hawthorn, Downy
Hawthorn, Green
Hawthorn, Little Hip
Hawthorn, Parsley
Hercules' Club
Hickory, Bitternut
Hickory, Black
Hickory, Mockernut

Hickory, Nutmeg
Hickory, Pignut
Hickory, Shagbark
Hickory, Water
Holly, American
Holly, Deciduous
Holly, Winterberry
Holly, Yaupon
Hop Hornbeam, Wooly
Hornbeam, American
Linden, Carolina
Locust, Honey
Locust, Water
Magnolia, Southern
Magnolia, Sweet Bay
Maple, Chalk
Maple, Red
Maple, Southern Sugar
Maple, Trident
Mayhaw
Mulberry, Red
Oak, Black
Oak, Blackjack
Oak, Bluejack
Oak, Bottomland Post
Oak, Diamond Leaf
Oak, Laurel
Oak, Nuttall
Oak, Overcup
Oak, Post
Oak, Shumard
Oak, Southern Red
Oak, Swamp Chestnut
Oak, Water
Oak, Willow
Palm, Louisiana
Pawpaw
Pecan
Persimmon
Pine, Loblolly
Pine, Longleaf
Pine, Shortleaf
Plum, Mexican
Red Bay
Redbud, Eastern

Sassafras
Silver Bell, Carolina
Silver Bell, Two Wing
Soapberry, Western
Sumac, Flameleaf
Swamp Privet
Sweet Leaf
Sweetgum
Sycamore, American
Titi
Tupelo, Water
Viburnum, Rusty Blackhaw
Wafer Ash
Walnut, Black
Waxmyrtle, Southern
Willow, Black

Region 2:
Gulf Prairies and Marshes

Anaqua
Ash, Berlandier
Ash, Green
Ash, White
Black Gum
Box Elder
Brazil
Buckeye, Mexican
Buckthorn, Carolina
Button Bush
Cedar, Southern Red
Cherry Laurel
Colima
Coma
Cottonwood, Eastern
Cypress, Bald
Devil's Walking Stick
Ebony, Texas
Elderberry
Elm, American
Elm, Cedar
Elm, Winged
Farkleberry
Fringe Tree
Guajillo
Gum Bumelia
Hackberry, Net Leaf
Hackberry, Sugar
Hawthorn, Cockspur
Hawthorn, Downy

Hawthorn, Green
Hawthorn, Little Hip
Hawthorn, Parsley
Hawthorn, Texas
Hercules' Club
Hickory, Bitternut
Hickory, Nutmeg
Hickory, Water
Holly, American
Holly, Deciduous
Holly, Winterberry
Holly, Yaupon
Hornbeam, American
Huisache
Huisachillo
Lime Prickly Ash
Locust, Honey
Locust, Water
Maple, Red
Mesquite, Honey
Mulberry, Red
Oak, Blackjack
Oak, Bluejack
Oak, Bottomland Post
Oak, Bur
Oak, Live
Oak, Overcup
Oak, Plateau Live
Oak, Post
Oak, Shumard
Oak, Southern Red
Oak, Swamp Chestnut
Oak, Water
Oak, Willow
Palm, Louisiana
Paloverde
Pecan
Persimmon, Texas
Pine, Loblolly
Pine, Longleaf
Pine, Shortleaf
Plum, Mexican
Red Bay
Redbud, Eastern
Retama
Silver Bell, Carolina
Silver Bell, Two Wing
Soapberry, Western
Spanish Dagger
Sumac, Flameleaf

Swamp Privet
Sweetgum
Sycamore, American
Tenaza
Tepeguaje
Titi
Viburnum, Rusty Blackhaw
Walnut, Black
Waxmyrtle, Southern
Willow, Black
Yellow Trumpet

Region 3:
Post Oak Savannah

Anaqua
Ash, Green
Ash, White
Birch, River
Black Gum
Box Elder
Brazil
Buckeye, Mexican
Buckeye, Red
Buckthorn, Carolina
Button Bush
Cedar, Eastern Red
Cherry Laurel
Cherry, Black
Cottonwood, Eastern
Cottonwood, Plains
Cypress, Bald
Devil's Walking Stick
Dogwood, Flowering
Dogwood, Rough Leaf
Elderberry
Elm, American
Elm, Cedar
Elm, Slippery
Elm, Winged
Farkleberry
Gum Bumelia
Hackberry, Net Leaf
Hackberry, Sugar
Hawthorn, Big Tree
Hawthorn, Cockspur
Hawthorn, Downy
Hawthorn, Green
Hawthorn, Little Hip
Hawthorn, Parsley

Hawthorn, Texas
Hercules' Club
Hickory, Bitternut
Hickory, Black
Hickory, Mockernut
Hickory, Nutmeg
Hickory, Pignut
Hickory, Water
Holly, American
Holly, Deciduous
Holly, Yaupon
Hop Hornbeam, Wooly
Hornbeam, American
Huisache
Linden, Carolina
Locust, Honey
Locust, Water
Maple, Red
Mesquite, Honey
Mulberry, Red
Oak, Black
Oak, Blackjack
Oak, Bluejack
Oak, Bottomland Post
Oak, Bur
Oak, Chinkapin
Oak, Live
Oak, Overcup
Oak, Plateau Live
Oak, Post
Oak, Shumard
Oak, Southern Red
Oak, Texas
Oak, Water
Oak, Willow
Osage Orange
Pecan
Persimmon
Persimmon, Texas
Pine, Loblolly
Pine, Shortleaf
Plum, Mexican
Redbud, Eastern
Retama
Sassafras
Soapberry, Western
Sumac, Flameleaf
Swamp Privet
Sweetgum
Sycamore, American

Viburnum, Rusty Blackhaw
Wafer Ash
Walnut, Black
Waxmyrtle, Southern
Willow, Black

Region 4:
Blackland Prairies

Anaqua
Ash, Green
Ash, White
Box Elder
Buckeye, Mexican
Buckeye, Red
Buckthorn, Carolina
Button Bush
Cedar, Eastern Red
Cottonwood, Eastern
Cottonwood, Plains
Dogwood, Rough Leaf
Elderberry
Elm, American
Elm, Cedar
Elm, Slippery
Elm, Winged
Eve's Necklace
Gum Bumelia
Hackberry, Net Leaf
Hackberry, Sugar
Hawthorn, Big Tree
Hawthorn, Cockspur
Hawthorn, Downy
Hawthorn, Green
Hawthorn, Little Hip
Hercules' Club
Hickory, Bitternut
Hickory, Black
Holly, Deciduous
Holly, Yaupon
Locust, Honey
Mesquite, Honey
Mulberry, Red
Oak, Blackjack
Oak, Bur
Oak, Chinkapin
Oak, Live
Oak, Plateau Live
Oak, Post
Oak, Shumard

Oak, Texas
Oak, White Shin
Osage Orange
Pecan
Persimmon, Texas
Plum, Mexican
Redbud, Eastern
Redbud, Texas
Retama
Soapberry, Western
Sumac, Flameleaf
Sycamore, American
Viburnum, Rusty Blackhaw
Wafer Ash
Walnut, Black
Willow, Black

Region 5:
Cross Timbers and Prairies

Acacia, Wright
Ash, Green
Box Elder
Buckeye, Mexican
Buckthorn, Carolina
Button Bush
Cedar, Eastern Red
Cottonwood, Eastern
Cottonwood, Plains
Dogwood, Rough Leaf
Elderberry
Elm, American
Elm, Cedar
Elm, Slippery
Elm, Winged
Eve's Necklace
Gum Bumelia
Hackberry, Net Leaf
Hackberry, Sugar
Hawthorn, Cockspur
Hawthorn, Downy
Hawthorn, Green
Hickory, Black
Holly, Deciduous
Juniper, Ashe
Lime Prickly Ash
Locust, Honey
Mesquite, Honey
Mulberry, Red
Oak, Blackjack

Oak, Bur
Oak, Chinkapin
Oak, Plateau Live
Oak, Post
Oak, Shumard
Oak, Texas
Oak, White Shin
Pecan
Persimmon
Persimmon, Texas
Plum, Mexican
Redbud, Eastern
Redbud, Texas
Retama
Soapberry, Western
Sumac, Prairie Flameleaf
Sycamore, American
Viburnum, Rusty Blackhaw
Wafer Ash
Walnut, Black
Walnut, Texas
Willow, Black

Region 6:
South Texas Plains

Acacia, Gregg
Acacia, Wright
Anacahuita
Anaqua
Ash, Berlandier
Ash, Green
Baretta
Brazil
Button Bush
Colima
Coma
Coral Bean Tree
Coyotillo
Cypress, Bald
Cypress, Montezuma Bald
Ebony, Texas
Elderberry
Elm, American
Elm, Cedar
Granjeno
Guajillo
Guayacan
Gum Bumelia
Hackberry, Sugar

Huisache
Huisachillo
Lime Prickly Ash
Mesquite, Honey
Mountain Laurel, Texas
Oak, Live
Oak, Plateau Live
Oak, Post
Palm, Sabal
Paloverde
Pecan
Persimmon, Texas
Poinciana, Mexican
Potato Tree
Retama
Soapberry, Western
Spanish Dagger
Tamaulipan Fiddlewood
Tenaza
Tepeguaje
Torchwood, Sierra Madre
Walnut, Texas
Willow, Black
Xylosma
Yellow Trumpet
Yucca, Torrey

Region 7:
Edwards Plateau

Acacia, Gregg
Acacia, Roemer
Acacia, Wright
Anacacho Bauhinia
Ash, Fragrant
Ash, Green
Ash, Texas
Box Elder
Brazil
Buckeye, Mexican
Buckeye, Red
Buckeye, Yellow
Buckthorn, Carolina
Button Bush
Chaparro Prieto
Cherry, Black
Coma
Cottonwood, Eastern
Crabapple, Texas
Cypress, Bald

Desert Willow
Dogwood, Rough Leaf
Elderberry
Elm, American
Elm, Cedar
Elm, Slippery
Eve's Necklace
Granjeno
Guayacan
Gum Bumelia
Hackberry, Lindheimer
Hackberry, Net Leaf
Hackberry, Sugar
Hawthorn, Cockspur
Hawthorn, Downy
Hawthorn, Green
Hawthorn, Mountain
Hickory, Black
Hickory, Nutmeg
Holly, Deciduous
Huisache
Huisachillo
Juniper, Ashe
Juniper, Redberry
Lead Tree, Golden Ball
Lime Prickly Ash
Linden, Carolina
Locust, Honey
Madrone, Texas
Mahogany, Mountain
Maple, Bigtooth
Mesquite, Honey
Mountain Laurel, Texas
Mulberry, Red
Oak, Blackjack
Oak, Bur
Oak, Chinkapin
Oak, Lacey
Oak, Live
Oak, Mohr
Oak, Plateau Live
Oak, Post
Oak, Texas
Oak, Vasey
Oak, White Shin
Paloverde
Pecan
Persimmon
Persimmon, Texas
Pistache, Texas

Plum, Mexican
Redbud, Texas
Retama
Smoke Tree, American
Soapberry, Western
Spanish Dagger
Sumac, Prairie Flameleaf
Sycamore, American
Tepeguaje
Viburnum, Rusty Blackhaw
Wafer Ash
Walnut, Arizona
Walnut, Black
Walnut, Texas
Willow, Black
Yellow Trumpet
Yucca, Torrey

Region 8:
Rolling Plains

Acacia, Roemer
Acacia, Wright
Ash, Green
Buckeye, Mexican
Button Bush
Cedar, Eastern Red
Cottonwood, Plains
Elm, American
Gum Bumelia
Hackberry, Net Leaf
Hackberry, Sugar
Juniper, Ashe
Juniper, Redberry
Mahogany, Mountain
Mesquite, Honey
Oak, Havard Shin
Oak, Mohr
Oak, Post
Oak, White Shin
Pecan
Persimmon
Redbud, Texas
Soapberry, Western
Sumac, Prairie Flameleaf
Walnut, Black
Walnut, Texas
Willow, Black

Region 9:
High Plains

Ash, Green
Button Bush
Cedar, Eastern Red
Hackberry, Net Leaf
Juniper, Redberry
Madrone, Texas
Mesquite, Honey
Oak, Havard Shin
Willow, Black

Region 10:
Trans-Pecos, Mountains
and Basins

Acacia, Gregg
Acacia, Roemer
Acacia, Wright
Ash, Fragrant
Ash, Velvet
Aspen, Quaking
Buckeye, Mexican
Button Bush
Chaparro Prieto
Cherry, Black
Cottonwood, Arizona
Cottonwood, Rio Grande
Coyotillo
Cypress, Arizona
Desert Willow
Douglas Fir
Elder, Mexican
Giant Dagger
Granjeno
Guayacan
Gum Bumelia
Hackberry, Net Leaf
Hackberry, Sugar
Hawthorn, Mountain
Huisache
Juniper, Alligator
Juniper, Ashe
Juniper, Redberry
Juniper, Roseberry
Lead Tree, Golden Ball
Madrone, Texas
Mahogany, Mountain

Maple, Bigtooth
Mesquite, Honey
Mesquite, Screwbean
Mountain Laurel, Texas
Oak, Chisos Red
Oak, Emory
Oak, Gambel
Oak, Gray
Oak, Lacey
Oak, Mexican
Oak, Mohr
Oak, Sandpaper
Oak, Scrub
Oak, Silver Leaf
Oak, Vasey
Oak, Wavy Leaf
Persimmon, Texas
Pine, Arizona
Pine, Mexican Pinyon
Pine, Pinyon
Pine, Ponderosa
Retama
Soapberry, Western
Sumac, Prairie Flameleaf
Viburnum, Rusty Blackhaw
Wafer Ash
Walnut, Arizona
Walnut, Texas
Willow, Black
Willow, Yew Leaf
Yellow Trumpet
Yucca, Beaked
Yucca, Soaptree
Yucca, Thompson
Yucca, Torrey

BUTTERFLY HOST TREES

Appendix E

Grasses, forbs, and shrubs are food for the larvae of many butterfly species, and certain trees are hosts to some of the more attractive kinds. Among the Texas trees that help perpetuate these "flying flowers" are the following:

The several kinds of hackberries (*Celtis* species) found around Texas are favored by the larvae of a number of butterfly species, and the oozing sap of the trees attracts some adult butterflies.

Sassafras (*Sassafras albidum*) is host to the spicebush swallowtail.

Hercules' club (*Zanthoxylum clava-herculis*) and trifoliate orange (*Poncirus trifoliata*) are food for the larvae of the giant swallowtail.

The various kinds of ash (*Fraxinus* species) and wild cherries (*Prunus* species) feed several kinds of butterfly larvae, including those of the tiger swallowtail.

Red bay (*Persea borbonia*) is the host for the Palamedes swallowtail.

Black willow (*Salix nigra*) is favored by the viceroy butterfly.

Pawpaw (*Asimina triloba*) is food for zebra swallowtail larvae.

The elms (*Ulmus* species) attract several kinds of butterflies.

Western soapberry (*Sapindus saponaria* var. *drummondii*), cottonwoods (*Populus* species), and some *Acacia* species are hosts for butterflies in Texas.

With the increasing interest in butterflies, a number of books and pamphlets have been written in recent years on this topic. A good web site is "Butterflies of Texas" (http://www.npsc.nbs.gov/index.htm). Click on the map of Texas, and you can get detailed information about your county and regional sightings plus host plants and flowers to attract the various species.

Appendix F LIGHT AND WATER REQUIREMENTS

The light and water requirements for cultivating the trees listed in this book are given by the following codes:

LIGHT REQUIREMENTS

FS   full sun
PSH   partial shade
S/PSH   sun or partial shade
S/SH   sun or shade

WATER REQUIREMENTS

W   normal watering
LW   likes watering often
MW   minimal water needed
X   xerophytic (drought tolerant)

A factor to consider is that many forest trees like partial shade when young but more sunshine as they grow and mature. Many xerophytic or desert species can be grown in wetter areas but need good drainage. The W (normal watering) category trees can thrive on the amount of water required to keep a lawn green.

This appendix does not include invasive pest species like Chinese tallow, salt cedar, or Chinese privet. We do not recommend their cultivation. Also not included are a few species that grow only in limited high altitude places in the state. More information is given in the text for trees that are especially worthy of cultivation.

Tree	Light	Water
Allegheny Chinquapin (*Castanea pumila*)	PSH	W
Alligator Juniper (*Juniperus deppeana*)	S/PSH	X
American Beech (*Fagus grandifolia*)	S/PSH	W
American Elm (*Ulmus americana*)	S/PSH	W
American Holly (*Ilex opaca*)	PSH	MW
American Hornbeam (*Carpinus caroliniana*)	PSH	LW
American Smoke Tree (*Cotinus obovatus*)	S/PSH	MW
American Sycamore (*Platanus occidentalis*)	S/PSH	LW
Anacacho Bauhinia (*Bauhinia lunarioides*)	FS	MW
Anacahuita (*Cordia boissieri*)	FS	X
Anaqua (*Ehretia anacua*)	FS	MW
Arizona Cottonwood (*Populus fremontii* var. *mesetae*)	S/PSH	LW
Arizona Cypress (*Cupressus arizonica*)	FS	MW
Arizona Pine (*Pinus arizonica* var. *stormiae*)	FS	MW
Arizona Walnut (*Juglans major*)	S/PSH	LW
Ashe Juniper (*Juniperus ashei*)	FS	X
Bald Cypress (*Taxodium distichum*)	S/PSH	LW
Baretta (*Helietta parvifolia*)	FS	MW
Beaked Yucca (*Yucca rostrata*)	FS	X
Berlandier Ash (*Fraxinus berlandieriana*)	FS	W
Big Tree Hawthorn (*Crataegus berberifolia*)	S/PSH	W
Bigtooth Maple (*Acer grandidentatum*)	FS/PSH	W
Bitternut Hickory (*Carya cordiformis*)	FS/PSH	MW
Black Cherry (*Prunus serotina*)	FS/PSH	W
Black Gum (*Nyssa sylvatica*)	PSH	W
Black Hickory (*Carya texana*)	FS/PSH	MW
Black Locust (*Robinia pseudoacacia*)	FS/PSH	W
Black Oak (*Quercus velutina*)	FS/PSH	W
Black Walnut (*Juglans nigra*)	FS/PSH	W
Black Willow (*Salix nigra*)	FS/PSH	LW
Blackjack Oak (*Quercus marilandica*)	FS/PSH	MW
Bluejack Oak (*Quercus incana*)	FS/PSH	MW
Bottomland Post Oak (*Quercus similis*)	FS/PSH	W
Box Elder (*Acer negundo*)	FS/PSH	LW
Brazil (*Condalia hookeri*)	FS/PSH	MW
Bur Oak (*Quercus macrocarpa*)	FS	W

Button Bush (*Cephalanthus occidentalis*)	FS/PSH	LW
Carolina Ash (*Fraxinus caroliniana*)	PSH	LW
Carolina Buckthorn (*Frangula caroliniana*)	FS/PSH	MW
Carolina Linden (*Tilia caroliniana*)	FS/PSH	W
Carolina Silver Bell (*Halesia caroliniana*)	PSH	W
Cedar Elm (*Ulmus crassifolia*)	FS/PSH	W
Chalk Maple (*Acer leucoderme*)	PSH	W
Chaparro Prieto (*Acacia rigidula*)	FS	X
Chaste Tree (*Vitex agnus-castus*)	FS/PSH	W
Cherry Laurel (*Prunus caroliniana*)	PSH	LW
Chinese Elm (*Ulmus parvifolia*)	S/PSH	W
Chinese Parasol Tree (*Firmiana simplex*)	FS	W
Chinese Pistache (*Pistacia chinensis*)	FS	W
Chinkapin Oak (*Quercus muhlenbergii*)	S/PSH	W
Chisos Red Oak (*Quercus gravesii*)	FS	W
Cockspur Hawthorn (*Crataegus crus-galli*)	S/PSH	W
Colima (*Zanthoxylum fagara*)	FS	W
Coma (*Sideroxylon celastrina*)	FS	MW
Coral Bean Tree (*Erythrina herbacea* var. *arborea*)	S/PSH	W
Coyotillo (*Karwinskia humboldtiana*)	FS	X
Crapemyrtle (*Lagerstroemia indica*)	FS/PSH	W
Deciduous Holly (*Ilex decidua*)	FS/PSH	W
Desert Willow (*Chilopsis linearis*)	FS	W
Devil's Walking Stick (*Aralia spinosa*)	S/SH	W
Diamond Leaf Oak (*Quercus obtusa*)	S/PSH	W
Downy Hawthorn (*Crataegus mollis*)	FS/PSH	W
Eastern Cottonwood (*Populus deltoides*)	FS	LW
Eastern Red Cedar (*Juniperus virginiana*)	FS/PSH	LW
Eastern Redbud (*Cercis canadensis*)	PSH	W
Elderberry (*Sambucus canadensis*)	FS/PSH	LW
Emory Oak (*Quercus emoryi*)	FS	W
Eve's Necklace (*Sophora affinis*)	FS	W
Farkleberry (*Vaccinium arboreum*)	PSH	W
Flameleaf Sumac (*Rhus copallina*)	S/PSH	W
Flowering Dogwood (*Cornus florida*)	PSH	W
Fragrant Ash (*Fraxinus cuspidata*)	FS	W
Fringe Tree (*Chionanthus virginica*)	S/PSH	W
Gambel Oak (*Quercus gambelii*)	FS	MW
Giant Dagger (*Yucca faxoniana*)	FS	X
Ginkgo (*Ginkgo biloba*)	S/PSH	W

Golden Ball Lead Tree *(Leucaena retusa)*	FS	W
Golden Rain Tree *(Koelreuteria paniculata)*	FS/PSH	W
Granjeno *(Celtis pallida)*	FS	X
Gray Oak *(Quercus grisea)*	FS	MW
Green Ash *(Fraxinus pennsylvanica)*	S/PSH	LW
Green Hawthorn *(Crataegus viridis)*	S/PSH	W
Gregg Acacia *(Acacia greggii)*	FS	X
Guajillo *(Acacia berlandieri)*	FS	X
Guayacan *(Guaiacum angustifolium)*	FS	X
Gum Bumelia *(Sideroxylon lanuginosum)*	S/PSH	W
Havard Shin Oak *(Quercus havardii)*	FS	MW
Hercules' Club *(Zanthoxylum clava-herculis)*	S/PSH	W
Honey Locust *(Gleditsia triacanthos)*	S/PSH	W
Honey Mesquite *(Prosopis glandulosa)*	FS	X
Huisache *(Acacia farnesiana) (A. smallii)*	FS	X
Huisachillo *(Acacia schaffneri)*	S/PSH	X
Lacey Oak *(Quercus laceyi)*	FS	MW
Laurel Oak *(Quercus laurifolia)*	S/PSH	W
Lime Prickly Ash *(Zanthoxylum hirsutum)*	FS	W
Lindheimer Hackberry *(Celtis lindheimeri)*	FS	MW
Little Hip Hawthorn *(Crataegus spathulata)*	S/PSH	W
Live Oak *(Quercus virginiana)*	S/PSH	W
Loblolly Pine *(Pinus taeda)*	S/PSH	W
Longleaf Pine *(Pinus palustris)*	FS	W
Loquat *(Eriobotrya japonica)*	S/PSH	W
Louisiana Palm *(Sabal louisiana)*	PSH	LW
Mayhaw *(Crataegus opaca)*	PSH	LW
Mexican Buckeye *(Ungnadia speciosa)*	FS	W
Mexican Elder *(Sambucus mexicana)*	FS	W
Mexican Oak *(Quercus polymorpha)*	FS	W
Mexican Pinyon Pine *(Pinus cembroides)*	FS	MW
Mexican Plum *(Prunus mexicana)*	S/PSH	W
Mexican Poinciana *(Caesalpinia mexicana)*	FS	W
Mimosa *(Albizia julibrissin)*	S/PSH	W
Mockernut Hickory *(Carya tomentosa) (Carya alba)*	S/PSH	W
Mohr Oak *(Quercus mohriana)*	FS	MW
Montezuma Bald Cypress *(Taxodium mucronatum)*	S/PSH	LW
Mountain Hawthorn *(Crataegus tracyi)*	S/PSH	W
Mountain Mahogany *(Cercocarpus montanus)*	FS	MW
Net Leaf Hackberry *(Celtis reticulata)*	FS	MW

Northern Catalpa (*Catalpa speciosa*)	FS	W
Nutmeg Hickory (*Carya myristiciformis*)	S/PSH	W
Nuttall Oak (*Quercus nuttallii*)	S/PSH	W
Osage Orange (*Maclura pomifera*)	FS	W
Overcup Oak (*Quercus lyrata*)	S/PSH	LW
Paloverde (*Parkinsonia texana* var. *macra*)	FS	X
Parsley Hawthorn (*Crataegus marshallii*)	S/PSH	W
Pawpaw (*Asimina triloba*)	PSH	W
Pecan (*Carya illinoinensis*)	S/PSH	W
Persimmon (*Diospyros virginiana*)	S/PSH	W
Pignut Hickory (*Carya glabra*)	S/PSH	W
Pinyon Pine (*Pinus edulis*)	FS	MW
Plains Cottonwood (*Populus sargentii*)	FS	LW
Plateau Live Oak (*Quercus fusiformis*)	FS	MW
Post Oak (*Quercus stellata*)	S/PSH	MW
Potato Tree (*Solanum erianthum*)	S/PSH	W
Prairie Flameleaf Sumac (*Rhus lanceolata*)	FS	W
Red Bay (*Persea borbonia*)	S/PSH	W
Red Buckeye (*Aesculus pavia* var. *pavia*)	FS	W
Red Maple (*Acer rubrum*)	PSH	LW
Red Mulberry (*Morus rubra*)	PSH	W
Redberry Juniper (*Juniperus pinchotii*)	FS	X
Retama (*Parkinsonia aculeata*)	FS	MW
Rio Grande Cottonwood (*Populus wislizeni*)	S/PSH	LW
River Birch (*Betula nigra*)	S/PSH	LW
Roemer Acacia (*Acacia roemeriana*)	FS	X
Roseberry Juniper (*Juniperus coahuilensis*)	FS	X
Rough Leaf Dogwood (*Cornus drummondii*)	S/PSH	W
Rusty Blackhaw Viburnum (*Viburnum rufidulum*)	S/PSH	W
Sabal Palm (*Sabal mexicana*)	S/PSH	MW
Sassafras (*Sassafras albidum*)	FS	W
Screwbean Mesquite (*Prosopis pubescens*)	FS	X
Scrub Oak (*Quercus turbinella*)	FS	X
Shagbark Hickory (*Carya ovata*)	S/PSH	W
Shortleaf Pine (*Pinus echinata*)	S/PSH	W
Shumard Oak (*Quercus shumardii*)	S/PSH	W
Sierra Madre Torchwood (*Amyris madrensis*)	FS	MW
Silver Maple (*Acer saccharinum*)	FS	W
Slippery Elm (*Ulmus rubra*)	S/PSH	W
Smooth Alder (*Alnus serrulata*)	S/PSH	LW

Soaptree Yucca *(Yucca elata)*	FS	X
Southern Crabapple *(Malus angustifolia)*	S/PSH	W
Southern Magnolia *(Magnolia grandiflora)*	S/PSH	LW
Southern Red Cedar *(Juniperus virginiana* var. *silicicola)*	S/PSH	W
Southern Red Oak *(Quercus falcata)*	S/PSH	W
Southern Sugar Maple *(Acer barbatum)*	S/PSH	W
Southern Waxmyrtle *(Myrica cerifera)*	S/PSH	LW
Spanish Dagger *(Yucca treculeana)*	FS	X
Sugar Hackberry *(Celtis laevigata)*	S/PSH	W
Swamp Chestnut Oak *(Quercus michauxii)*	S/PSH	W
Swamp Privet *(Forestiera acuminata)*	S/PSH	LW
Sweet Bay Magnolia *(Magnolia virginiana)*	S/PSH	LW
Sweetgum *(Liquidambar styraciflua)*	S/PSH	W
Sweet Leaf *(Symplocos tinctoria)*	PSH	W
Tamaulipan Fiddlewood *(Citharexylum berlandieri)*	FS	MW
Tenaza *(Pithecellobium pallens)*	FS	MW
Tepeguaje *(Leucaena pulverulenta)*	FS	MW
Texas Ash *(Fraxinus texensis)*	S/PSH	W
Texas Crabapple *(Malus ioensis* var. *texana)*	S/PSH	W
Texas Ebony *(Pithecellobium flexicaule)*	FS	MW
Texas Hawthorn *(Crataegus texana)*	PSH	W
Texas Madrone *(Arbutus xalapensis)*	S/PSH	W
Texas Mountain Laurel *(Sophora secundiflora)*	FS	W
Texas Oak *(Quercus buckleyi)*	S/PSH	W
Texas Persimmon *(Diospyros texana)*	S/PSH	MW
Texas Pistache *(Pistacia texana)*	S/PSH	MW
Texas Redbud *(Cercis canadensis* var. *texensis)*	FS	W
Texas Walnut *(Juglans microcarpa)*	S/PSH	W
Thompson Yucca *(Yucca thompsoniana)*	FS	X
Titi *(Cyrilla racemiflora)*	S/PSH	LW
Tobacco Tree *(Nicotiana glauca)*	S/PSH	MW
Torrey Yucca *(Yucca torreyi)*	FS	X
Trident Maple *(Acer rubrum* var. *tridens)*	S/PSH	W
Tung Oil Tree *(Aleurites fordii)*	S/PSH	W
Two Wing Silver Bell *(Halesia diptera)*	PSH	W
Vasey Oak *(Quercus vaseyana)*	FS	MW
Velvet Ash *(Fraxinus velutina)*	S/PSH	W
Wafer Ash *(Ptelea trifoliata)*	S/PSH	W
Washington Palm *(Washingtonia filifera)*	FS	W
Water Hickory *(Carya aquatica)*	S/PSH	W

Water Locust (Gleditsia aquatica)   S/PSH
LW

Water Oak (*Quercus nigra*)	S/PSH	W
Water Tupelo (*Nyssa aquatica*)	S/PSH	LW
Wavy Leaf Oak (*Quercus undulata*)	FS	MW
Western Soapberry (*Sapindus saponaria* var. *drummondii*)	S/PSH	W
White Ash (*Fraxinus americana*)	S/PSH	W
White Mulberry (*Morus alba*)	S/PSH	W
White Oak (*Quercus alba*)	S/PSH	W
White Shin Oak (*Quercus sinuata* var. *breviloba*)	FS	MW
Willow Oak (*Quercus phellos*)	S/PSH	W
Winged Elm (*Ulmus alata*)	S/PSH	W
Winterberry Holly (*Ilex verticillata*)	PSH	LW
Wooly Hop Hornbeam (*Ostrya virginiana*)	PSH	W
Wright Acacia (*Acacia wrightii*)	FS	X
Xylosma (*Xylosma flexuosa*)	S/PSH	W
Yaupon Holly (*Ilex vomitoria*)	S/SH	W
Yellow Buckeye (*Aesculus pavia* var. *flavescens*)	FS	W
Yellow Trumpet (*Tecoma stans*)	S/PSH	W
Yew Leaf Willow (*Salix taxifolia*)	S/PSH	LW

RECIPES FOR WILD EDIBLES

Appendix G

Although some plants have toxic properties, many others prove edible and tasty. The recipes that follow provide just a small sampling intended to pique your interest. If you want to explore further, we recommend that you check out a good book on the subject, such as Marilyn Kruger's *The Wild Flavor* (Boston: Houghton Mifflin, 1984) or Lee Allen Peterson's *A Field Guide to Wild Edible Plants* (Boston: Houghton Mifflin, 1977). Never experiment on your own.

Black Walnut Cake

Ingredients
1 cup black walnuts, finely ground
½ cup shortening or cooking oil
1 cup sugar
1 cup flour
1½ tsp. baking powder
½ cup milk
2 eggs, separated
¼ tsp. salt
½ tsp. vanilla extract

Gather enough black walnuts to extract 1 cup of finely ground nuts. Mix the shortening and sugar. Add the milk, egg yolks, and vanilla. Beat well. Sift the flour, baking powder, and salt and add to mixture. Beat the egg whites until stiff. Gently cut in the egg whites and nuts with the batter. Pour into a 9-inch, lightly greased pan, and bake at 350° for about 20 minutes. A toothpick inserted into the cake will come out clean when the cake is done. Set on oven rack to cool.

Persimmon Cookies

Ingredients
1 cup persimmon pulp
½ cup butter or margarine
1 cup sugar
1 egg
1 tsp. baking soda
2 cups flour
salt
cloves
cinnamon
raisins (optional)
pecans (optional)

Pick and wash ripe persimmons. (Persimmons are ripe when they feel soft and separate easily from the twigs. You may also use persimmons after they have dropped from the tree on their own, as long as they remain fresh.) Hand-press enough persimmons through a colander—removing skins and seeds—to yield about 1 cup of pulp. Set aside.

Blend butter or margarine with sugar until smooth. Mix in the egg and baking soda. Set aside.

Sift flour with a pinch of salt, and a touch of ground cloves and cinnamon. Add raisins and pecans if desired. Blend all ingredients with the persimmon pulp and drop by the teaspoonful on a greased cookie sheet.

Bake at 350° for about 15 minutes. Makes two dozen cookies.

Pecan Pie

Ingredients
One 8-inch pie shell
1 cup brown sugar
¼ cup butter
3 eggs
½ cup corn syrup
1 cup crumbled pecan bits
¼ cup pecan halves
1 tsp. vanilla extract
½ tsp. salt

Lightly brown the pie shell for about 5 minutes in a hot oven. Cream the sugar and butter. Work in the eggs, then the other ingredients. Pour mix into pie shell, lay the pecan halves over the top, and bake about 45 minutes at 350°. Test for doneness with a knife. The pie should be firm, not runny.

Elderberry Wine

Ingredients
1 gallon elderberries
1 gallon cold water
10 lb. sugar

Gather 1 gallon of ripe elderberries. Wash them, and mash them in a stone crock. Add ½ a gallon of water. Cover with a cheesecloth, and allow to ferment for 4 to 5 days, stirring lightly each day. Strain juice. Add the sugar and the rest of the water to the juice. Stir, and allow to ferment for one more day. Pour mixture into bottles. Cap tightly, and store in a cool place for about 6 months to allow it to age. If kept unopened in a cool place, the wine should keep for several years.

Hickory Nut Brittle

Ingredients
  2 cups hickory nuts
  2 cups sugar
  1 cup corn syrup
  1 tsp. salt
  ¼ tsp. baking soda
  2 Tbsp. butter
  1 cup water

Bring water to a boil. Remove from heat and stir in the sugar until dissolved. Add corn syrup, nuts, and salt. Return to stove. Boil at medium heat, stirring occasionally, for about 10 minutes. Stir in butter and baking soda. Pour into well-buttered pan. Spread the mixture evenly until it is very thin. When it is cool, break into small pieces.

Mayhaw Jelly

Ingredients
  4 cups mayhaw fruits
  5½ cups sugar
  1 box fruit pectin
  water

Collect 4 cups of fruit. To make the juice, bring 2 quarts of water and the fruits to a boil in a large saucepan. Lower heat and simmer for 45 minutes to an hour. Strain liquid through cheese-cloth or sieve. Discard skins and seeds.

Pour juice back into pan. Stir in pectin and place over high heat, stirring in sugar. Stir continually until mixture comes to a rolling boil that cannot be stirred down. Let it boil for 1½–2 minutes. Skim off foam, and pour mixture into hot sterilized jars. Do not fill jars completely. Seal jars according to manufacturer's instructions.

Set in boiling water bath for 10 minutes, let cool, then store in refrigerator. Enjoy!

Acorn Bread

Ingredients
  1 cup acorn meal
  1 cup flour
  3 tsp. baking powder
  1½ tsp. salt
  4 Tbsp. sugar
  1 egg
  1 cup milk
  3 Tbsp. vegetable oil

Collect a quantity of acorns from the white oak group. We recommend those of bur oak because they are the largest. *Do not use acorns from the red oak group;* they contain too much tannic acid.

Using a sharp knife and a great deal of caution, peel the tough outer shell off the acorns. Remove the papery inner shell, leaving only the off-white kernels. Chop the kernels into smaller pieces and boil them. The water in which you boil them will turn a brownish color due to the tannic acid present in the nuts. Drain off the water and replace with fresh water. Repeat the boiling and draining process until the water remains nearly clear, indicating that most of the tannic acid has been removed.

Run the chopped, boiled kernels through a blender to produce acorn meal. Preheat oven to 400°. Mix together 1 cup of the acorn meal with the flour, baking powder, salt, and sugar. Set aside.

In a separate bowl, beat the egg. Add milk and vegetable oil. Add to acorn meal mixture. Stir. Pour mixture into greased bread pan and bake at 400° for approximately 30 minutes. Serve warm.

Sumacade

Ingredients
  Sumac fruits
  (*see Tree Profiles, pp. 180, 181*)
  water
  2/3 cup suger

Pick two or three clusters of sumac fruits when they are red and ripe. Wash them, then wrap them in cheesecloth and boil in ½ a gallon of water. Remove from heat, and allow to steep for about 15 minutes. Strain the liquid through a layer of cheesecloth to remove seeds and skins. Add sugar and serve. The drink will resemble pink lemonade, with a special tang of its own. You can experiment with various concentrations of fruit and different amounts of sugar to find the taste you prefer.

Yaupon Tea

Ingredients
  Yaupon leaves
  water

Gather a mix of young and older yaupon leaves. Pick out and discard any that look brown or insect-damaged. *Do not use yaupon berries;* they are purgative. Spread the leaves out evenly on a cookie sheet and place in the oven at a low temperature (150–200°). Stir the leaves occasionally with a fork to ensure even toasting. When they look olive-brown and feel crisp and brittle, they are ready.

Bring water to a boil. Remove from heat and set aside. Steep about 1 teaspoon of crumbled leaves in 1 cup of water. Strain the tea. Sweeten to taste, and serve.

acorn The nut of an oak tree.

anther The part of a flower that contains the pollen.

arboreal Like a tree.

berry A fleshy or pulpy fruit with the seed or seeds embedded in the tissue; cf. drupe.

bonsai A tree grown in a shallow container and dwarfed by pruning.

bract A modified leaf; the leaflike part of a plant growing below the flower or flower cluster.

cannabis Marijuana.

carcinogen A cancer-causing substance.

compound leaf A leaf with its blade subdivided into leaflets.

cone The scaly fruit of a conifer.

conifer A cone-bearing tree or shrub, usually evergreen, such as a pine.

cultivar A distinctive form of a plant perpetuated by deliberate means.

curandero A folk healer or herbalist.

deciduous Characterized by the annual shedding of leaves.

dehiscent Possessing definite seams which open to discharge seeds.

dendrology The study of trees.

drupe A fleshy or pulpy fruit with the seed or seeds enclosed in a stony layer; cf. berry.

epiphyte A plant that grows on another plant but does not take nutrients from the host.

flower The seed-producing organ of a plant.

frond The divided leaf of a palm or fern.

fruit The seed-bearing part of a plant.

gall The abnormal swelling of plant tissue, often caused by insects.

gallinaceous Chickenlike, pertaining to birds, such as quail or turkeys.

genus A classification of related plants or animals more general than a species; a group of closely related species.

graft To insert or transplant a shoot of one plant into another living plant.

gum A sticky substance found in certain trees.

herbivorous Pertaining to animals, the characteristic of eating plants.

horticulture The art or science of growing plants.

hybridize To cross breed.

indigenous Native to; originating in or growing naturally in a particular habitat or region.

invertebrate An animal without a backbone.

key The fruiting structure of certain trees, such as ash and maple.

knee A root formation of certain trees, particularly cypresses, resembling the bent knee of a person.

leaf A usually flattened, usually green structure of a plant consisting of one or more broad blades set on a leaf stem; the organ of a plant where photosynthesis occurs.

leaf scar The mark left behind on a twig at the point of attachment of a leaf after the leaf has dropped off or been removed.

leaflet The leaflike segment of a compound leaf.

lichen A composite organism consisting of fungus and algae that forms a crusty- or mossy-looking growth on rocks or tree trunks.

lobe The rounded or pointed projecting part of a leaf.

midrib The central supporting structure of a leaf blade contiguous with the leaf stem or petiole; the main vein of a leaf.

mucilaginous Characterized by production of a viscous, mucouslike substance.

GLOSSARY

nectar Sweet liquid produced by flowers apparently to attract insects for pollination and used by bees to produce honey.

needle A thin, stiff, elongated leaf of a conifer.

nut A fruit consisting of a hard shell surrounding a kernel.

palmate Shaped like the palm of a hand; pertaining to leaves, the characteristic of having lobes or leaflets protruding, fingerlike, from a central point.

panicle A flower cluster that is branched more than once.

parasite An organism, such as a plant, that grows in or on another and takes nutrients from it without any benefit to the host.

petiole The leaf stem; the stalk between a branch and a leaf.

photosynthesis The biochemical process whereby a plant uses sunlight to convert carbon dioxide and water into carbohydrates.

pinnate Characterized by the arrangement of veins, lobes, or leaflets perpendicular to the midrib, or main vein, of a leaf.

pitch A sticky substance found in certain trees, particularly pines.

pith The soft, spongy substance in the center of certain fruits (also in the center of some branches or stems).

pollination The act of transferring pollen to the stigma of a flower; fertilization.

pome A specific kind of fleshy fruit such as an apple; a fleshy false fruit enclosing the true fruit.

prickle A sharp, pointed plant structure not a modification of another plant part, not containing a vein, and not growing from the wood of the plant.

purgative Causing vomiting or evacuation of the bowels.

raceme An elongated flower cluster with many small flowers arranged along a central, unbranched stalk.

resin A sticky substance exuded by some trees and used to produce varnish.

rhizome A usually horizontal underground stem that sends roots downward and sends shoots upward.

rootstock The root portion of a plant to which another plant is grafted or which is propagated by division.

samara The fruiting structure of certain trees, such as elms.

saponin A plant substance with properties similar to soap in its ability to produce lather.

seed The ripe ovule of a plant; a plant embryo.

semi-evergreen Partially deciduous; characterized by the annual shedding of only some of the leaves.

signature tree A tree typifying a particular region or habitat.

species A specific classification of plants or animals; a group of animals or plants ranking below a genus or subgenus and sharing certain permanent characteristics.

spine A sharp, pointed plant structure formed by the modification of a plant organ, especially leaves, as for example in holly leaves.

stigma The part of a flower on which pollen is deposited for fertilization.

tannin A substance derived from certain plants used for tanning leather; tannic acid.

taxonomy The systematic classification of plants and animals according to their natural relationships.

temperate zone The moderate climatic region between arctic and tropical zones of the earth.

thorn A sharp, pointed plant structure formed by the modification of a plant organ, especially a hard side stem in which a sharp tip replaces the growing point.

trifoliate Characterized by compound leaves consisting of three leaflets set on a single leaf stem.

understock A plant to which another related plant is grafted.

understory A lower layer of forest, below the canopy.

variety A plant possessing characteristics that differ from the norm but not sufficiently for the plant to classify as a separate species.

BIBLIOGRAPHY

BOOKS

Cabeza de Vaca's Adventures in the Unknown Interior of America. Translated by Cyclone Covey, epilogue by William T. Pilkington. Albuquerque: University of New Mexico Press, 1997.

Cook, William. *The Physiomedical Dispensatory.* Cincinnati: William H. Cook, 1869.

Cox, Paul W., and Patty Leslie. *Texas Trees: A Friendly Guide.* San Antonio: Corona Publishing Company, 1988.

Erichsen-Brown, Charlotte. *Use of Plants for the Past 500 Years.* Aurora, Ontario: Breezy Creeks Press, 1979.

Gould, Frank W. *Texas Plants: A Checklist and Ecological Summary.* College Station: Texas A&M University Press, 1962.

Kruger, Marilyn. *The Wild Flavor.* Boston: Houghton Mifflin, 1984.

Nixon, Elray S. *Trees, Shrubs and Woody Vines of East Texas.* Nacogdoches: Bruce Lyndon Cunningham Productions, 1985.

Peattie, Donald Culross. *A Natural History of Texas.* Boston: Houghton Mifflin Company, 1950.

———. *The Road of a Naturalist.* Boston: Houghton Mifflin Company, 1941.

Peterson, Lee Allen. *A Field Guide to Wild Edible Plants.* Boston: Houghton Mifflin, 1977.

Powell, A. Michael. *Trees and Shrubs of the Trans-Pecos and Adjacent Areas.* Austin: University of Texas Press, 1998.

Simpson, Benny J. *A Field Guide to Texas Trees.* Houston: Gulf Publishing Company, 1988.

Vines, Robert A. *Trees, Shrubs and Woody Vines of the Southwest.* Austin: University of Texas Press, 1960.

ELECTRONIC SOURCES

A Modern Herbal: retrieved December 27, 2001, http://www.botanical.com/botanical/mgmh/mgmh.html

A Nomenclatural Morass: retrieved February 8, 2002, http://www.lewis-clark.org/REVEAL/tr_jrdf1.htm

Alexander von Humboldt: retrieved January 6, 2002, http://stat.tamu.edu/ecomod/alexhumb.html

APIS, Volume 2, Number 3, March 1984, Poisonous Plants in Florida: retrieved December 24, 2001, http://apis.ifas.ufl.edu/index.htm

Asimina Genetic Resources: retrieved February 20, 2002, http://www.ars-grin.gov/ars/PacWest/Corvallis/ncgr/minor/asiinfo.html

Aus den Berliner Museen: retrieved January 29, 2002, http://www.diegeschichteberlins.de/archiv/014/04.html

Australian Botany Pages, Collectors & Artists, Archibald Menzies: retrieved February 8, 2002, http://www.anbg.gov.au/index.html

Author data – D: Deppe, Wilhelm: retrieved January 29, 2002, http://www.zoonomen.net/bio/biod.html

Bernheim Arboretum and Research Forest, PLANT PROFILES: retrieved February 18, 2002, http://www.bernheim.org/profiles.htm

Biography.com, Jean Nicot: retrieved December 2, 2002, http://www.biography.com/

Books on Nova Scotia, Kalm, Peter: retrieved January 30, 2002, http://www.blupete.com/Library/History/NovaScotia/K.htm

Boone County Arboretum at Central Park: retrieved January 5, 2002, http://www.bcarboretum.org/index.asp

California Plant Names, Word Meanings and Name Derivations: retrieved January 6, 2002, http://www.calflora.net/botanicalnames/index.html

CATHOLIC ENCYCLOPEDIA, History of Medicine: retrieved January 15, 2002, http://www.newadvent.org/cathen/10122a.htm

Center for Wood Anatomy Research, Technology Transfer Fact Sheet: retrieved February 8, 2002, http://pc37.fpl.fs.fed.us/TechSheets/SoftwoodNA/PDF%20files/taxiodiumeng.pdf

Center for Wood Anatomy Research, Technology Transfer Fact Sheet: retrieved December 27, 2001, http://www2.fpl.fs.fed.us/TechSheets/HardwoodNA/htmlDocs/magnol2.html

City of Rocks State Park: retrieved February 19, 2002, http://www.emnrd.state.nm.us/nmparks/PAGES/brochures/parks/CITYROCK.pdf

Clemson Extension: retrieved December 27, 2001, http://www.clemson.edu/extension/

Conservation New England: retrieved January 3, 2002, http://omega.cc.umb.edu/~conne/index.html

Dendrology at Virginia Tech: retrieved February 18, 2002, http://www.cnr.vt.edu/dendro/dendrology/main.htm

Der Amerikanischer Amberbaum—Liquidamber styraciflua: retrieved December 30, 2001, http://www.bgbm.fu-berlin.de/BGBM/pr/zurzeit/papers/liquidam.htm

Explorer Andre Michaux: retrieved December 29, 2001, http://www.grandfather.com/museum/michaux.htm

Fire Effects Information: retrieved February 14, 2002, http://www.fs.fed.us/database/feis/index.html

Floridata: retrieved December 30, 2001, http://www.floridata.com/

Flowers, Pollination & Ocean Disbursal In Coral Trees (Erythrina): retrieved January 13, 2002, http://waynesword.palomar.edu/coraltr1.htm

Forests of Illinois: retrieved January 11, 2002, http://www.museum.state.il.us/muslink/forest/

Gernot Katzer's Spice Pages, Sassafras: retrieved December 29, 2001, http://www-ang.kfunigraz.ac.at/~katzer/engl/generic_frame.html?Sass_alb.html

Golden Gate Audubon Society, Early Birds, Gambel's Life: Brief But Brilliant: retrieved December 29, 2001, http://www.goldengateaudubon.org/

Harvard University Herbaria, Library of the Gray Herbarium Archives: retrieved December 30, 2001, http://www.huh.harvard.edu/libraries/Grayarc.htm

Herbal Research Review, Vitex agnus castus Clinical Monograph: retrieved January 14, 2002, http://www.thorne.com/townsend/oct/herbal.html

Hong Kong Zoological & Botanical Gardens, History: retrieved December 30, 2001, http://www.lcsd.gov.hk/LEISURE/LP/hkzbg/engindex.html

Improving Availability Of Under-Utilized Small Trees For Texas: retrieved January 10, 2002, http://www.hcs.ohio-state.edu/METRIA/arnold/arnold.htm

JC Raulston Arboretum at NC State University: retrieved February 8, 2002, http://www.ncsu.edu/jcraulstonarboretum/

John C. Fremont / Sen. Thomas H. Benton: retrieved December 30, 2001, http://www.kcmuseum.com/explor09.html

Kentucky Trees: retrieved February 20, 2002, http://www.uky.edu/Ag/Horticulture/kytreewebsite/welcome.htm

Lefalophodon, An Informal History of Evolutionary Biology Web Site: retrieved February 19, 2002, http://www.nceas.ucsb.edu/~alroy/lefa/lophodon.html

Locations of State Environmental Historical Markers, Pennsylvania Historical & Museum Commission, The Woodlands: retrieved January 4, 2002, http://www.dep.state.pa.us/dep/pa_env-her/historicalmarkers.htm

Lost Maples State Natural Area in Texas: retrieved December 30, 2001, http://www.tpwd.state.tx.us/park/lostmap/lostmap.htm

Lower Rio Grande Valley Development Council, Integrated Water Resource Plan,m—Phase II: retrieved November 21, 2002, http://www.lrgvdc.org/PLANNING/HTM%20Folder/IWRP%20Report/Repsumm.htm

Medicinal Plants of the Southwest: retrieved February 8, 2002, http://medplant.nmsu.edu/

Mexico, National Symbols: retrieved February 8, 2002, http://www.caribeinside.com/countryemblems.do?country=201

Migrations: American Indian Art & Crafts: retrieved February 19, 2002, http://www.migrations.com/welcome.html

Missouri Botanical Garden, Horticulture Division: retrieved December 27, 2001, http://www.mobot.org/hort/

Missouri Department of Conservation Online: retrieved December 29, 2001, http://www.conservation.state.mo.us/

Native Plants of South Texas: retrieved December 29, 2001, http://uvalde.tamu.edu/herbarium/index.html

Native Trees of Texas: retrieved December 30, 2001, http://aggie-horticulture.tamu.edu/ornamentals/natives/indexcommon.htm

Northern Prairie Wildlife Research Center, Butterflies of North America: retrieved December 17, 2001, http://www.npsc.nbs.gov/index.htm

Oklahoma Biological Survey: retrieved December 24, 2001, http://www.biosurvey.ou.edu/

Ornamental Plants for Far West Texas: retrieved December 27, 2001, http://aggie-horticulture.tamu.edu/ornamentals/elpasoplants/index.html

Pinchot Institute for Conservation: retrieved January 29, 2002, http://www.pinchot.org/

Poisonous Plants of North Carolina: retrieved February 26, 2002, http://www.ces.ncsu.edu/depts/hort/consumer/poison/poison.htm

Purdue University Center for New Crops & Plant Products: retrieved February 20, 2002, http://www.hort.purdue.edu/newcrop/Default.html

Samuel Mills Tracy: retrieved December 29, 2001, http://www.csdl.tamu.edu/FLORA/taes/tracy/TRACY.htm

Searching for Dr. Vasey: retrieved December 30, 2001, http://www.chicagowildernessmag.org/issues/winter2001/vasey.html

Shagbark Hickory: retrieved January 13, 2002, http://www.na.fs.fed.us/spfo/pubs/silvics_manual/Volume_2/carya/ovata.htm

Stephen F. Austin State University Arboretum: retrieved February 8, 2002, http://www.sfasu.edu/ag/arboretum/index.htm

Table Mountains Conservation Fund, Inc.: retrieved February 19, 2002, http://www.tablemountains.org/index.htm

Texas Fast Facts and Trivia: retrieved January 3, 2002, http://www.50states.com/facts/texas.htm

The Arnold Arboretum of Harvard University, History: retrieved December 30, 2001, http://www.arboretum.harvard.edu/

The Dallas Morning News Extra: retrieved December 27, 2001, http://archive.dallasnews.com/

The Handbook of Texas Online: retrieved December 29, 2001, http://www.tsha.utexas.edu/handbook/online/index.new.html

The History of the Santa Barbara Mission Archive-Library: retrieved January 29, 2002, http://www.ca-missions.org/olmstead.html

The Longwood Herbal Task Force: retrieved January 14, 2002, http://www.mcp.edu/herbal/

The Ohio State University Plant Dictionary: retrieved February 20, 2002, http://hcs.osu.edu/plants.html

The Physiomedical Dispensatory: retrieved December 30, 2001, http://www.ibiblio.org/herbmed/eclectic/cook/main.htm

The Texas A&M University System, Texas Agricultural Extension Service, What We Know About Coyotillo: retrieved November 21, 2001, http://agpublications.tamu.edu/pubs/rem/e23.pdf

The University of Chicago, The ARTFL Project, Webster's Revised Unabridged Dictionary, Sassafras: retrieved December 29, 2001, http://humanities.uchicago.edu/orgs/ARTFL/

The Woodlands: retrieved January 4, 2002, http://www.fieldtrip.com/pa/53862181.htm

Travis Audubon Society, Think Trees & Shrubs This Winter: retrieved December 27, 2001, http://www.travisaudubon.org/Backyard/habtrees.htm

TreeGuide: retrieved December 30, 2001, http://www.treeguide.com/index.asp

Trees of the Pacific Northwest: retrieved February 8, 2002, http://www.orst.edu/instruct/for241/index.html

Types: retrieved December 29, 2001, http://www.biosci.ohio-state.edu/~herb/types.htm

U.S. Forest Service History: retrieved December 30, 2001, http://www.lib.duke.edu/forest/usfscoll/

UConn Plant Database of Trees, Shrubs & Vines: retrieved December 24, 2001, http://www.hort.uconn.edu/plants/index.html

University at Albany Libraries, The Two Millionth Volume and Commemorative Volumes, Spring 2001: retrieved January 30, 2002, http://library.albany.edu/speccoll/2millionth/

University of Arizona Cooperative Extension: retrieved February 24, 2002, http://ag.arizona.edu/pima/gardening/

University of Arizona Plant Walk: retrieved December 30, 2001, http://ag.arizona.edu/arboretum/pwalk/mappw.htm

University of Florida Center for Aquatic and Invasive Plants: retrieved February 25, 2002, http://aquat1.ifas.ufl.edu/welcome.html

University of Florida Extension, Institute of Food and Agricultural Sciences: retrieved February 21, 2002, http://edis.ifas.ufl.edu/

University of Western Ontario, Department of Plant Sciences, Guide to Plant Collection & Identification: retrieved January 6, 2002, http://www.botany.utoronto.ca/courses/BOT307/B_How/janeTOC.html

Untitled document: retrieved February 21, 2002, http://www.hort.purdue.edu/hort/courses/HORT217/etymology

Vascular Plant Herbarium: retrieved February 18, 2002, http://lsvl.la.asu.edu/herbarium/index.html

Volcanism and the Davis Mountains, Texas: retrieved December 29, 2001, http://www.cdri.org/Discovery/News.html

Welcome to Jimmo Helps, Karl Theodor Mohr: retrieved February 24, 2002, http://www.jimmo.com/

Yucca & Yucca Moth: retrieved February 15, 2002, http://waynesword.palomar.edu/ww0902a.htm

INDEX

Common names used for tree profiles appear in parentheses.

Acacia berlandieri (Guajillo), 155
    farnesiana (Huisache), 148
    greggii (Gregg Acacia), 144
    rigidula (Chaparro Prieto), 152
    roemeriana (Roemer Acacia), 146
    schaffneri (Huisachillo), 149
    smallii (Huisache), 148
    wrightii (Wright Acacia), 145
Acacia, Berlandier (Guajillo), 155
    Blackbrush (Chaparro Prieto), 152
    False (Black Locust), 168
    Gregg, 144
    Medusa (Huisachillo), 149
    Roemer, 146
    Schaffner's (Huisachillo), 149
    Sweet (Huisache), 148
    Twisted (Huisachillo), 149
    Wright, 145
Acer barbatum (Southern Sugar
    Maple), 121
    grandidentatum (Bigtooth Maple),
    118
    leucoderme (Chalk Maple), 120
    negundo (Box Elder), 203
    rubrum (Red Maple), 117
    rubrum var. *tridens* (Trident Maple),
    119
    saccharinum (Silver Maple), 115
Aesculus pavia var. *pavia* (Red Buck-
    eye), 210–11
    pavia var. *flavescens* (Yellow
    Buckeye), 210–11
Ague Tree (Sassafras), 102
Ahueheute (Montezuma Bald Cypress),
    220
Ailanthus altissima (Tree of Heaven),
    177
Alamo (Eastern Cottonwood), 136
    (Rio Grande Cottonwood), 135
    blanco (Quaking Aspen), 133
Albizia julibrissin (Mimosa), 154
Alder Buckthorn (Carolina Buckthorn),
    71
Alder, Black (Smooth Alder), 78
    (Winterberry Holly), 28
    Common (Smooth Alder), 78

Hazel (Smooth Alder), 78
    Smooth, 78
    Tag (Smooth Alder), 78
Aleurites fordii (Tung Oil Tree), 130–31
Algaroba (Honey Mesquite), 158–59
Allegheny Chinquapin, 63
Alligator Juniper, 218
    Tree (Sweetgum), 116
Alnus serrulata (Smooth Alder), 78
American Beech, 53
    Black Walnut (Black Walnut), 184
    Cotton Palm (Washington Palm),
    240–41
    Cyrilla (Titi), 5
    Elder (Elderberry), 190
    Elm, 52
    Holly, 103
    Hop Hornbeam (Wooly Hop
    Hornbeam), 57
    Hornbeam, 56
    Pistachio (Texas Pistache), 172
    Plane Tree (American Sycamore),
    124–25
    Silver Bell (Two Wing Silver Bell),
    58
    Smoke Tree, 70
    Sweetgum, 116
    Sycamore, 124–25
Amole (Soaptree Yucca), 230
Amyris madrensis (Sierra Madre
    Torchwood), 173
Anacacho Bauhinia, 142
Anacahuita, 72
    (Anaqua), 65
Anaqua (*a/k/a Anacua*), 65
Angelica Tree (Devil's Walking Stick),
    143
Anstwood (Coma), 14
Apache Oak (Emory Oak), 104
Ape's Earring (Tenaza), 150
    (Texas Ebony), 151
Apple Haw (Mayhaw), 20
Aralia (Devil's Walking Stick), 143
Aralia spinosa (Devil's Walking Stick),
    143
Arbutus xalapensis (Texas Madrone), 69

Arizona Ash (Berlandier Ash), 193
    (Velvet Ash), 195
    Cottonwood, 134
    Cypress, 219
    Pine, 227
    Rough Cypress (Arizona Cypress),
    219
    Walnut (*a/k/a Arizona Black
    Walnut*), 185
Arkansas Pine (Shortleaf Pine), 225
Arrowwood (Flowering Dogwood), 38
Ash, Arizona (Berlandier), 193
    (Velvet Ash), 195
    Berlandier, 193
    Biltmore (White Ash), 191
    Cane (White Ash), 191
    Carolina, 194
    Darlington (Green Ash), 192
    Desert (Velvet Ash), 195
    Florida (Carolina Ash), 194
    Flowering (Fragrant Ash), 175
    (Fringe Tree), 30
    Fragrant, 175
    Green, 192
    Leather Leaf (Velvet Ash), 195
    Mexican (Berlandier Ash), 193
    Modesto (Velvet Ash), 195
    Mountain (Texas Ash), 192
    Poison (Fringe Tree), 30
    Poppy (Carolina Ash), 194
    Red (Green Ash), 192
    River (Green Ash), 192
    Smallseed White (White Ash), 191
    Smooth (Velvet Ash), 195
    Standley (Velvet Ash), 195
    Swamp (Carolina Ash), 194
    (Green Ash), 192
    Texas, 192
    Toumey (Velvet Ash), 195
    Velvet, 195
    Wafer, 208
    Water (Carolina Ash), 194
    (Green Ash), 192
    White, 191
Ashe Juniper, 213
Ashleaf Maple (Box Elder), 203

Asimina triloba (Pawpaw), 22–23
Aspen, Golden (Quaking Aspen), 133
    Quaking, 133

Bald Cypress, 221
Barberry Hawthorn (Big Tree Hathorn), 27
Baretta, 206
Barron Oak (Blackjack Oak), 94–95
Basket Elm (Cedar Elm), 86
    Oak (Swamp Chestnut Oak), 92
Baton Rouge (Eastern Red Cedar), 214
Basswood, Carolina (Carolina Linden), 137
    Florida (Carolina Linden), 137
Bauhinia, Anacacho, 142
Bauhinia lunarioides (Anacacho Bauhinia), 142
Bay (Sweet Bay Magnolia), 73
Bay, Red, 6
    Silk (Red Bay), 6
    Sweet (Red Bay), 6
Bayberry, Southern (Southern Waxmyrtle), 24
Beaked Yucca, 231
Bearberry (Deciduous Holly), 25
Beaver Tree (Sweet Bay Magnolia), 73
Beech Nut (American Beech), 53
Beech, American, 53
    Blue (American Hornbeam), 56
    Red (American Beech), 53
    Ridge (American Beech), 53
    Water (American Hornbeam), 56
    White (American Beech), 53
Bellota (Emory Oak), 104
Berlandier Acacia (Guajillo), 155
    Ash, 193
    Fiddlewood (Tamaulipan Fiddlewood), 35
Betula nigra (River Birch), 79
Big Bend Yucca (Beaked Yucca), 231
    Laurel (Southern Magnolia), 74–75
    (Sweet Bay Magnolia), 73
    Tree Hawthorn, 27
    Plum (Mexican Plum), 49
Bigbud Hickory (Mockernut Hickory), 198–99
Bigelow Oak (White Shin Oak), 90
Bigtooth Maple, 118
Biltmore Ash (White Ash), 191
Birch, Black (River Birch), 79
    Red (River Birch), 79

River, 79
    Water (River Birch), 79
Bird of Paradise, Mexican (Mexican Poinciana), 153
Bitter Hickory (Water Hickory), 202
    Orange (Trifoliate Orange), 207
    Pecan (Bitternut Hickory), 189
    (Water Hickory), 202
    Walnut (Bitternut Hickory), 189
    Water Hickory (Nutmeg Hickory), 187
    Waternut (Nutmeg Hickory), 187
Bitternut Hickory, 189
Black Alder (Smooth Alder), 78
    (Winterberry Holly), 28
    Birch (River Birch), 79
    Cherry, 47
    Gum, 44
    Hickory, 188
    Hill Ponderosa Pine (Ponderosa Pine), 229
    Lin (Sweet Bay Magnolia), 73
    Locust, 168
    Oak, 109
        (Blackjack Oak), 94–95
        (Emory Oak), 104
    Persimmon (Texas Persimmon), 15
    Sumac (Flameleaf Sumac), 181
    Titi (Titi), 5
    Tupelo (Black Gum), 44
    Walnut, 184
    Willow, 11
Blackbrush Acacia (Chaparro Prieto), 152
Blackhaw, Southern (Rusty Blackhaw Viburnum), 81
Blackhaw Viburnum, Rusty, 81
Blackjack Oak, 94–95
Blanco Crab Apple (Texas Crab Apple), 80
Blisted (Sweetgum), 116
Blue Beech (American Hornbeam), 56
    Douglas Fir (Douglas Fir), 224
    Elderberry (Mexican Elder), 190
    Oak (Lacey Oak), 89
Bluehaw (Rusty Blackhaw Viburnum), 81
Bluejack Oak, 13
Bluewood Condalia (Brazil), 16
Bodark (Osage Orange), 40
Bois d'Arc (Osage Orange), 40
Border Paloverde (Paloverde), 147

Bottle Tree (Chinese Parasol Tree), 112–23
Bottomland Post Oak, 97
    Red Oak (Southern Red Oak), 110
Bow Willow (Desert Willow), 10
    Wood (Osage Orange), 40
Box Elder, 203
Boxwood (Flowering Dogwood), 38
Brazil, 16
Break Cedar (Ashe Juniper), 213
Broom Hickory (Pignut Hickory), 201
Buckeye, Hill Country (Yellow Buckeye), 210–11
    Mexican, 186
    Red, 210–11
    Texas (Mexican Buckeye), 186
    Yellow, 210–11
Buckley Hickory (Black Hickory), 188
    Oak (Texas Oak), 112
Buckthorn, Alder (Carolina Bucthorn), 71
    Carolina, 71
    False (Gum Bumelia), 18
    Milk (Coma), 14
    Southern (Carolina Buckthorn), 71
    Tropical (Coma), 14
    Yellow Buckthorn (Carolina Buckthorn), 71
Bull Bay Magnolia (Southern Magnolia), 74–75
    (Sweet Bay Magnolia), 73
Bullnut (Mockernut Hickory), 198–99
Bumelia, Gum, 18
    Wooly (a/k/a Woolybucket Bumelia) (Gum Bumelia), 18
Bumelia celastrina (Coma), 14
    lanuginosa (Gum Bumelia), 18
Burnwood Bark (Titi), 5
Bur Oak, 100–101
Buttonball Tree (American Sycamore), 124–25
Button Bush (a/k/a Button Willow), 42
Buttonwood (American Sycamore), 124–25

Caesalpinia mexicana (Mexican Poinciana), 153
Caesalpinia, Mexican (Mexican Poinciana), 153
California Fan Palm (Washington Palm), 240–41

Camphor Tree (*a/k/a Camphor Laurel*), 34

Candleberry (Southern Waxmyrtle), 24

Cane Ash (White Ash), 191

Canyon Maple (Bigtooth Maple), 118
Oak (Lacey Oak), 89

Capul negro (Brazil), 16

Capulin (Brazil), 16

Cardinal Spear (Coral Bean Tree), 204–205

Carolina Ash, 194
Basswood (Carolina Linden), 137
Buckthorn, 71
Cedar (Eastern Red Cedar), 214
Cherry Laurel (*a/k/a Carolina Cherry*), 36
Hickory (Shagbark Hickory), 200
Linden, 137
Poplar (Eastern Cottonwood), 136
Silver Bell, 59

Carpinus caroliniana (American Hornbeam), 56

Carya alba (Mockernut Hickory), 198–99
aquatica (Water Hickory), 202
cordiformis (Bitternut Hickory), 189
glabra (Pignut Hickory), 201
illinoinensis (Pecan), 183
myristiciformis (Nutmeg Hickory), 187
ovata (Shagbark Hickory), 200
texana (Black Hickory), 188
tomentosa (Mockernut Hickory), 198–99

Cassie (Huisache), 148

Cassine Holly (Yaupon Holly), 82

Cassio Berry Bush Tea (Yaupon Holly), 82

Castanea pumila (Allegheny Chinquapin), 63

Catalpa, Desert (Desert Willow), 10
Northern, 128–29
Southern (*see Northern Catalpa*), 128–29
Willowleaf (Desert Willow), 10

Catalpa bignonioides (Southern Catalpa). *See* Northern Catalpa, 128–29

Catalpa speciosa (Northern Catalpa), 128–29

Catalpa Willow (Desert Willow), 10

Catawba (Northern or Southern Catalpa), 128–29

Catclaw, Texas (Wright Acacia), 145

Catclaw (Chaparro Prieto), 152
(Gregg Acacia), 144
(Roemer Acacia), 146

Cedar, Break (Ashe Juniper), 213

Cedar (Ashe Juniper), 213
(Redberry Juniper), 217
(Roseberry Juniper), 216

Cedar Elm, 86

Carolina (Eastern Red Cedar), 214
Eastern Red, 214
Mountain (Alligator Juniper), 218
(Ashe Juniper), 213
Oakbark (Alligator Juniper), 218
Pencil (Eastern Red Cedar), 214
Post (Ashe Juniper), 213
Rock (Ashe Juniper), 213
Salt, 212
Sand (Southern Red Cedar), 215
Southern Red, 215
Texas (Ashe Juniper), 213
Thickbark (Alligator Juniper), 218

Cedro blanco (Arizona Cypress), 219

Celtis laevigata (Sugar Hackberry), 33
lindheimeri (Lindheimer Hackberry), 32
pallida (Granjeno), 83
reticulata (Netleaf Hackberry), 31

Cephalanthus occidentalis (Button Bush), 42

Cercidium macrum (Paloverde), 147

Cercis canadensis (Eastern Redbud), 127
canadensis var. *texensis* (Texas Redbud), 126

Cercocarpus montanus (Mountain Mahogany), 19

Chalk Maple, 120

Chaparral (Brazil), 16

Chaparro Prieto, 152

Chapote negro (Texas Persimmon), 15

Chaste Berry (Chaste Tree), 209
Tree, 209

Checkerbark (Alligator Juniper), 218

Cherokee Bean (Coral Bean Tree), 204–205

Cherry Laurel (*a/k/a Carolina Cherry Laurel*), 36

Cherry, Black, 47

Escarpment Black, 47
Indian (Carolina Buckthorn), 71
Laurel (Cherry Laurel), 36
Rum (Black Cherry), 47
Southwestern Choke, 47
Wild (*a/k/a Wild Black Cherry*) (Black Cherry), 47

Cherrybark Oak (Southern Red Oak), 110

Chestnut Oak (Chinkapin Oak), 62
Oak, Swamp, 92

Chilopsis linearis (Desert Willow), 10

China Plum (Loquat), 8

Chinaberry, 161
Wild (Western Soapberry), 178

Chinatree, Wild (Western Soapberry), 178

Chinese Citron (Trifoliate Orange), 207
Elm, 55
Parasol Tree, 122–23
Pistache, 179
Privet, 66
Tallow Tree, 132

Chinkapin Oak, 62

Chinquapin, Allegheny, 63

Chionanthus virginica (Fringe Tree), 30

Chisos Red Oak, 114

Chittamwood (American Smoke Tree), 70
(Gum Bumelia), 18

Choke Cherry, Southwestern, 47

Christmas Berry Juniper (Redberry Juniper), 217
Holly (American Holly), 103

Cigar Tree (Northern or Southern Catalpa), 128–29

Cinnamon Oak (Bluejack Oak), 13

Cinnamomum camphora (Camphor Tree), 34

Cipres (Montezuma Bald Cypress), 220

Citharexylum berlandieri (Tamaulipan Fiddlewood), 35

Citron, Chinese (Trifoliate Orange), 207

Coahuilla Oak (Mexican Oak), 91

Coast Juniper (Southern Red Cedar), 215
Live Oak (Live Oak), 77
Pignut Hickory (Pignut Hickory), 201

Cockspur Hawthorn (*a/k/a Cockspur Thorn*), 29

Colima, 169
Colorado Douglas Fir (Douglas Fir), 224
    Pinyon Pine (Pinyon Pine), 222
Coma, 14
Coma (Gum Bumelia), 18
Common Alder (Smooth Alder), 78
    Buttonbush (Buttonbush), 42
    Elder (Elderberry), 190
    Elm (American Elm), 52
    Persimmon (Persimmon), 41
    Winterberry (Winterberry Holly), 28
Condalia hookeri (Brazil), 16
Condalia, Bluewood (Brazil), 16
Coral Bean Tree, 204–205
Coralberry (Winterberry Holly), 28
Cordia boisieri (Anacahuita), 72
Cork Elm (Winged Elm), 54
Cornus drummondii (Rough Leaf Dogwood), 39
    florida (Flowering Dogwood), 38
Coronilla (Xylosma), 61
Cotinus obovatus (American Smoke Tree), 70
Cotton Gum (Water Tupelo), 45
    Palm (Washington Palm), 240–41
Cottonwood, Arizona, 134
    Eastern, 136
    Meseta (Arizona Cottonwood), 134
    Northern (Plains Cottonwood), 136
    Plains, 136
    Rio Grande, 135
    Southern (Eastern Cottonwood), 136
    Texas (Plains Cottonwood), 136
    Valley (Rio Grande Cottonwood), 135
    Wislizenus (Rio Grande Cottonwood), 135
Cow Oak (Swamp Chestnut Oak), 92
Cowlicks (Two Wing Silver Bell), 58
Coyotillo, 4
Crabapple, Blanco (Texas Crabapple), 80
    Narrow Leaf (Southern Crabapple), 48
    Prairie (Texas Crabapple), 80
    Southern, 48
    Texas, 80
    Western (Texas Crabapple), 80
Crapemyrtle, 64
Crataegus berberifolia (Big Tree Hawthorn), 27

crus-galli (Cockspur Hawthorn), 29
marshallii (Parsley Hawthorn), 140
mollis (Downy Hawthorn), 84
opaca (Mayhaw), 20
spathulata (Little Hip Hawthorn), 21
texana (Texas Hawthorn), 26
tracyi (Mountain Hawthorn), 85
viridis (Green Hawthorn), 50
Cross Oak (Post Oak), 96
Cucumberwood (Sweet Bay Magnolia), 73
Cupressus arizonica (Arizona Cypress), 219
Custard Apple (Pawpaw), 22–23
Cypress, Arizona (*a/k/a Arizona Rough Cypress*), 219
    Bald, 221
    Gulf (Bald Cypress), 221
    Mexican (Montezuma Bald Cypress), 220
    Montezuma Bald, 220
    Red (Bald Cypress), 221
    Rough Bark Arizona (Arizona Cypress), 219
    Southern (Bald Cypress), 221
    Swamp (Bald Cypress), 221
    Tidewater Red (Bald Cypress), 221
    White (Bald Cypress), 221
    Yellow (Bald Cypress), 221
Cyrilla racemiflora (Titi), 5
Cyrilla, American (Titi), 5

Dagger, Giant, 235
    Spanish, 234
        (Giant Dagger), 235
        (Torrey Yucca), 233
Darlington Ash (Green Ash), 192
    Oak (Laurel Oak), 9
Date Plum (Persimmon), 41
Deciduous Holly, 25
Deerwood (Wooly Hop Hornbeam), 57
Delta Post Oak (Bottomland Post Oak), 97
Desert Ash (Velvet Ash), 195
    Catalpa (Desert Willow), 10
    Fan Palm (Washington Palm), 240–41
    Hackberry (Granjeno), 83
    Live Oak (Emory Oak), 104
    Willow, 10
Devil's Claw (Gregg Acacia), 144
    Walking Stick, 143

Diamond Leaf Oak (Laurel Oak), 9
Diospyros texana (Texas Persimmon), 15
    virginiana (Persimmon), 41
Dogwood, Florida (Flowering Dogwood), 38
    Flowering, 38
    Rough Leaf, 39
    Virginia (Flowering Dogwood), 38
Douglas Fir, 224
Downward Plum (Coma), 14
Downy Hawthorn, 84
Drummond Red Maple (Red Maple), 117
Duck Oak (Water Oak), 17
Dwarf Huisache (Huisachillo), 149

Eastern Black Walnut (Black Walnut), 184
    Coral Bean (Coral Bean Tree), 204–205
    Cottonwood, 136
    Hop Hornbeam (Wooly Hop Hornbeam), 57
    Ironwood (Wooly Hop Hornbeam), 57
    Persimmon, 41
    Poplar (Eastern Cottonwood), 136
    Red Cedar, 214
    Redbud, 127
    Sycamore (American Sycamore), 124–25
Ebony, Texas (*a/k/a Ebano*), 151
Ebony Blackbeard (Texas Ebony), 151
Ehretia anacua (Anaqua), 65
Elder, American (Elderberry), 190
    Box, 203
    Common (Elderberry), 190
    Mexican, 190
    Sweet (Elderberry), 190
Elderberry, 190
    Blue (Mexican Elder), 190
Elm, American, 52
    Basket (Cedar Elm), 86
    Cedar, 86
    Chinese, 55
    Common (American Elm), 52
    Cork (Winged Elm), 54
    Indian (Slippery Elm), 51
    Lace Bark (Chinese Elm), 55
    Lime (Cedar Elm), 86
    Moose (Slippery Elm), 51

Elm *(continued)*
    Red (Slippery Elm), 51
    Rock (Slippery Elm), 51
    Scrub (Cedar Elm), 86
    Slippery, 51
    Soft (American Elm), 52
    Southern Rock (Cedar Elm), 86
    Sweet (Slippery Elm), 51
    Texas (Cedar Elm), 86
    Wahoo (Winged Elm), 54
    Water (American Elm), 52
    White (American Elm), 52
    Winged, 54
    Witch (Winged Elm), 54
Emetic Holly (Yaupon Holly), 82
Emory Oak, 104
Encino (Live Oak), 77
    (Mexican Oak), 91
    (Sandpaper Oak), 108
    (Scrub Oak), 107
    (Wavy Leaf Oak), 105
Encino prieta (Gray Oak), 87
Eriobotrya japonica (Loquat), 8
Erythrina herbacea var. *arborea* (Tree
    Coral Bean), 204–205
Escarpment Live Oak (Plateau Live
    Oak), 76
    Black Cherry, 47
Esperanza (Yellow Trumpet), 196
Evergreen Holly (American Holly), 103
    (Yaupon Holly), 82
Magnolia (Southern Magnolia), 74–75
    (Sweet Bay Magnolia), 73
Eve's Necklace, 171

Fagus grandifolia (American Beech), 53
False Acacia (Black Locust), 168
    Box (Flowering Dogwood), 38
    Buckthorn (Gum Bumelia), 18
    Willow (Desert Willow), 10
Farkleberry, 67
Faxon Yucca (Giant Dagger), 235
Fiddlewood, Tamaulipan (*a/k/a*
    Berlandier Fiddlewood), 35
Fir, Douglas, 224
Firecracker Plant (Red Buckeye), 210–
    11
Firmiana simplex (Chinese Parasol
    Tree), 122–23
Flameleaf Sumac, 181
    Prairie, 180
Flor de mimbre (Desert Willow), 10

Florida Ash (Carolina Ash), 194
    Basswood (Carolina Linden), 137
    Dogwood (Flowering Dogwood), 38
    Linden (Carolina Linden), 137
    Maple (Southern Sugar Maple), 121
Flowering Ash (Fragrant Ash), 175
    (Fringe Tree), 30
    Dogwood, 38
    Willow (Desert Willow), 10
Forestiera acuminata (Swamp Privet), 60
Fork Leaf White Oak (White Oak), 93
Fragrant Ash, 175
    Hickory (Mockernut Hickory), 198–
    99
Frangula caroliniana (Carolina
    Buckthorn), 71
Fraxinus americana (White Ash), 191
    berlandieriana (Berlandier Ash), 193
    caroliniana (Carolina Ash), 194
    cuspidata (Fragrant Ash), 175
    pennsylvanica (Green Ash), 192
    texensis (Texas Ash), 192
    velutina (Velvet Ash), 195
Fremont Screwbean (Screwbean
    Mesquite), 158–59
French Tamarisk (Salt Cedar), 212
Fresno (Berlandier Ash), 193
    (Fragrant Ash), 175
    (Velvet Ash), 195
Frijolito (Texas Mountain Laurel), 176
Fringe Tree, 30

Gambel Oak, 99
Giant Dagger, 235
Ginkgo, 141
Ginkgo biloba (Ginkgo), 141
Glandular Mesquite (Honey Mesquite),
    158–59
Gleditsia aquatica (Water Locust), 166–
    67
    triacanthos (Honey Locust), 164–65
Golden Aspen (Quaking Aspen), 133
    Ball Lead Tree, 156
    Rain Tree, 162–63
Gooding Willow (Black Willow), 11
Grandfather Graybeard (Fringe Tree),
    30
Granjeno (*a/k/a Granjeno Huasteco*), 83
Graves Oak (Chisos Red Oak), 114
Graybeard Tree (Fringe Tree), 30
Gray Oak, 87

Great Laurel Magnolia (Southern
    Magnolia), 74–75
    Lead Tree (Tepeguaje), 157
    Leucaena (Tepeguaje), 157
Green Ash, 192
    Hawthorn, 50
    Locust (Black Locust), 168
Gregg Acacia (*a/k/a Gregg Catclaw*), 144
Guaiacum angustifolium (Guyacan), 170
Guajillo, 155
Guayacan, 170
Gulf Black Willow (Black Willow), 11
    Cypress (Bald Cypress), 221
Gum Bumelia, 18
    Elastic (Gum Bumelia), 18
    Woolybucket (Gum Bumelia), 18
Gum, Black, 44
    Cotton (Water Tupelo), 45
    Red (Sweetgum), 116
    Sour (Black Gum), 44
    (Water Tupelo), 45
    Starleaved (Sweetgum), 116
    Water (Water Tupelo), 45
    White (Sweetgum), 116
Gumbo Filé (Sassafras), 102

Hackberry, Desert (Granjeno), 83
    Granjeno, 83
    Lindheimer, 32
    Lowland (Sugar Hackberry), 33
    Net Leaf, 31
    Southern (Sugar Hackberry), 33
    Spiney (Granjeno), 83
    Sugar, 33
    Western (Net Leaf Hackberry), 31
Halesia diptera (Two Wing Silver Bell),
    58
    caroliniana (Carolina Silver Bell), 59
Hard Maple (Southern Sugar Maple),
    121
    Pine (Longleaf Pine), 228
Hardbark Hickory (Mockernut
    Hickory), 198–99
Hardy Orange (Trifoliate Orange), 207
Havard Shin Oak, 88
Hawthorn, Barberry (Big Tree Haw-
    thorn), 27
    Big Tree, 27
    Cockspur, 29
    Downy, 84
    Green, 50
    Little Hip, 21

Mayhaw (*a/k/a May Hawthorn*), 20
Mountain, 85
Parsley (*a/k/a Parsley Leaf Hawthorn*), 140
Riverflat (Mayhaw), 20
Small Fruit Hawthorn (Little Hip Hawthorn), 21
Southern (Green Hawthorn), 50
Texas, 26
Tracy (Mountain Hawthorn), 85
Hazel Alder (Smooth Alder), 78
Heart Pine (Longleaf Pine), 228
Hedge Apple (Osage Orange), 40
Helietta parvifolia (Baretta), 206
Hemp Tree (Chaste Tree), 209
Hercules' Club, 197
(Devil's Walking Stick), 143
Hercules' Club, Texas (Lime Prickly Ash), 174
Hickory, Bigbud (Mockernut Hickory), 198–99
Bitter (Water Hickory), 202
Bitter Water (Nutmeg Hickory), 187
Bitternut, 189
Black, 188
Broom (Pignut Hickory), 201
Buckley (Black Hickory), 188
Carolina (Shagbark Hickory), 200
Coast Pignut (Pignut Hickory), 201
Fragrant (Mockernut Hickory), 198–99
Hardbark (Mockernut Hickory), 198–99
Mockernut, 198–99
Nutmeg, 187
Pignut, 201
(Bitternut Hickory), 189
(Black Hickory), 188
Red (Bitternut Hickory), 189
(Pignut Hickory), 201
Scalybark (Shagbark Hickory), 200
Shagbark, 200
Shellbark (Shagbark Hickory), 200
Smoothbark (Pignut Hickory), 201
Swamp (Bitternut Hickory), 189
(Nutmeg Hickory), 187
(Pignut Hickory), 201
(Water Hickory), 202
Switch (Pignut Hickory), 201
Texas (Black Hickory), 188
Upland (Shagbark Hickory), 200
Water, 202

White (Bitternut Hickory), 189
(Mockernut Hickory), 198–99
Whiteheart (Mockernut Hickory), 198–99
Hill Country Buckeye (Yellow Buckeye), 210–11
Pine (Longleaf Pine), 228
Hog Apple (Cockspur Hawthorn), 29
Hognut (Mockernut Hickory), 198–99
Holly Oak (Emory Oak), 104
Holly, American, 103
Cassine (Yaupon Holly), 82
Christmas (American Holly), 103
Deciduous, 25
Emetic (Yaupon Holly), 82
Evergreen (American Holly), 103
(Yaupon Holly), 82
Meadow (Deciduous Holly), 25
Michigan (Winterberry Holly), 28
Prairie (Deciduous Holly), 25
Prickly (American Holly), 103
Swamp (Deciduous Holly), 25
Welk (Deciduous Holly), 25
White (American Holly), 103
Winterberry, 28
Yaupon, 82
Yule (American Holly), 103
Honey Bells (Button Bush), 42
Locust (*a/k/a Honey Shucks Locust*), 164–65
Mesquite, 158–59
Honeyball (Button Bush), 42
Hop Tree (Wafer Ash), 208
Hornbeam, American, 56
American Hop (Wooly Hop Hornbeam), 57
Eastern Hop (Wooly Hop Hornbeam), 57
Wooly Hop, 57
Horse Apple (Osage Orange), 40
Bean (Retama), 160
Sugar (Sweet Leaf), 7
Huckleberry (Farkleberry), 67
Huisache, 148
Huisache, Dwarf (Huisachillo), 149
Little (Huisachillo), 149
Huisachillo, 149
Humboldt Coyotillo (Coyotillo), 4

Ilex decidua (Deciduous Holly), 25
opaca (American Holly), 103

verticillata (Winterberry Holly), 28
vomitoria (Yaupon Holly), 82
Inch Plum (Mexican Plum), 49
Indian Bark (Sweet Bay Magnolia), 73
Bean (Northern or Southern Catalpa), 128–29
Blackdrink (Yaupon Holly), 82
Cherry (Carolina Buckthorn), 71
Elm (Slippery Elm), 51
Soap Plant (Western Soapberry), 178
Inland Douglas Fir (Douglas Fir), 224
Interior Douglas Fir (Douglas Fir), 224
Ponderosa Pine (Ponderosa Pine), 229
Iowa Crab (Texas Crabapple), 80
Iron Oak (Blackjack Oak), 94–95
(Post Oak), 96
Ironwood, Eastern (Wooly Hop Hornbeam), 57
Roughbark (Wooly Hop Hornbeam), 57
Ironwood (American Hornbeam), 56
(Gum Bumelia), 18

Jaboncillo (Western Soapberry), 178
Jack Oak (Blackjack Oak), 94–95
Jano (Desert Willow), 10
Japanese Ligustrum, 37
Plum (Loquat), 8
Privet (Japanese Ligustrum), 37
Varnish Tree (Chinese Parasol Tree), 112–23
Jerusalem Thorn (Retama), 160
Jove's Fruit (Persimmon), 41
Judas Tree (Eastern Redbud), 127
Juglans major (Arizona Walnut), 185
microcarpa (Texas Walnut), 182
nigra (Black Walnut), 184
Juniper, Alligator, 218
Ashe, 213
Coast (Southern Red Cedar), 215
Christmas Berry (Redberry Juniper), 217
Mexican (Ashe Juniper), 213
Pinchot (Redberry Juniper), 217
Red (Eastern Red Cedar), 214
Redberry, 217
Roseberry, 216
Texas (Redberry Juniper), 217
Virginia (Eastern Red Cedar), 214
Western (Alligator Juniper), 218

Juniperus ashei (Ashe Juniper), 213
  coahuilensis (Roseberry Juniper), 216
  deppeana (Alligator Juniper), 218
  pinchotii (Redberry Juniper), 217
  virginiana (Eastern Red Cedar), 214
  virginiana var. *silicicola* (Southern
    Red Cedar), 215

Karwinskia humboldtiana (Coyotillo), 4
Knockaway (Anaqua), 65
Koelreuteria paniculata (Golden Rain
    Tree), 162–63

Lace Bark Elm (Chinese Elm), 55
Lacey Oak, 89
La coma (Coma), 14
Lady's Legs (Texas Madrone), 69
Lagerstroemia indica (Crapemyrtle), 64
Lampassas Mulberry (Red Mulberry),
    138
Lance-leaved Sumac (Prairie Flameleaf
    Sumac), 180
Laurel, Big (Southern Magnolia), 74–75
    (Sweet Bay Magnolia), 73
  Swamp (Sweet Bay Magnolia), 73
  Texas Mountain, 176
  White (Sweet Bay Magnolia), 73
  Wild (Sweet Leaf), 7
Laurel Cherry (Cherry Laurel), 36
  Magnolia (Sweet Bay Magnolia), 73
  Oak (*a/k/a Laurel Leaf Oak*), 9
  Tree (Red Bay), 6
Lead Tree, Golden Ball, 156
  Great (Tepeguaje), 157
  Little Leaf (Golden Ball Lead Tree),
    156
  Mexican (Tepeguaje), 157
Leather Leaf Ash (Velvet Ash), 195
Leatherwood (Titi), 5
Lemonball (Golden Ball Lead Tree), 156
Lentisco (Texas Pistache), 172
Leucaena, Great (Tepeguaje), 157
  Little (Golden Ball Lead Tree), 156
Leucaena pulverulenta (Tepeguaje), 157
  retusa (Golden Ball Lead Tree), 156
Leverwood (Wooly Hop Hornbeam), 57
Ligustrum, Japanese, 37
  Wax Leaf, 37
Ligustrum japonicum (Japanese
    Ligustrum), 37
  lucidum (Wax Leaf Ligustrum), 37
  sinense (Chinese Privet), 66

Lilacs of the South (Crapemyrtle), 64
Lime, Wild (Colima), 169
Lime Elm (Cedar Elm), 86
  Prickly Ash, 174
    (Colima), 169
  Tree (Carolina Linden), 137
Limestone Sumac (Prairie Flameleaf
    Sumac), 180
Limoncillo (Lime Prickly Ash), 174
Linden, Carolina, 137
  Florida (Carolina Linden), 137
Lindheimer Black Willow (Black
    Willow), 11
  Hackberry, 32
Liquidamber styraciflua (Sweetgum),
    116
Little Hip Hawthorn, 21
  Huisache (Huisachillo), 149
  Leaf Lead Tree (Golden Ball Lead
    Tree), 156
  Leucaena (Golden Ball Lead Tree),
    156
  Silver Bell (Carolina Silver Bell), 59
  Walnut (Texas Walnut), 182
Live Oak, Coast (Live Oak), 77
  Desert (Emory Oak), 104
  Escarpment (Plateau Live Oak), 76
  Plateau, 76
  Scrub (Plateau Live Oak), 76
    (Wavy Leaf Oak), 105
  Shrub (Sandpaper Oak), 108
    (Scrub Oak), 107
  Southern (Live Oak), 77
  Spanish (Plateau Live Oak), 76
  Virginia (Live Oak), 77
  West Texas (Plateau Live Oak), 76
Loblolly Magnolia (Southern Magnolia),
    74–75
  Pine, 226
Locust, Black, 168
  Green (Black Locust), 168
  Honey (*a/k/a Honey Shucks Locust*),
    164–65
  Post (Black Locust), 168
  Ship Mast (Black Locust), 168
  Swamp (Water Locust), 166–67
  Sweet (Honey Locust), 164–65
  Thorny (Honey Locust), 164–65
  Water, 166–67
  White (Black Locust), 168
  Yellow (Black Locust), 168

Locust Tree (Black Locust), 168
Logwood (Brazil), 16
Long Straw Pine (Longleaf Pine), 228
Longleaf Pine, 228
Longtag Pine (Shortleaf Pine), 225
Loquat, 8
Louisiana Palm, 236–37
Lowland Hackberry (Sugar Hackberry),
    33

Maclura pomifera (Osage Orange), 40
Madrone, Texas (*a/k/a Madroña or
    Madroño*), 69
Magnolia, Bull Bay (Southern Magno-
    lia), 74–75
    (Sweet Bay Magnolia), 73
  Evergreen (Southern Magnolia), 74–
    75
    (Sweet Bay Magnolia), 73
  Great Laurel (Southern Magnolia),
    74–75
  Laurel (Sweet Bay Magnolia), 73
  Loblolly (Southern Magnolia), 74–75
  Mountain (Sweet Bay Magnolia), 73
  Small (Sweet Bay Magnolia), 73
  Southern, 74–75
  Swamp Bay (*a/k/a Swamp Magnolia*)
    (Sweet Bay Magnolia), 73
  Sweet Bay (*a/k/a Sweet Magnolia*), 73
  Virginia (Sweet Bay Magnolia), 73
  White Bay (Sweet Bay Magnolia), 73
Magnolia grandiflora (Southern
    Magnolia), 74–75
  virginiana (Sweet Bay Magnolia), 73
Mahogany, Mountain, 19
Maidenhair Tree (Ginkgo), 141
Malus angustifolia (Southern
    Crabapple), 48
  ioensis var. *texana* (Texas
    Crabapple), 80
Mamou (Coral Bean Tree), 204–205
Manna Plant (Salt Cedar), 212
Manzanillo (*a/k/a Manzanita*) (Anaqua),
    65
    (Xylosma), 61
Maple, Ashleaf (Box Elder), 203
  Bigtooth, 118
  Canyon (Bigtooth Maple), 118
  Chalk, 120
  Drummond Red (Red Maple), 117
  Florida (Southern Sugar Maple), 121

Hard (Southern Sugar Maple), 121
Red, 117
  (Trident Maple), 119
Red River (Box Elder), 203
Sabinal (Bigtooth Maple), 118
Scarlet (Red Maple), 117
  (Trident Maple), 119
Silver, 115
Soft (Red Maple), 117
  (Silver Maple), 115
  (Trident Maple), 119
Southern Sugar, 121
Southwestern Bigtooth Maple
  (Bigtooth Maple), 118
Sugar, Southern, p, 121
Swamp (Red Maple), 117
  (Silver Maple), 115
  (Trident Maple), 119
Trident, 119
Uvalde Bigtooth (Bigtooth Maple),
  118
Water (Red Maple), 117
  (Trident Maple), 119
Western Sugar Maple (Bigtooth
  Maple), 118
White (Silver Maple), 115
Whitebark (Chalk Maple), 120
Mayhaw (*a/k/a May Hawthorn*), 20
Meadow Holly (Deciduous Holly), 25
Medusa Acacia (Huisachillo), 149
Melia azedarach (Chinaberry), 161
Mescalbean (Texas Mountain Laurel),
  176
Meseta Cottonwood (Arizona Cotton-
  wood), 134
Mesquite, Glandular (Honey Mesquite),
  158–59
  Honey, 158–59
  Screwbean (*a/k/a Screwpod Mes-
  quite*), 158–59
Mexican Ash (Berlandier Ash), 193
  Bird of Paradise (Mexican Poinciana),
  153
  Buckeye, 186
  Caesalpinia (Mexican Poinciana), 153
  Cypress (Montezuma Bald Cypress),
  220
  Elder, 190
  Juniper (Ashe Juniper), 213
  Lead Tree (Tepeguaje), 157
  Oak, 91
  Olive (Anacahuita), 72

Palmetto (Sabal Palm), 238–39
Paloverde (Retama), 160
Persimmon (Texas Persimmon), 15
Pinyon Pine, 223
Plum, 49
Poinciana, 153
  Torchwood (Sierra Madre Torch-
  wood), 173
  White Oak (Mexican Oak), 91
Michigan Holly (Winterberry Holly), 28
Milk Buckthorn (Coma), 14
Mimbre (Desert Willow), 10
Mimosa, 154
Mississippi Valley Oak (Bottomland
  Post Oak), 97
Mockernut Hickory, 198–99
Mock Orange (Cherry Laurel), 36
  (Trifoliate Orange), 207
Modesto Ash (Velvet Ash), 195
Mohr Oak, 46
Monillo (Mexican Buckeye), 186
Monk's Pepper (Chaste Tree), 209
Monterrey Oak (Mexican Oak), 91
Montezuma Bald Cypress, 220
Moose Elm (Slippery Elm), 51
Moral (Red Mulberry), 138
  blanco (White Mulberry), 139
Morus alba (White Mulberry), 139
  rubra (Red Mulberry), 138
Mossycup Oak (Bur Oak), 100–101
Mountain Ash (Texas Ash), 192
  Cedar (Alligator Juniper), 218
  (Ashe Juniper), 213
  Hawthorn, 85
  Laurel, Texas, 176
  Magnolia (Sweet Bay Magnolia), 73
  Mahogany, 19
  Oak (Chisos Red Oak), 114
  Sumac (Flameleaf Sumac), 181
  Torchwood (Sierra Madre Torch-
  wood), 173
  Walnut (Arizona Walnut), 185
Mulberry, Lampassas (Red Mulberry),
  138
  Red, 138
  Russian (White Mulberry), 139
  Silkworm (White Mulberry), 139
  White, 139
Mullein (Potato Tree), 43
Muscle Wood (American Hornbeam), 56
Myrica cerifera (Southern Waxmyrtle),
  24

Naked Indian (Texas Madrone), 69
Namboca (Texas Walnut), 182
Nannyberry, Rusty (Rusty Blackhaw
  Viburnum), 81
  Southern (Rusty Blackhaw Vibur-
  num), 81
Nannyberry (Rusty Blackhaw Vibur-
  num), 81
Naranjo chino (Osage Orange), 40
Narrow Leaf Crabapple (Southern
  Crabapple), 48
Necklace Poplar (Eastern Cottonwood),
  136
  Tree (Eve's Necklace), 171
Negrito (Tamaulipan Fiddlewood), 35
Net Leaf Hackberry (*a/k/a Net Leaf
  Sugar Hackberry*), 31
New Mexico Pinyon Pine (Pinyon Pine),
  222
Newcastle Thorn (Cockspur Hawthorn),
  29
Nicotiana glauca (Tobacco Tree), 68
Nogal silvestre (Arizona Walnut), 185
Nogalito (Texas Walnut), 182
Northern Catalpa, 128–29
  Cottonwood (Plains Cottonwood),
  136
Nutmeg Hickory, 187
Nut Pine (Mexican Pinyon Pine), 223
  (Pinyon Pine), 222
Nuttall Oak, 111
Nyssa aquatica (Water Tupelo), 45
  sylvatica (Black Gum), 44

Oak, Apache (Emory Oak), 104
  Barron (Blackjack Oak), 94–95
  Basket (Swamp Chestnut Oak), 92
  Bigelow (White Shin Oak), 90
  Black, 109
  (Blackjack Oak), 94–95
  (Emory Oak), 104
  Blackjack, 94–95
  Blue (Lacey Oak), 89
  Bluejack, 13
  Bottomland Post, 97
  Bottomland Red (Southern Red
  Oak), 110
  Buckley (Texas Oak), 112
  Bur, 100–101
  Canyon (Lacey Oak), 89
  Cherrybark (Southern Red Oak), 110

Oak (continued)
Chestnut (Chinkapin Oak), 62
Chinkapin, 62
Chisos Red, 114
Cinnamon (Bluejack Oak), 13
Coahuila (Mexican Oak), 91
Coast Live (Live Oak), 77
Cow (Swamp Chestnut Oak), 92
Cross (Post Oak), 96
Darlington (Laurel Oak), 9
Delta Post (Bottomland Post Oak), 97
Desert Live (Emory Oak), 104
Diamond Leaf, 9
Duck (Water Oak), 17
Emory, 104
Escarpment Live (Plateau Live Oak), 76
Fork Leaf White Oak (White Oak), 93
Gambel, 99
Graves (Chisos Red Oak), 114
Gray, 87
Havard Shin, 88
Holly (Emory Oak), 104
Iron (Blackjack Oak), 94–95
(Post Oak), 96
Jack (Blackjack Oak), 94–95
Lacey, 89
Laurel (a/k/a Laurel Leaf Oak), 9
Live, Desert (Emory Oak), 104
Live, Plateau, 76
Live, Scrub (Plateau Live Oak), 76
(Wavy Leaf Oak), 105
Live, Shrub (Sandpaper Oak), 108
(Scrub Oak), 107
Live, Southern (Live Oak), 77
Mexican, 91
Mississippi Valley (Bottomland Post Oak), 97
Mohr, 46
Monterrey (Mexican Oak), 91
Mossycup (Bur Oak), 100–101
Mountain (Chisos Red Oak), 114
Nuttall, 111
Obtusa (Diamond Leaf Oak), 9
Overcup, 98
Pagoda (Southern Red Oak), 110
Peach (Willow Oak), 3
Pin (Nuttall Oak), 111
(Water Oak), 17
(Willow Oak), 3
Plateau Live, 76
Possum (Water Oak), 17

Post, 96
Post, Bottomland, 97
Post, Delta (Bottomland Post Oak), 97
Post, Swamp (Bottomland Post Oak), 97
(Overcup Oak), 98
Prairie (Bur Oak), 100–101
Punk (Water Oak), 17
Red, Bottomland (Southern Red Oak), 110
Red, Chisos, 114
Red, Shumard (Shumard Oak), 113
Red, Southern, 110
Red, Swamp (Shumard Oak), 113
(Southern Red Oak), 110
Red, Texas (Chisos Red Oak), 114
(Texas Oak), 112
Red, Three Lobe (Southern Red Oak), 110
Red (Nuttall Oak), 111
Red River (Nuttall Oak), 111
Ridge White (White Oak), 93
Rock Chestnut Oak (Chinkapin Oak), 62
Rock (Chinkapin Oak), 62
(Chisos Red Oak), 114
(Lacey Oak), 89
Sand Shin (Havard Shin Oak), 88
Sandjack (Bluejack Oak), 13
Sandpaper, 108
Scalybark (White Shin Oak), 90
Scrub, 107
(Mohr Oak), 46
(Sandpaper Oak), 108
(Vasey Oak), 106
(Wavy Leaf Oak), 105
(White Shin Oak), 90
Scrub Live (Plateau Live Oak), 76
(Wavy Leaf Oak), 105
Shin (Bluejack Oak), 13
(Mohr Oak), 46
(Sandpaper Oak), 108
(Vasey Oak), 106
(Wavy Leaf Oak), 105
Shin, Havard, 88
Shin, Sand (Havard Shin Oak), 88
Shin, White, 90
Shrub Live (Sandpaper Oak), 108
(Scrub Oak), 107
Shumard, 113
Silver Leaf, 3

Smokey (Lacey Oak), 89
Smoothbark Oak (Black Oak), 109
Southern Live (Live Oak), 77
Southern Red, 110
Spanish Live (Plateau Live Oak), 76
Spanish (Southern Red Oak), 110
(Texas Oak), 112
Spotted (Shumard Oak), 113
(Texas Oak), 112
(Water Oak), 17
Stave (White Oak), 93
Striped (Nuttall Oak), 111
Swamp Chestnut, 92
Swamp Laurel (Laurel Oak), 9
Swamp Post (Bottomland Post Oak), 97
(Overcup Oak), 98
Swamp Red (Shumard Oak), 113
(Southern Red Oak), 110
Swamp Spanish (Southern Red Oak), 110
Swamp White (Overcup Oak), 98
Swamp Willow (Willow Oak), 3
Swamp White (Overcup Oak), 98
(Swamp Chestnut Oak), 92
Texas, 112
Texas Red (Chisos Red Oak), 114
(Texas Oak), 112
Three Lobe Red (Southern Red Oak), 110
Turbinella (Scrub Oak), 107
Turkey (Bluejack Oak), 13
Upland Willow (Bluejack Oak), 13
Vasey, 106
Virginia Live (Live Oak), 77
Water, 17
Water White (Overcup Oak), 98
Wavy Leaf, 105
West Texas Live (Plateau Live Oak), 76
Western Black (Emory Oak), 104
White, 93
White, Mexican (Mexican Oak), 91
White, Swamp (Overcup Oak), 98
White, Water (Overcup Oak), 98
White Leaf (Silver Leaf Oak), 2
White Shin, 90
Willow, 3
Yellow (Black Oak), 109
(Bottomland Post Oak), 97
(Chinkapin Oak), 62

Yellow Chestnut (Chinkapin Oak), 62
Yellowbark (Black Oak), 109
Oakbark Cedar (Alligator Juniper), 218
Obtusa Oak (Diamond Leaf Oak), 9
Oldfield Pine (Loblolly Pine), 226
Old Man's Beard (Fringe Tree), 30
　　Shag (Torrey Yucca), 233
Olive, Mexican (Anacahuita), 72
　　Texas (Anacahuita), 72
　　Wild (Anacahuita), 72
Olmo (Cedar Elm), 86
Orange, Bitter (Trifoliate Orange), 207
　　Hardy (Trifoliate Orange), 207
　　Mock (Trifoliate Orange), 207
　　Osage, 40
　　Trifoliate, 207
Orchid Tree (Anacacho Bauhinia), 142
Osage Orange, 40
Ostrya virginiana (Wooly Hop Horn-
　　beam), 57
Overcup Oak, 98

Pagoda Oak (Southern Red Oak), 110
Palm, American Cotton (Washington
　　Palm), 240–41
　　California Fan (Washington Palm),
　　　240–41
　　　Cotton (Washington Palm), 240–
　　　41
　　Desert Fan (Washington Palm),
　　　240–41
　　Louisiana, 236–37
　　Petticoat (Washington Palm), 240–41
　　Sabal, 238–39
　　Washington, 240–41
Palma (Giant Dagger), 235
　　(Torrey Yucca), 233
Palma de datil (Spanish Dagger), 234
Palma de micharos (Sabal Palm), 238–39
Palma pita (Spanish Dagger), 234
Palmera de abanicos (Washington
　　Palm), 240–41
Palmetto, (Louisiana Palm), 236–37
　　Mexican (Sabal Palm), 238–39
　　Rio Grande (Sabal Palm), 238–39
　　Texas (Sabal Palm), 238–39
　　Victoria (Sabal Palm), 238–39
Palmilla (Soaptree Yucca), 230
　　(Thompson Yucca), 232
Palmita (Beaked Yucca), 231
Palmito (Spanish Dagger), 234

Palo blanco (Net Leaf Hackberry), 31
　　(Sugar Hackberry), 33
Paloverde, 147
Paloverde (Retama), 160
Panicled Golden Rain Tree (Golden
　　Rain Tree), 162–63
Parasol Tree, Chinese, 112–23
Parkinsonia (Retama), 160
Parkinsonia aculeata (Retama), 160
　　texana var. *macra* (Paloverde), 147
Parsley Hawthorn (*a/k/a Parsley Leaf
　　Hawthorn*), 140
Pasture Haw (Little Hip Hawthorn), 21
Pawpaw, 22–23
Peach Oak (Willow Oak), 3
Pecan, 183
　　Bitter (Bitternut Hickory), 189
　　　(Water Hickory), 202
　　Wild (Water Hickory), 202
Pencil Cedar (Eastern Red Cedar), 214
Pepperbark (Hercules' Club), 197
Pepperidge (Black Gum), 44
Persea borbonia (Red Bay), 6
Persimmon, Black (Texas Persimmon),
　　15
　　Common (Persimmon), 41
　　Eastern (Persimmon), 41
　　Mexican (Texas Persimmon), 15
　　Texas, 15
Petticoat Palm (Washington Palm),
　　240–41
Phoenix Tree (Chinese Parasol Tree),
　　122–23
Pigeon Tree (Devil's Walking Stick), 143
Pignut Hickory, 201
　　(Bitternut Hickory), 189
　　(Black Hickory), 188
Pinchot Juniper (Redberry Juniper), 217
Pine, Arizona, 227
　　Arkansas (Shortleaf Pine), 225
　　Colorado Pinyon (Pinyon Pine), 222
　　Hard (Longleaf Pine), 228
　　Heart (Longleaf Pine), 228
　　Hill (Longleaf Pine), 228
　　Loblolly, 226
　　Long Straw (Longleaf Pine), 228
　　Longleaf, 228
　　Longtag (Shortleaf Pine), 225
　　Mexican Pinyon, 223
　　New Mexico Pinyon (Pinyon Pine),
　　　222
　　Nut (Pinyon Pine), 222

Oldfield (Loblolly Pine), 226
　　Pinyon, 222
　　Pitch (Longleaf Pine), 228
　　Ponderosa, 229
　　Short Straw (Shortleaf Pine), 225
　　Shortleaf, 225
　　Southern Yellow (Longleaf Pine),
　　　228
　　　(Shortleaf Pine), 225
　　Yellow (Longleaf), 228
　　　(Shortleaf), 225
Pink Sophora (Eve's Necklace), 171
Pin Oak (Nuttall Oak), 111
　　(Water Oak), 17
　　(Willow Oak), 3
Pino real colorado (Douglas Fir), 224
Piñón (Mexican Pinyon Pine), 223
　　(Pinyon Pine), 222
Pinus arizonica var. *stormiae* (Arizona
　　Pine), 227
　　cembroides (Mexican Pinyon Pine),
　　　223
　　echinata (Shortleaf Pine), 225
　　edulis (Pinyon Pine), 222
　　palustris (Longleaf Pine), 228
　　ponderosa var. *scopulorum* (Arizona
　　　Pine), 227
　　　(Ponderosa Pine), 229
　　taeda (Loblolly Pine), 226
Pinyon, Two Leaf (Pinyon Pine), 222
Pinyon Pine, 222
　　Colorado (Pinyon Pine), 222
　　Mexican, 223
　　New Mexico (Pinyon Pine), 222
Pistache, Chinese, 179
　　Texas, 172
Pistacia chinensis (Chinese Pistache),
　　179
　　texana (Texas Pistache), 172
Pistachio, American (Texas Pistache),
　　172
　　Wild (Texas Pistache), 172
Pitch Pine (Longleaf Pine), 228
Pithecellobium flexicaule (Texas Ebony),
　　151
　　pallens (Tenaza), 150
Plains Cottonwood, 136
Plane Tree, American (American
　　Sycamore), 124–25
Plantanus occidentalis (American
　　Sycamore), 124–25

Plateau Live Oak, 76
Plum, Big Tree (Mexican Plum), 49
    China (Loquat), 8
    Date (Persimmon), 41
    Downward (Coma), 14
    Inch (Mexican Plum), 49
    Japanese (Loquat), 8
    Mexican, 49
    Saffron (Coma), 14
    Winter (Persimmon), 41
Plumero (Berlandier Ash), 193
Poinciana, Mexican, 153
Poison Ash (Fringe Tree), 30
Poncirus trifoliata (Trifoliate Orange), 207
Ponderosa Pine, 229
Poplar, Carolina (Eastern Cottonwood), 136
    Eastern (Eastern Cottonwood), 136
    Necklace Poplar (Eastern Cottonwood), 136
    Trembling (Quaking Aspen), 133
Poppy Ash (Carolina Ash), 194
Populus deltoides (Eastern Cottonwood), 136
    fremontii var. *mesetae* (Arizona Cottonwood), 134
    sargentii (Plains Cottonwood), 136
    tremuloides (Quaking Aspen), 133
    wislizenii (Rio Grande Cottonwood), 135
Porlieria, Texas (Guayacan), 170
Possum Haw (Deciduous Holly), 25
    Oak (Water Oak), 17
Possumwood (Persimmon), 41
Post Cedar (Ashe Juniper), 213
    Locust (Black Locust), 168
    Oak, 96
    Oak, Bottomland, 97
    Oak, Delta (Bottomland Post Oak), 97
    Oak, Swamp (Bottomland Post Oak), 97
    (Overcup Oak), 98
Potato Tree, 43
Powderpuff Tree (Mimosa), 154
Prairie Crabapple (Texas Crabapple), 80
    Flameleaf Sumac, 180
    Holly (Deciduous Holly), 25
    Oak (Bur Oak), 100–101
    Shining Sumac (Prairie Flameleaf Sumac), 180

Prickly Ash, Lime, 174
    (Colima), 169
    Elder (Devil's Walking Stick), 143
    Holly (American Holly), 103
Prickly Ash (Devil's Walking Stick), 143
    (Hercules' Club), 197
Privet Berry (Japanese Ligustrum), 37
Privet, Chinese, 66
    Japanese (Japanese Ligustrum), 37
    Swamp, 60
    Texas (Swamp Privet), 60
    Tree (Wax Leaf Ligustrum), 37
Prosopis glandulosa (Honey Mesquite), 158–59
    pubescens (Screwbean Mesquite), 158–59
Prunus caroliniana (Cherry Laurel), 36
    mexicana (Mexican Plum), 49
    serotina (Black Cherry), 47
    serotina var. *eximia* (Escarpment Black Cherry), 47
    serotina var. *virens* (Southwestern Choke Cherry), 47
Pseudotsuga menziesii (Douglas Fir), 224
Ptelea trifoliata (Wafer Ash), 208
Punk Oak (Water Oak), 17
Purple Haw (Brazil), 16

Quaking Aspen, 133
Quercitron (Black Oak), 109
Quercus alba (White Oak), 93
    buckleyi (Texas Oak), 112
    emoryi (Emory Oak), 104
    falcata (Southern Red Oak), 110
    fusiformis (Plateau Live Oak), 76
    gambelii (Gambel Oak), 99
    gravesii (Chisos Red Oak), 114
    grisea (Gray Oak), 87
    havardii (Havard Shin Oak), 88
    hypoleucoides (Silver Leaf Oak), 2
    incana (Bluejack Oak), 13
    laceyi (Lacey Oak), 89
    laurifolia (Laurel Oak), 9
    lyrata (Overcup Oak), 98
    macrocarpa (Bur Oak), 100–101
    marilandica (Blackjack Oak), 94–95
    michauxii (Swamp Chestnut Oak), 92
    mohriana (Mohr Oak), 46
    muehlenbergii (Chinkapin Oak), 62
    nigra (Water Oak), 17

    nuttallii (Nuttall Oak), 111
    obtusa (Diamond Leaf Oak), 9
    phellos (Willow Oak), 3
    polymorpha (Mexican Oak), 91
    prinus (Swamp Chestnut Oak), 92
    pungens (Sandpaper Oak), 108
    pungens var. *vaseyana* (Vasey Oak), 106
    shumardii (Shumard Oak), 113
    similis (Bottomland Post Oak), 97
    sinuata var. *breviloba* (White Shin Oak), 90
    stellata (Post Oak), 96
    turbinella (Scrub Oak), 107
    undulata (Wavy Leaf Oak), 105
    vaseyana (Vasey Oak), 106
    velutina (Black Oak), 109
    virginiana (Live Oak), 77

Rain Tree, Golden, 162–63
Red Ash (Green Ash), 192
    Bay (a/k/a Red Bay Persea), 6
    Beech (American Beech), 53
    Birch (River Birch), 79
    Buckeye, 210–11
    Cardinal (Coral Bean Tree), 204–205
    Cypress (Bald Cypress), 221
    Elm, 51
    Gum (Sweetgum), 116
    Haw (Downy Hawthorn), 84
    Hickory (Bitternut Hickory), 189
    (Pignut Hickory), 201
    Juniper (Eastern Red Cedar), 214
Maple, 117
    (Trident Maple), 119
Mulberry, 138
Oak, (Nuttall Oak), 111
Oak, Bottomland (Southern Red Oak), 110
Oak, Chisos, 114
Oak, Shumard (Shumard Oak), 113
Oak, Southern, 110
Oak, Swamp (Shumard Oak), 113
    (Southern Red Oak), 110
Oak, Texas (Chisos Red Oak), 114
    (Texas Oak), 112
Oak, Three Lobe (Southern Red Oak), 110
River Maple (Box Elder), 203
River Oak (Nuttall Oak), 111
Savin (Eastern Red Cedar), 214
Titi (Titi), 5

Redberry Juniper, 217
Redbud, Eastern, 127
    Texas, 126
Retama, 160
    China (Paloverde), 147
Rhamnus caroliniana (Carolina
        Buckthorn), 71
Rhus copallina (Flameleaf Sumac), 181
    lanceolata (Prairie Flameleaf
        Sumac), 180
Ridge Beech (American Beech), 53
    White Oak (White Oak), 93
Rio Grande Cottonwood, 135
    Palmetto (Sabal Palm), 238–39
River Ash (Green Ash), 192
    Birch, 79
    Walnut (Arizona Walnut), 185
        (Texas Walnut), 182
Riverflat Hawthorn (Mayhaw), 20
Robinia pseudoacacia (Black Locust),
        168
Roble negro (Emory Oak), 104
Rock Cedar (Ashe Juniper), 213
    Chestnut Oak (*a/k/a Rock Oak*)
        (Chinkapin Oak), 62
    Elm (Slippery Elm), 51
    Oak (Chinkapin Oak), 62
        (Chisos Red Oak), 114
        (Lacey Oak), 89
Rocky Mountain Douglas Fir (Douglas
        Fir), 224
    Mountain Ponderosa Pine (Ponde-
        rosa Pine), 229
Roemer Acacia, 146
Rootbeer Tree (Sassafras), 102
Rose Lantern (Golden Rain Tree), 162–
        63
Roseberry Juniper, 216
Rough Bark Arizona Cypress (Arizona
        Cypress), 219
    Leaf Dogwood, 39
Roughbark Ironwood (Wooly Hop
        Hornbeam), 57
Rum Cherry (Black Cherry), 47
Russian Mulberry (White Mulberry), 139
Rusty Blackhaw Viburnum, 81
    Nannyberry (Rusty Blackhaw
        Viburnum), 81

Sabal louisiana (Louisiana Palm), 236–37
    mexicana (Sabal Palm), 238–39

Sabal Palm, 238–39
Sabinal Maple (Bigtooth Maple), 118
Sabino (Ashe Juniper), 213
        (Montezuma Bald Cypress), 220
Saffron Plum (Coma), 14
Salix nigra (Black Willow), 11
    taxifolia (Yew Leaf Willow), 12
Saloop (Sassafras), 102
Salt Cedar, 212
Sambucus canadensis (Elderberry), 190
    mexicana (Mexican Elder), 190
Sand Cedar (Southern Red Cedar), 215
Shin Oak (Havard Shin Oak), 88
Sandjack Oak (Bluejack Oak), 13
Sandpaper Oak, 108
    Tree (Anaqua), 65
Sapindus saponaria var. *drummondii*
        (Western Soapberry), 178
Sapium sebiferum (Chinese Tallow
        Tree), 132
Sassafras albidum (Sassafras), 102
Sassafras, 102
Sassafras, Southern (Sweet Bay
        Magnolia), 73
    Swamp (Sweet Bay Magnolia), 73
Satin Walnut (Sweetgum), 116
Sauz (Black Willow), 11
Scalybark Hickory (Shagbark Hickory),
        200
    Oak (White Shin Oak), 90
Scarlet Maple (Red Maple), 117
        (Trident Maple), 119
Schaffner's Acacia (Huisachillo), 149
    Wattle (Huisachillo), 149
Screwbean Mesquite (*a/k/a Screwpod
        Mesquite*), 158–59
Scrub Elm (Cedar Elm), 86
    Live Oak (Plateau Live Oak), 76
        (Wavy Leaf Oak), 105
    Oak, 107
        (Mohr Oak), 46
        (Sandpaper Oak), 108
        (Vasey Oak), 106
        (Wavy Leaf Oak), 105
        (White Shin Oak), 90
Shagbark Hickory, 200
Shavings (Fringe Tree), 30
Shellbark Hickory (Shagbark Hickory),
        200
Shining Sumac (Flameleaf Sumac), 181
Shinnery (Havard Shin Oak), 88
        (Vasey Oak), 106

Shin Oak, Havard, 88
    White, 90
Shin Oak (Bluejack Oak), 13
        (Mohr Oak), 46
        (Sandpaper Oak), 108
        (Vasey Oak), 106
        (Wavy Leaf Oak), 105
Ship Mast Locust (Black Locust), 168
        (White Shin Oak), 90
Shittamwood (Gum Bumelia), 18
Shortleaf Pine, 225
Short Straw Pine (Shortleaf Pine), 225
Shotbush (Devil's Walking Stick), 143
Shrub Live Oak (Sandpaper Oak), 108
        (Scrub Oak), 107
    Nightshade (Potato Tree), 43
Shumard Oak (*a/k/a Shumard Red
        Oak*), 113
Sideroxylon celestrina (Coma), 14
    lanuginosum (Gum Bumelia), 18
Sierra Madre Torchwood, 173
Silk Bay (Red Bay), 6
    Tree (Mimosa), 154
Silkworm Mulberry (White Mulberry),
        139
Silver Bell, American (Two Wing Silver
        Bell), 58
    Carolina, 59
    Little (Carolina Silver Bell), 59
    Two Wing, 58
Silver Leaf Oak, 2
    Maple, 115
    Mountain Mahogany (Mountain
        Mahogany), 19
Skunk Bush (Wafer Ash), 208
Slippery Elm, 51
Small Fruit Hawthorn (Little Hip
        Hawthorn), 21
    Magnolia (Sweet Bay Magnolia), 73
Smallseed White Ash (White Ash), 191
Smokebush (American Smoke Tree), 70
Smoke Tree, American, 70
    Wild (American Smoke Tree), 70
Smokey Oak (Lacey Oak), 89
Smooth Alder, 78
    Ash (Velvet Ash), 195
Smoothbark Hickory (Pignut Hickory),
        201
    Oak (Black Oak), 109
Snow Bell (Two Wing Silver Bell), 58
    Drop Tree (Two Wing Silver Bell), 58

Snowflower Tree (Fringe Tree), 30
Soapberry, Western, 178
Soapbush (Guayacan), 170
Soaptree Yucca (*a/k/a Soapweed Yucca*), 230
Soft Elm (American Elm), 52
    Maple (Red Maple), 117
        (Silver Maple), 115
        (Trident Maple), 119
Solanum erianthum (Potato Tree), 43
Sophora, Pink (Eve's Necklace), 171
    Texas (Eve's Necklace), 171
Sophora affinis (Eve's Necklace), 171
    secundiflora (Texas Mountain Laurel), 176
Sour Gum (Black Gum), 44
    (Water Tupelo), 45
Southern Bayberry (Southern Waxmyrtle), 24
    Blackhaw (Rusty Blackhaw Viburnum), 81
    Buckthorn (Carolina Buckthorn), 71
    Catalpa (*see Northern Catalpa*), 128–29
    Cottonwood (Eastern Cottonwood), 136
    Crabapple, 48
    Cypress (Bald Cypress), 221
    Hackberry (Sugar Hackberry), 33
    Hawthorn (Green Hawthorn), 50
    Live Oak (Live Oak), 77
    Magnolia, 74–75
    Nannyberry (Rusty Blackhaw Viburnum), 81
    Red Cedar, 215
    Red Oak, 110
    Rock Elm (Cedar Elm), 86
    Sassafras (Sweet Bay Magnolia), 73
    Sugar Maple, 121
    Sweetbay (Sweet Bay Magnolia), 73
    Waxmyrtle, 24
    Yellow Pine (Longleaf Pine), 228
        (Shortleaf Pine), 225
Southwestern Bigtooth Maple (Bigtooth Maple), 118
    Black Willow (Black Willow), 11
    Choke Cherry, 47
Soyate (Beaked Yucca), 231
Spanish Bayonet (Giant Dagger), 235
    (Spanish Dagger), 234
    (Torrey Yucca), 233
    Dagger, 234

    (Giant Dagger), 235
    (Torrey Yucca), 233
Live Oak (Plateau Live Oak), 76
Oak (Southern Red Oak), 110
    (Texas Oak), 112
Pincushion (Button Bush), 42
Sparkleberry (Farkleberry), 67
Spiny Hackberry (Granjeno), 83
Spotted Oak (Texas Oak), 112
Standley Ash (Velvet Ash), 195
Star Leaved Gum (Sweetgum), 116
Stave Oak (White Oak), 93
Striped Oak (Nuttall Oak), 111
Sugarberry (Anaqua), 65
    (Net Leaf Hackberry), 31
Sugar Hackberry (*a/k/a Sugarberry*), 33
    Maple, Southern, 121
Sumac, Black (Flameleaf Sumac), 181
    Flameleaf, 181
    Lance-leaved (Prairie Flameleaf Sumac), 180
    Limestone (Prairie Flameleaf Sumac), 180
    Mountain (Flameleaf Sumac), 181
    Prairie Flameleaf (*a/k/a Prairie Shining Sumac*), 180
    Shining (Flameleaf Sumac), 181
    Texas (Prairie Flameleaf Sumac), 180
    Tree (Prairie Flameleaf Sumac), 180
    Upland (Flameleaf Sumac), 181
    Wing Rib (Flameleaf Sumac), 181
Sunflower Tree (Fringe Tree), 30
Swamp Ash (Carolina Ash), 194
    (Green Ash), 192
    Bay Magnolia (Sweet Bay Magnolia), 73
    Chestnut Oak, 92
    Cypress (Bald Cypress), 221
    Cyrilla (Titi), 5
    Hickory (Bitternut Hickory), 189
        (Nutmeg Hickory), 187
        (Pignut Hickory), 201
        (Water Hickory), 202
    Holly (Deciduous Holly), 25
    Laurel (Sweet Bay Magnolia), 73
    Laurel Oak (Laurel Oak), 9
    Locust (Water Locust), 166–67
    Magnolia (Sweet Bay Magnolia), 73
    Maple (Red Maple), 117
        (Silver Maple), 115
        (Trident Maple), 119

Post Oak (Bottomland Post Oak), 97
    (Overcup Oak), 98
Privet, 60
Red Oak (Shumard Oak), 113
    (Southern Red Oak), 110
Sassafras (Sweet Bay Magnolia), 73
Spanish Oak (Southern Red Oak), 110
Tupelo (Water Tupelo), 45
White Oak (Overcup Oak), 98
    (Swamp Chestnut Oak), 92
Willow (Black Willow), 11
Willow Oak (Willow Oak), 3
Sweet Acacia (Huisache), 148
    Bay (Red Bay), 6
    Bay Magnolia, 73
    Bean Tree (Honey Locust), 164–65
    Elder (Elderberry), 190
    Elm (Slippery Elm), 51
    Leaf, 7
    Locust (Honey Locust), 164–65
    Magnolia (Sweet Bay Magnolia), 73
    Pignut (Pignut Hickory), 201
Sweetgum, American, 116
Switch Hickory (Pignut Hickory), 201
Sycamore, American, 124–25
    Eastern (American Sycamore), 124–25
Symplocos tinctoria (Sweet Leaf), 7

Tag Alder (Smooth Alder), 78
Tallow Shrub (Southern Waxmyrtle), 24
    Tree, Chinese, 132
Tamarindo (Salt Cedar), 212
Tamarisk (*a/k/a Tamarisco*) (Salt Cedar), 212
Tamarix gallica (Salt Cedar), 212
Tamaulipan Fiddlewood, 35
Tascate (Alligator Juniper), 218
Taxodium distichum (Bald Cypress), 221
    mucronatum (Montezuma Bald Cypress), 220
Tecoma stans (Yellow Trumpet), 196
Tenaza, 150
Tepeguaje, 157
Texas Arbutus (Texas Madrone), 69
    Ash, 192
    Black Walnut (Texas Walnut), 182
    Buckeye (Mexican Buckeye), 186
    Catclaw (Gregg Acacia), 144
        (Wright Acacia), 145
    Cedar (Ashe Juniper), 213

Cottonwood (Plains Cottonwood), 136
Crabapple, 80
Ebony, 151
Elm (Cedar Elm), 86
Hawthorn, 26
Hercules' Club (Lime Prickly Ash), 174
Hickory (Black Hickory), 188
Huisache (Huisache), 148
Juniper (Redberry Juniper), 217
Madrone, 69
Mountain Laurel, 176
Oak, 112
Olive (Anacahuita), 72
Palmetto (Sabal Palm), 238–39
Paloverde (Paloverde), 147
Persimmon, 15
Pistache, 172
Porlieria (Guayacan), 170
Privet (Swamp Privet), 60
Red Oak (Chisos Red Oak), 114
    (Texas Oak), 112
Redbud, 126
Sophora (Eve's Necklace), 171
Sugarberry (Sugar Hackberry), 33
Sumac (Prairie Flameleaf Sumac), 180
Walnut, 182
Thickbark Cedar (Alligator Juniper), 218
Thompson Yucca, 232
Thorny Locust (Honey Locust), 164–65
Three Lobe Red Oak (Southern Red Oak), 110
Tickle Tongue (Hercules' Club), 197
    (Lime Prickly Ash), 174
Tidewater Red Cypress (Bald Cypress), 221
Tilia caroliniana (Carolina Linden), 137
Titi, 5
Tobacco Tree, 68
Toothache Tree (Devil's Walking Stick), 143
    (Hercules' Club), 197
    (Lime Prickly Ash), 174
Torchwood, Mexican (Sierra Madre Torchwood), 173
    Mountain (Sierra Madre Torchwood), 173
    Sierra Madre, 173
Tornillo (Screwbean Mesquite), 158–59

Torrey Yucca, 233
Toumey Ash (Velvet Ash), 195
Tracy Hawthorn (Mountain Hawthorn), 85
Trecul Yucca (Spanish Dagger), 234
Trembling Poplar (Quaking Aspen), 133
Tree Coral Bean, 204–205
    Huckleberry (Farkleberry), 67
    of Heaven, 177
    Privet (Wax Leaf Ligustrum), 37
    Sumac (Prairie Flameleaf Sumac), 180
    Tobacco (*a/k/a Yellow Tree Tobacco*) (Tobacco Tree), 68
Trident Maple, 119
Trifoliate Orange, 207
Tropical Buckthorn (Coma), 14
True Mountain Mahogany (Mountain Mahogany), 19
Trumpet Bush (Yellow Trumpet), 196
Tung Oil Tree, 130–31
Tupelo, Black (Black Gum), 44
    Swamp (Water Tupelo), 45
    Water, 45
Turbinella Oak (Scrub Oak), 107
Turkey Oak (Bluejack Oak), 13
Twisted Acacia (Huisachillo), 149
    Bean (Screwbean Mesquite), 158–59
Two Leaf Pinyon (Pinyon Pine), 222
    Wing Silver Bell, 58

Ulmus alata (Winged Elm), 54
    americana (American Elm), 52
    crassifolia (Cedar Elm), 86
    parvifolia (Chinese Elm), 55
    rubra (Slippery Elm), 51
Umbrella Tree (Chinaberry), 161
Ungnadia speciosa (Mexican Buckeye), 186
Uña de gato (Gregg Acacia), 144
    (Wright Acacia), 145
Upland Hickory (Shagbark Hickory), 200
    Sumac (Flameleaf Sumac), 181
    Willow Oak (Bluejack Oak), 13
Uvalde Bigtooth Maple, 118

Vaccinium arboreum (Farkleberry), 67
Valley Cottonwood (Rio Grande Cottonwood), 135
Varnish Tree (Chinese Parasol Tree), 122–23

(Golden Rain Tree), 162–63
(Tung Oil Tree), 130–31
Vasey Oak, 106
Velvet Ash, 195
Viburnum, Rusty Blackhaw, 81
Viburnum rufidulum (Rusty Blackhaw Viburnum), 81
Victoria Palmetto (Sabal Palm), 238–39
Virginia Dogwood (Flowering Dogwood), 38
    Juniper (Eastern Red Cedar), 214
    Live Oak (Live Oak), 77
    Magnolia (Sweet Bay Magnolia), 73
Vitex (Chaste Tree), 209
Vitex agnus-castus (Chaste Tree), 209
Vogelbeerbaum (Anaqua), 65

Wafer Ash, 208
Wahoo Elm (Winged Elm), 54
    Tree (Golden Ball Lead Tree), 156
Walnut, Arizona (*a/k/a Arizona Black Walnut*), 185
    Bitter (Bitternut Hickory), 189
    Black, 184
    Little (Texas Walnut), 182
    Mountain (Arizona Walnut), 185
    River (Arizona Walnut), 185
    (Texas Walnut), 182
    Satin (Sweetgum), 116
    Texas (*a/k/a Texas Black Walnut*), 182
Washingtonia filifera (Washington Palm), 240–41
Washington Palm, 240–41
Water Ash (Carolina Ash), 194
    (Green Ash), 192
    Beech (American Hornbeam), 56
    Birch (River Birch), 79
    Elm (American Elm), 52
    Gum (Water Tupelo), 45
    Hickory, 202
    Locust, 166–67
    Maple (Red Maple), 117
    (Trident Maple), 119
    Oak, 17
    Pignut (Water Hickory), 202
    Tupelo, 45
    White Oak (Overcup Oak), 98
Waternut, Bitter (Nutmeg Hickory), 187
Wavy Leaf Oak, 105
Wax Leaf Ligustrum, 37

Waxmyrtle, Southern, 24
Welk Holly (Deciduous Holly), 25
West Texas Live Oak (Plateau Live
Oak), 76
Western Black Oak (Emory Oak), 104
Black Willow (Black Willow), 11
Crabapple (Texas Crabapple), 80
Hackberry (Net Leaf Hackberry), 31
Juniper (Alligator Juniper), 218
Mayhaw (Mayhaw), 20
Soapberry, 178
Sugar Maple (Bigtooth Maple), 118
White Ash, 191
Bay Magnolia (Sweet Bay Magnolia),
73
Beech (American Beech), 53
Cornel (Flowering Dogwood), 38
(Rough Leaf Dogwood), 39
Cypress (Bald Cypress), 221
Elm (American Elm), 52
Fringe Tree (Fringe Tree), 30
Gum (Sweetgum), 116
Hickory (Bitternut Hickory), 189
(Mockernut Hickory), 198–99
Holly (American Holly), 103
Laurel (Sweet Bay Magnolia), 73
Leaf Oak (Silver Leaf Oak), 2
Locust (Black Locust), 168
Maple (Silver Maple), 115
Mulberry, 139
Oak, 93
Sassafras (Sassafras), 102
Shin Oak, 90
Titi (Titi), 5
Whitebark Maple (Chalk Maple), 120
Whiteheart Hickory (Mockernut
Hickory), 198–99
Wild Banana (Pawpaw), 22–23
Cherry (*a/k/a Wild Black Cherry*)
(Black Cherry), 47
Chinaberry (Western Soapberry), 178
Chinatree (Western Soapberry), 178
Laurel (Sweet Leaf), 7
Lime (Colima), 169
Olive (Anacahuita), 72
Peach (Cherry Laurel), 36
Pecan (Water Hickory), 202
Pistachio (Texas Pistache), 172
Smoke Tree (American Smoke
Tree), 70
Oak, 3

Willow, Black, 11
Bow (Desert Willow), 10
Button (Button Bush), 42
Catalpa (Desert Willow), 10
Desert, 10
False (Desert Willow), 10
Flowering (Desert Willow), 10
Gooding (Black Willow), 11
Gulf Black (Black Willow), 11
Lindheimer Black (Black Willow), 11
Southwestern Black (Black Willow),
11
Swamp (Black Willow), 11
Western Black (Black Willow), 11
Yew Leaf (*a/k/a Yew Willow*), 12
Willow Leaf Catalpa (Desert Willow), 10
Winged Elm, 54
Wing Rib Sumac (Flameleaf Sumac), 181
Winterberry (Deciduous Holly), 25
Winterberry Holly, 28
Winter Huckleberry (Farkleberry), 67
Plum (Persimmon), 41
Wislizenus Cottonwood (Rio Grande
Cottonwood), 135
Witch Elm (Winged Elm), 54
Woolybucket Bumelia (Gum Bumelia),
18
Wooly Buckthorn (*a/k/a Wooly
Bumelia*) (Gum Bumelia), 18
Hop Hornbeam, 57
Wright Acacia, 145

Xylosma, 61
Xylosma flexuosa (Xylosma), 61

Yaupon Holly, 82
Yellowbark Oak (Black Oak), 109
Yellow Bells (Yellow Trumpet), 196
Buckeye, 210–11
Buckthorn (Carolina Buckthorn), 71
Chestnut Oak (Chinkapin Oak), 62
Cypress (Bald Cypress), 221
Locust (Black Locust), 168
Oak (Black Oak), 109
(Bottomland Post Oak), 97
(Chinkapin Oak), 62
Pine (Longleaf Pine), 228
(Shortleaf Pine), 225
Tree Tobacco (Tobacco Tree), 68
Trumpet, 196
Wood (Carolina Buckthorn), 71

(Osage Orange), 40
(Sweet Leaf), 7
Yew Leaf Willow (*a/k/a Yew Willow*), 12
Yucca, Beaked, 231
Big Bend Yucca (Beaked Yucca), 231
Faxon (Giant Dagger), 235
Giant Dagger, 235
Soaptree (*a/k/a Soapweed Yucca*), 230
Spanish Dagger, 234
Thompson, 232
Torrey, 233
Trecul (Spanish Dagger), 234
Yucca elata (Soaptree Yucca), 230
faxonia (Giant Dagger), 235
rostrata (Beaked Yucca), 231
thompsoniana (Thompson
Yucca), 232
torreyi (Torrey Yucca), 233
treculeana (Spanish Dagger), 234
Yule Holly (American Holly), 103

Zanthoxylum clava-herculis (Hercules'
Club), 197
fagara (Colima), 169
hirsutum (Lime Prickly Ash), 174
Zitherwood (Tamaulipan Fiddlewood),
35